AF248786

INDIAN LIFE
IN
THE SUKLA-YAJURVEDA

DR. SITANATH DEY

FIRMA KLM PRIVATE LIMITED

CALCUTTA   ●   ●   1985

Published by
Firma KLM Private Limited
257-B, B. B. Ganguly Street
Calcutta-700 012
INDIA

First Published, Calcutta, 1985
© Dr. Sitanath Dey

Price Rs. 90.00

Printed by : 'ALPHABET' 2/1, Dr. A. K. Pal Road, Calcutta-34

Dedicated to

The Memory of my revered

Acharyya

Dr. Jogiraj Basu

M. A. (Tripple) Ph. D.

PEACE INVOCATION

(शान्ति-पाठः)

* * * * * * *

आ ब्रह्मन्ब्राह्मणो ब्रह्मवर्चसी जायतामा राष्ट्रे राजन्यः शूरः

इष्व्योऽतिव्याधी महारथो जायतां दोग्ध्री धेनुर्वोढानड्वानाशुः सप्तिः

पुरन्धिर्योषा जिष्णु रथेष्ठाः सभेयो युवास्य यजमानस्य वीरो जायताम्

निकामे निकामे नः पर्जन्यो वर्षतु फलवत्यो न ओषधयः पच्यन्तां यागक्षेमो

नः कल्पताम् ॥

ओ३म् शान्तिः शान्तिः शान्तिः—यजु २२.२२

"Oh Brahman, may the Brāhmaṇa in our nation overflow
with Brahmanical lustre and shine. May the Kṣatriya be brave,
skilled in archery, efficient in shooting and warrior of highest
degree. May the cow yield (abundant) milk, the bullocks (strong
enough) to carry (the burden of the yoke) and the horse speedy.
May the young woman be a respectable matron. May the youthful
son of this host be a hero, ever victorious, moving in magnificent
chariot and worthy of an assembly. May the rains shower regularly
for us in seasons. May the trees bear fruits for us. May we be
contented (by acquisition of our needs and by preservation of the
acquired wealth)"—S. Yv. XXII.22

ACKNOWLEDGEMENT

At the outset I do pay my homage and heartfelt gratitude to the hallowed memory of my revered Acharya, the Late Prof. Dr. Jogiraj Basu, M.A. (Triple) Ph.D., a saintly personality and noted Indologist under whose guidance I had the privilege to undertake this Research work entitled "SUKLA-YAJURVEDA : A STUDY" (in all available aspects) and got the registration of the same in the University of Dibrugarh in 1974. But unfortunate as I was, premature death snatched him away from us at a time when my research work was nearing its completion. I am much indebted to him as he found time to go through the manuscripts of the first two books and a part of the last book of my thesis. I beseech his blessings from the other world. I am thankful to the University of Dibrugarh which after the death of Dr. Basu permitted me to continue my research work under Dr. P. P. Upadhyaya M.A. Ph.D of the Gauhati University. Dr. Upadhyaya, through his scholarly aptitude has kindly acted as my guide up to the completion of my thesis. I owe a deep debt of gratitude to him also. My sincere thanks are due to Dr. B. C. Das, M.A. Ph.D and Prof. B. P. Mukherjee, M.A. of M.B.B. College, Agartala, who were good enough to inspire me through their constant encouragement.

ABBREVIATIONS

A. A.	—	Aitareya Āraṇyaka
A. B.	—	Aitareya Brāhmaṇa
A. S. S.	—	Āśvalāyana Śrauta-sūtra
A. V.	—	Atharva Veda
B. U.	—	Bṛhadāraṇyakopaniṣad
C. U.	—	Chāndogyopaniṣad
K. S.	—	Kāṭhaka Saṃhitā
K. U.	—	Kaṭhopaniṣad
M. S.	—	Maitrāyaṇī Saṃhitā
M. U.	—	Muṇḍakopaniṣad
Mbh.	—	Mahābhārata
R. V.	—	Ṛgveda
S. V.	—	Sāmaveda
S. Yv.	—	Śukla-Yajurveda
S. B.	—	Śatapatha Brāhmaṇa
S. U.	—	Śvetāśvataropaniṣad
T. S.	—	Taittirīya Saṃhitā
T. A.	—	Taittirīya Āraṇyaka
T. B.	—	Taittirīya Brāhmaṇa
V. S.	—	Vājasaneyī Saṃhitā
Y. V.	—	Yajurveda

TRANSLITERATION

The following are the main points to be noted in the scheme of transliteration followed in this work.

a	अ	k	क्	ṇ	ण	v	व
ā	आ	kh	ख्	t	त्	ś	श्
i	इ	g	ग्	th	थ्	ṣ	ष्
ī	ई	gh	घ्	d	द्	s	स्
u	उ	ṅ	ङ्	dh	ध्	h	ह्
ū	ऊ	c	च्	n	न्	Anusvara · ṃ	
ṛ	ऋ	ch	छ्	p	प	Visarga : ḥ	
e	ए	j	ज्	ph	फ		
ai	ऐ	jh	झ्	b	ब		
o	ओ	ñ	ञ्	bh	भ		
au	औ	ṭ	ट	m	म		
		ṭh	ठ	y	य		
		ḍ	ड	r	र		
		ḍh	ढ	l	ल		

PREFACE

Ancient India's contribution to the world culture and civilisation in various branches of knowledge—spiritual and material (parā vidyā and aparā vidyā), have been handed over down the centuries through the Vedas, the Saṃhitas, the Brāhmaṇas, the Āraṇyakas, the Upaniṣads, the Purāṇas, the Epics and numerous other works all of which constitute our great cultural heritage. This vast store house of knowledge has naturally undergone significant changes marking stages of development in the course of its long literary tradition. Some of them were evolved long before the art of writing was invented. The formulations of the precocious grammarian Pāṇini (c. 5th Century B.C.) are usually taken as the great watershed. The post-Pāṇinian works are termed as the classical Sanskrit literature while the Vedic literature is treated as Pre-Pāṇinian.

Vedic literature in its turn has several branches and divisions. The Śukla-Yajurveda Saṃhitā belongs to one of the four Vedas. It is also known as the Vājasaneyī Saṃhitā after its seer, the famous Yājñabalkya, the son of Vājasani. The only available recensions (Śākhās) of the Śukla-Yajurveda Saṃhitā are Kānva and Mādhyandina. In both the Śākhās, the Saṃhitā consists of 40 chapters (Adhyāyas) the last Chapter (Ch. XL) being known as the famous Īśopaniṣad.

The present work 'Indian life in the Śukla-Yajurveda' being the out-come of my doctoral thesis, introduces an analytical study of the Śukla-Yajurveda. An attempt has been made here to analyse the ancient Indian life and culture as depicted in the Śukla-Yajurveda. What follows is divided into four major parvans or books, each of which is again sub-divided into a few chapters. In all, there are twenty chapters which are preceded by an introduction and followed by a conclusion.

The first book deals at some length with the Socio-economic aspect wherein are discussed such topics as education, caste-system, dress and decoration, food & drink, agriculture, trade and commerce etc. The second book is devoted to the aspects of public administration including the origin and types of kingship, the cabinet and the administrative organisation etc. While the first and second books are about mundane affairs, the third book deals with such supramundane affairs as religion, philosophy, bhakti cult, popular religious cults, eschatology & cosmogony etc. The fourth book describes miscellaneous topics like flora & fauna, calendar, language & literature etc.

To our sainty Acharya Dr. Jagiraj Basu, my indebtedness is incalculable. I have the privilege of starting the work under Professor Basu but he could not see it in the present form as he had left the world before its completion. I would like to record my gratitude to Dr. Sitanath Goswami of Jadavpur University and and Dr. P. P. Upadhyaya of Gauhati University for their valuable suggestions. I am thankful to Dr. B. C. Das, Dr. B. P. Mukhapadhyaya and Dr. J. Ganchowdhuri of Agartala, who were good enough to inspire and encourage me. My thanks are also due to Sri Tapan Bhattacharyya who helped in varifying the Type-scripts with the original. Firma KLM Pvt. Ltd. of Calcutta deserves my congratulation for publishing this work within a reasonable time.

Ommissions and commissions as well as constructive suggestions, if kindly pointed out, will be given due consideration in the next edition.

CONTENTS

BOOK I

THE SOCIAL AND ECONOMIC ASPECT

(xii)

BOOK II

THE POLITICAL AND MILITARY ASPECT

BOOK III

THE RELIGIO-PHILOSOPHICAL ASPECT

BOOK IV

MISCELLANEOUS

INTRODUCTION

The object of this work as its very title indicates, is a thorough study of the ŚUKLA-YAJURVEDA SAMHITĀ, otherwise known as the Vājasaneyī Saṃhitā. The study has been made from the view point of all major aspects such as—social, economic, political, religious, theological-cum-philosophical etc. Accordingly, the work has been divided into several books, each dealing with a particular aspect and comprising several chapters. Certain aspects not falling into the groups mentioned above have been included in a separate book under the heading 'Miscellaneous'. Thus an attempt has been made to undertake an all-round investigation of this Saṃhitā in all its available aspects. The study mainly concerns this particular Saṃhitā no doubt, but an attempt has been made to present a comparative study with a view to bring out the references to other Saṃhitās, Brāhmaṇas, Āraṇyakas and Upaniṣads.

Before we enter into discussion of the Śukla-Yajurveda in particular, it is necessary to discuss first the import of the term 'Veda' and its different classes in general. The term 'Veda' primarily means knowledge par excellence i.e. the sacred, religious knowledge. Secondly, the term denotes works containing the most sacred and authoritative knowledge.

According to Sāyana,[1] Āpastamba[2] and the Pūrvamīmāṃsā,[3] 'Veda' is the name given to Mantra and Brāhmaṇa jointly. The authority of the Veda is claimed on the ground that it is the final tribunal in matters of dispute concerning religion or philosophy or social customs. 'Veda is the fountain-head of all religions or duties'—observes the Manusaṃhitā.[4]

The Vedic literature consists of three different classes of literary works and to these different classes belongs a greater or smaller number of works. The three different classes of Vedic literature are :—

(i) SAMHITĀ i.e. collections—collections of hymns, prayers, incantations, benedictions, sacrificial formulas and litanies.

(ii) BRĀHMAṆAS which contain theological matters—especially observations on sacrifice and the practical and mystical significance of the separate sacrificial rites and ceremonies.

iii) *ĀRAṆYAKAS & UPANIṢADS* which are partly included in the Brāhmaṇas themselves or attached to them but partly are also independent works. They contain the meditations of forest hermits and ascetics and god, the world and mankind and there is contained in them a good deal of the oldest Indian philosophy.

There are, however, four Samhitās which differ clearly from one another and which have been preserved in one or more recensions :-

1. The Ṛgveda Samhitā—the collection of ṛcas i.e. cf the knowledge of songs and praise.

2. The Atharvaveda Samhitā—the collection of the Atharvans i.e. of the knowledge of the magic formulas.

3. The Sāmaveda Samhitā—the collection of the sāmans i.e. of the knowledge of the melodies.

4. The Yajurveda Samhitā—the collection of the Yajus i.e. of the knowledge of the sacrificial formulas. This Samhitā has been handed down in two forms :-

i) The one is the Śukla (White) Yajurveda which is also known as the Vājasaneyī Samhitā. It contains only the sacrificial formulas.

ii) The other is the Kṛṣṇa (Black) Yajurveda in which sacrificial formulas are intermingled with their explanations.

Every work that belongs to the class of the Brāhmaṇas, of the Āraṇyakas or of the Upaniṣads, belongs to one of the four enumerated above. Each Samhitā has, therefore, its own Brāhmaṇas, Āraṇyaka and Upaniṣads.

Generally the word 'Trayī' is used as a synonym for Veda. By the word 'Trayī' we should mean not only the three Vedas—Ṛg,

Sāma, Yajus, but also the threefold characteristics of vedic hymns. Thus, the hymns affixed with certain metres and feet are known as ṚK. When tunes are applied to them, the ṚK. verses attain the character of Sāma. The rest of the hymns which do not possess the above-mentioned characteristics are designated as Yajus. Nigada mantras are also included in the Yajus. This is the way of classifying the vedic mantras.

Now, let us pass on to the discussion of the Yajurveda. It has been stated that the mantras not belonging to ṚK and Sāma are known as Yajus. In the Ṛgveda and Sāmaveda prose is not to be met with ; the contents of the Yajurveda, on the other hand, consist partly of prose and partly of verse. Only 75 mantras of the Sāmaveda are claimed to be original by its own ; other mantras are borrowed from the Ṛgveda. The Yajurveda, on the other hand, though it borrows some mantras from the Ṛgveda, has most of the mantras of its own. The Yajurveda resembles the Sāmaveda in having been compiled for ritual application.

But while the Sāmaveda deals solely with one part of the ritual, the 'Soma sacrifice', the Yajus supplies the formulas for the whole sacrifice. The Yajurveda is directly connected with the sacrificial acts. All the rules and regulations relating to sacrifices are met with in this veda. Hence, knowledge of the Yajurveda is essential for the correct performance of any vedic sacrifice.

The Yajurveda has two main divisions viz : Śukla (White) Yajurveda (Vājasaneyī Saṃhitā) and Kṛṣṇa (Black) Yajurveda (Taittirīya Saṃhitā). The Śukla-Yajurveda has only one recension while the Kṛṣṇa Yajurveda has four important recensions such as :-

      i)   Kāṭhaka Saṃhitā
      ii) Kapisthala-Kaṭha Saṃhitā.
      iii) Maitrāyaṇī Saṃhitā
      iv) Taittirīya Saṃhitā.

All these recensions of the Kṛṣṇa Yajurveda agree in arranging their subject-matter according to a common principle different from that of the Śukla-Yajurveda or Vājasaneyī Saṃhitā. The first anuvāka of the Taittirīya Saṃhitā corresponds with the first kandikā or the Vājasaneyī Saṃhitā but all the rest differ and so does the arrangement of the subjects. Many of the topics are, indeed, alike in both the Saṃhitās but they are differently placed and differently treated.

As regards the two divisions (Krṣna and Śukla) of the Yajurveda, an interesting story is alluded to in the Vāyu and Viṣṇu Purāṇa. We shall first refer to that story and then find out other possible explanations of the terms Krṣna and Śukla. The story runs thus :-

For maintaining the integrity of the Vedic knowledge as well as for its wide publicity, Lord Vyāsa, the great compiler of Vedic Saṃhitās imparted lessons in the four Saṃhitās viz. ṚK, Sāma, Yaju and Atharva respectively to his four wellknown disciples such as Paila, Vaiśampāyana, Jaiminī and Sumantu. Among them, Vaiśampāyana learnt the Yajurveda well and taught the same to his disciple Yājñavalkya and others. It was a prevalent custom with the sages to assemble without fail once in a year on the peak of the mount Meru for the purpose of religious discourse. In case, one failed to attend the same, he had to be involved in grave sin. Once failing to attend such an important conference, Vaiśampāyana violated the custom and thus sinned. He asked his disciples if they could relieve him of sin through due austerity. At this, his foremost disciple Yājñavalkya pointed out the incapacity of his mates and expressed that none but he could alone relieve him of that sin of Brahmicide. That arrogant speech of Yājñabalkya evoked his preceptor's wrath. As a result he was cancelled from discipleship. Not only that, the preceptor asked him to give back whatever he had learnt so long from him. In order to abide by his preceptor's order, Yājñabalkya had no other alternative but to vomit whatever he had learnt. The preceptor then advised his other disciples to swallow that vomited knowledge. As it was impossible and indecent to swallow the vomit, the disciples took the same turning themselves into 'Tittiri' birds and began to preach the same vedic knowledge to their own community. The vedic knowledge being vomited was impure and therefore, named as Krṣna. And as the sages took the same in the form of Tittiri birds, it came to be known as Taittirīya Saṃhitā. Here, sage Yājñabalkya being devoid of vedic knowledge and discarded by his preceptor was spending his time in a sorrowful mind. Suddenly he was awakened with such a thought that the self-effulgent Sun-god presides over different vedas in different parts of the day. So, he was determined to learn the Vedic knowledge from the Sun and began to eulogise him with certain prayers. The Sun being pleased at his devotion, appeared before him in the form of a 'Vāji' (horse) and preached to him his cherished knowledge of vedas. As this veda was revealed from the sun as illumined (Vāji—horse), it came to be known as Vājasaneyī Saṃhitā or Śukla-Yajurveda. The term 'Vāja' again means the Sun-rays and 'Sani' means treasure. The veda which came out from the white sun-rays in the form of a great treasure was called Vājasaneyī Saṃhitā or White Yajurveda. Again, the Vājasaneyī Saṃhitā is so named after its master seer Yājñavalkya whose patronymic was Vājasaneya.

The above legend regarding the division of Yajus into Kṛṣṇa and Śukla is admitted by Kātyāyana, the author of Anukra-manikā as well as by Mahīdhara, the commentator of the S. Yv. Others, however, think this legend as a mere tale without any basis and try to bring out the separate meanings of these two apparently contradictory terms—Kṛṣṇa and Śukla. Sāyanācārya in the commencement of his commentary of the Taittirīya Saṃhitā opines that the Veda was so named as it was learnt by a seer named Tittiri from his teacher seer Ukhā who himself learnt it from Vaiśampāyana. Pāṇini also connects this name with a seer named Tittiri. Sāyana, however, gives another explanation of Śukla & Kṛṣṇa. According to him Kṛṣṇa-Yajurveda is so named as it overwhelms the intellect. Because in it there is no clear and separate injunction regarding the duties of Advharyu and Hotr priests—the duties of both of them being laid down together. Śukla-Yajurveda, on the otherhand, distinctly refers to the duties of Adhvaryu priests only. On account of this purity and clear injunction, it is named Śukla. But the most widely celebrated opinion regarding these two divisions is that the Śukla Yajur-veda is pure as it is not intermingled with explanatory prose passages and is known for its well-arranged plan of the hymns. On the other hand, the Kṛṣṇa-Yajurveda is intermingled with the explanatory prose passages about the performance of the sacrificial rites and its contents are not properly arranged. That which is mixed is known as Kṛṣṇa and as in it the sacrificial formulas (mantras) are immediately followed by their explanations (brāhmaṇas), it is rightly designated as Kṛṣṇa. In the Śukla-Yajurveda, on the contrary, the sacrificial formulas and their explanations are entirely separated from one another—the first being assigned to the Saṃhitā proper and their explanations and the rituals to the Brāhmaṇa as in the case of the Ṛgveda and Sāmaveda.

In the Bṛhadāraṇyakopaniṣad it is amply stated that Yājñabalkya, the son of Vājasani, is the author of the S. Yv. He taught these white Yajus after receiving them from Āditya (Sun-god).[5] This Yājñavalkya is mentioned at the end of Book XIV of the S. B. as the author of that Brāhmaṇa of white Yajus. And in the first five books (I-V) of that Brāhmaṇa he is referred to as the teacher whose authority is conclusive.[6] The authority of Yājñabalkya is also ascribed to the famous B. U. and to the Yājñabalkya Smṛti.[7] He was a reputed scholar. From the Purāṇas,[8] it is evident that he taught three Vedas to Śatānika I, the son of Janmejay[9] Pārikṣit. In the B. U. we find that Yājñabalkya and Janaka, the sage-like king of Videha were close friends and Janaka learnt much about the Self from Yājñabalkya. In the Upaniṣad we also find that Janaka performed a great sacrifice and on that occasion a great debate was held in Mithilā. In that debate scholars like Aśvala, Yājñabalkya, Artabhāga, the son of Jaratkāru, Uṣasta, Cākrāyāṇa, Vidagdha Śākalya, Uddālaka Āruṇi, the preceptor of Yājñabalkya etc. took part. By his erudite scholarship, Yājñabalkya defeated them all and obtained a number of cows from the king as prizes. Not only that, once king Janaka was so pleased at the instructions of Yājñabalkya that he was ready to offer him the whole Videha country and even himself at his service.[10] In the same upaniṣad we find a beautiful dialogue between Yājñabalkya and his learned wife Maitreyee. Yājñabalkya was about to renounce the world in order to spend the rest of his life as a hermit in the solitude of a forest. So he wanted to distribute his earthly resources between his two wives—Maitreyee and Kātyāyanī. At this Maitreyee refused to take earthly treasures but begged from her husband for the way of cognition by which alone she would be able to attain immortality. In a beautiful manner Yājñavalkya instructed her how the Self (Ātman) is the source of everything and through Self alone all is known.

Yājñabalkya preached the mantras of the S. Yv. to his fifteen disciples viz. Jābālā, Gaudheya, Kaṇva, Madhyandina etc. Kaṇva and Madhyandina were his two prominent disciples and through them arose the two important and wellknown recensions (Śākhā) of this Veda viz. Kāṇva recension and Mādhyandina recension. In the Caraṇabyūha, however, there is mention of fifteen recensions of the S. Yv. These are as follows :—Kāṇva, Mādhyandina, Śāpeya, Stāpanīya, Kāpāla, Pauṇḍravatsa, Avatika, Paramāvatika, Parā-śarya, Vaidheya, Vaineya, Audheya, Gālava, Baijava and Kātyā-yanīya. Again, according to Brahmāṇḍa-Purāṇa and Skanda Purāṇa, there are 107 recensions of the Yajurveda while according to Patañjali this Veda has 101 recensions, but the only available recensions for the Kṛṣṇa Yajurveda are—Taittirīya, Maitrāyanīya, Kāṭhaka & Kaṭha and for the S. Yv. are Kāṇva and Mādhyandina. As regards the origin of the title Mādhyandina two opinions are prevalent. According to some it is called Mādhyandina because all Śrauta rites prescribed by this recension are generally performed in the mid-day. According to others, this recension is so named after the sage Mādhyandina who learnt it from Yājñabalkya. Kāṇva recension is named after the famous seer Kaṇva. These two recensions were preached for the first time in Videha and then spread to Northern, Eastern and Western India. In subject matter and arrangement these two recensions are almost identical. Minor divergences exist in prose part. These differences are due to geo-graphical changes since each has its own peculiarities of spelling. The Saṃhitā of the S. Yv. is extent in both recensions in 40 Adhyā-yas. In the Mādhyandina recension these are divided into 303 Anuvākas and 1975 Kaṇḍikās.

The Brāhmaṇa, Āraṇyaka and Upaniṣads belonging to the two existing recensions of the S. Yv. are shown in the table below.

Recension (Śākhā)	Brāhmaṇa	Āraṇyaka	Upaniṣad
1. Kāṇva	Śatapatha	Bṛhadāraṇyaka (=Brāhmaṇa Kāṇḍa XVII)	1. Īśa (=Samhitā Ch. 40) 2. Bṛhadāraṇyaka Upaniṣad (=Āraṇyaka Ch. 3-8).
2. Mādhyandina	Śatapatha	Bṛhadāraṇyaka (=Brāhmaṇa Kāṇḍa XIV).	i) Īśa (=Samhitā Ch. 40) ii) Bṛhadāraṇyaka Upa.(=Āraṇyaka Ch. 4-9.)

Now, we shall bring out the contents of the S. Yv. Samhita in brief :-

Among the total 40 chapters of this Samhitā, the last 15 are of later date. The first 25 chapters contain the prayers for the most important sacrifices. The first two adhyāyas contain the prayers for the New and Full moon sacrifices (Darśa paurṇamāsa) and the oblations to the fathers (Piṇḍapitṛ-yajña). The third chapter gives the prayers for the Agnihotra sacrifice which has to be offered every morning and evening and the sacrifices of the seasons which have to be offered every four months of a year (Cāturmāsya).

The prayers for the Soma sacrifices (Agniṣṭoma) in general including the animal sacrifices are to be found in chapters IV to VIII. The prayers for the Vājapeya and Rājasūya sacrifices are contained in chapters IX and X. In the Xth chapter, there are also the prayers for the Sautrāmaṇi sacrifice. Then, in chapter XI to XVIII are given prayers for the Agnicayana or 'construction of altars for the sacred fire'. The Chapters XI to XXI contain the prayers for the Sautrāmaṇi celebration which is recommended to expiate the evil effects of too much indulgence in soma drink. The prayers for the great Aśvamedha (Horse sacrifice) are contained in chapters XXI to XXV with which the old part of the S. Yv.

ends. Chapters XXVI to XXIX are of a supplementary character because they contain only appendices to the prayers relating to sacrifices dealt with in previous chapters. Chapters XXX to XXXIX deal with altogether new sacrifices e.g. Puruṣamedha (Human sacrifice), Sarvamedha (All-sacrifice) Pitṛmedha and Pravargya. The last chapter (Ch. XL) contains an Upaniṣad—the famous Īśa Upaniṣad. As it is included in the Sṃahitā portion, this Upaniṣad is also named as Saṃhitopaniṣad. According to Macdonell,[11] the original portion of the S. Yv. contains the first 18 adhyāyas only : the remaining adhyāyas are late additions. In support of this view he has indicated some external and internal evidences which are worth-mentioning.

EXTERNAL EVIDENCE

a) The first eighteen chapters alone contain verses and prose formulas which almost recur in the Taittirīya Saṃhitā.

b) The contents of the last twenty two chapters are found again only in the Brāhmaṇa and the Āraṇyaka belonging to the Taittirīya Saṃhitā.

c) Moreover, only the mantras of the first eighteen adhyāyas of Vājasaneyī Saṃhitā are completely given word for word in its own Brāhmaṇa (S. B.).

d) According to the ancient index of the S. Yv. attributed to Kātyāyana, the ten chapters (XXVI to XXXV) form a supplement (Khila). Uvaṭa and Mahīdhara also subscribe to this view.

INTERNAL EVIDENCE

a) Ch. XXVI to XXIX are supplementary chapters because they contain mantras relating to ceremonies dealt with in the previous chapters.

b) Ch. XXX to XXXIX contain prayers for altogether new sacrifices such as—the Puruṣamedha, the Sarvamedha and the Pitṛmedha.

c) Ch. XL must be a late addition because it has no direct relation to the sacrificial ceremonials but bears the character of an upaniṣad.

d) Ch. XXXIX makes mention of two additional epithets of Rudra viz. Iśāna and Mahādeva. These are absent in Ch. XVI in which a number of epithets of Rudra are alluded to.

e) Again, Ch. XXX specifies most of the Indian mixed castes while the Ch. XVI mentions only a few of them.

From what is stated above, the following four chronological strata of the S. Yv. may be deduced.

Stage I   Ch. I—XVIII—Original
   „   II   Ch. XIX—XXV   } Dealing with the OLD
   „   III   Ch. XXVI—XXXIX   } (XXVI-XXIX) & NEW (XXX-
                                      XXXIX) ceremonies.
   „   IV   Ch. XI....................Īśopaniṣad.

The Śatapatha Brāhmaṇa is the most voluminous Brāhmaṇa belonging to the S. Yv. This Brāhmaṇa occupies undoubtedly the most significant position of all the Brāhmaṇas. The Bṛhadāraṇyaka Upaniṣad belonging to the S. Yv. is the largest and besides the Chāndogya Upaniṣad is the most important of all Upaniṣads. The concluding chapter (Ch. XL) of the S. Yv. is known as Īśopaniṣad. This Upaniṣad is also known as Īśābāsyopaniṣad after the two initial words 'Īśābāsyam' of the first verse of this Upaniṣad. It is again known as Saṃhitopaniṣad as belonging to the Saṃhitā portion of the S. Yv. Besides the Brāhmaṇa and Upaniṣads, the Sūtras belonging to the S. Yv. are the Śrauta-Sutra of Kātyāyana and the Gṛhyasūtra of Pāraskara.

The Yajurveda Saṃhitā in general may be placed sometimes after, sometimes before the Sāmaveda, before the Atharva Veda and in all cases after the Ṛgveda. Of the different recensions of the Yajurveda Samhitā, again, it is generally admitted that the youngest is the Vājasaneyī Saṃhitā (S. Yv.). The arrangement itself, the connection with the R. V. and certain linguistic characters show this.

It may be observed that even the original portion of the S. Yv. (Ch. I to XVIII) must have assumed shape somewhat later than any of the recensions of the Kṛṣṇa-Yajurveda as appears from its more systematic division and distribution of the subject matter. In the treatment of the Ṛgvedic mantras, the S. Yv. shows much less independence than the Kṛṣṇa Yajurveda and conforms much more to the Ṛgvedic text tradition. As a result, the Kāṇva recension of the white Yajus agrees with the R. V. in the peculiar rotation of the cerebral sound 'ḍ' by 'ḷ'. In language, the S. Yv. comes closer to the Brāhmaṇas and on this basis some assert that this Saṃhitā is almost contemporary to the Brāhmaṇas (nearly 2000 B.C.)

The two wellknown commentators of the Mādhyandina recension of the S. Yv. are Uvaṭa and Mahīdhara. Uvaṭa, the son of Vajrata of Anandapura wrote his commentary while residing at Avanti—the country that was reigned by king Bhoja at that time. So his time might have been the middle part of the 11th century. His commentary composed in short syllabic words is very lucid, simple and at the same time most authoritative. Mahīdhara, a nāgara brahmin was a resident of Venaras. His commentary on the S. Yv. is known as Veda-dīpa which is mainly based on the commentary of Uvaṭa. His speciality lies in the fact that he has made the elaboration of meanings and explained the sacrificial rituals in the easier way by quoting illustrations from Nirukta and Śrauta-sūtra. He also composed a tāntrik scripture named Mantramahodadhi in 1588 A.D. So his period might be the later part of the 16th century A. D. The commentators of the Kāṇva recension of the S. Yv. are—Halāyudha, Sāyanācārya, Anantācārya and Ānandabodha.

IMPORTANCE OF THE S. Yv.

For the study of the history of the Vedic culture and civilisation, the importance of the S. Yv. cannot be overlooked. We came across so much necessary as well as important information relating to caste-system, names of different non-aryan tribes, different professions, the origin of Rudra-Śiva cult etc. In the symbolical offering of the Puruṣamedha mentioned in the XXXth chapter of this Veda, at least 58 varieties of professions are alluded to and out of them seven professions are marked for women. We view with wonder how this veda of such an antiquity (at least on 2000 B. C.) depicts a highly civilised society having so many varieties of professions and small scale industries. Such varieties are not met with in any other Veda. Not only do we find the four castes firmly established as the main division of Indian Society in the period of the S. Yv. but most of the mixed castes known in later times are already found to exist. Concerning the origin of the Rudra-Śiva Cult and of Śaivaite religion, the importance of the S. Yv has been generally admitted by Vedic scholars. For the proper understanding of the later religions and philosophical thought also, the knowledge of this S. Yv. Saṃhitā along with other Saṃhitās of the Yajurveda is indispensible. The later religious knowledge depends on the Brāhmaṇas and the philosophical knowledge on the Upaniṣads. 'Without Yajurveda' observed Dr. Winternitz[12] 'we can not understand the Brahmanas & without these we cannot understand Upaniṣads.'

PLAN OF THE THESITS & ORIGINALITY CLAIMED :

This thesis, as it has already been stated, presents an overall picture of the period of the S. Yv. Examination of the Saṃhitā has been made from all possible aspects and angles of vision. Every effort has been made to support the fact and observation with references available from either original or secondary sources. Most of the pages of the work contain references which are placed at the end of the chapter concerned. Original and other sources of references have been mentioned in the Bibliography. Of the two recensions of the S. Yv. mainly the Mādhyandina recension with commentaries of Uvaṭa and Mahīdhara has been followed and occasionally, the Kāṇva recension with Sāyana's commentary. For English rendering of original verses, translations of Yajurveda by Dr. Griffith and Devichand have been consulted. Besides the four books, a short conclusion has been added at the end of the work.

The Synopsis of the thesis is given below :—

It will be a study of the Śukla-Yajurveda in all its available aspects, viz. social, economic, political, religious, philosophical and miscellaneous. The work will be divided into four books—(i) Social and Economic aspect, (ii) Political aspect, (iii) Religious and

Philosophical aspect and (iv) Miscellaneous. Under the social and economic aspect will discussed the geographical & historical background, the caste-system, education of women, dress and decorations, occupation and industries, food and drink, utensils and tools, agriculture, transport, trade etc. The political aspect will comprise topics of kingship, cabinet, warfare etc. The religio-philosophical aspect will take into account topics regarding emergence of popular religious cults, the Rudra-Śiva cult, the Viṣṇu-cult, the Vedic pantheon, theology, origin of Bhakti-cult, philosophical conception behind the worship of deities and sacrifice, cosmogony and allied topics. Topics which do not come under the purview of other aspects will be treated in the fourth section of the book entitled 'Miscellaneous'. This book will take note of such topics as flora and fauna, language and literature, metrical analysis, calendar etc. The work starts with an introduction and will round of with a conclusion.

Now, a succinct gist of each book is presented in the following lines :-

Book I : Deals with Socio-economic aspect. The book starts with the geographical and historical background. The Aryan civilisation in this era spread from the Indus valley to the eastern direction. The geographical data of the S. Yv. refer to the territory in the middle of Northern India occupied by the neighbouring people of the Kuru and Pāñcāla. This period embodies some tribes and territories like Kuru Pāñcālas and Magadhas which are unheard of in the R. V. Certain mixed castes and castes of lower origin are also met with. They are : the Niṣādas, Kaivarta, Maināla, Puñjiṣṭha, Paulkasa, Caṇḍāla, Kirāta, Baindas etc.

There were four main castes viz Brāhmaṇa, Kṣatriya, Vaiśya and Śūdra. The caste system was not rigid and there was no sign of caste-hatred. Caste-system was based on division of labour. Thus the Brāhmaṇas were in charge of propagation of learning, Kṣatriyas or the ruling class were entrusted with the duties of protecting the country and people. The Vaiśyas were entrusted with the duties of manning agriculture, trade and commerce and lastly the Śūdras were the labour class on whose toil and industry, the progress of the society depended. The harmonious relation among the four castes strengthened the social body. Besides the four main castes, certain mixed castes and fifth caste (Pañcajanaḥ) are heard of.

Marriage within the same caste was highly laudable. But intercaste marriage and marriage even with lower caste were sanctioned. For example, Nisāda which was treated as the fifth caste, was born of Brāhmaṇa male and Śūdra female. The three wives of a King viz. Mahiṣī, Vāvātā and Parivṛktā represented the three castes—Kṣatriya, Vaiśya and Śūdra respectively.

Education for higher three castes was compulsory. The syllabus for study was extensive. Aryans of the Śukla-Yajurvedic period were well versed in the science of Arithmetic as well as in the science of Grammar. Debates and discourses based on intellectual topics were in vogue. The relation between the teacher and the student was very cordial. Women folk were not debarred from learning. Though no female savant is mentioned in this Veda, mention of the goddess of learning by such terms as : Iḍā, Bhāratī and Sarasvatī is met with.

More than seventy types of professions were mentioned. These were practised by people belonging to various castes, sub-castes and mixed castes. Some of these professions were set apart for women.

Music both vocal and instrumental was widely practised. Dancing was practised publicly both by male and female artists. Horse racing and chariot-racing were the most popular items of amusement. Dicing was another favourite pastime.

The garments worn by the people were made of wool, cotton or silk. They were fastidious in dresses and decorations.

Staple food of the Aryans of this period was wheat and rice. Various edibles such as : roasted grains, gruel, barley, grain of roasted rice, milk, curd, mingled milk, whey and honey etc. are mentioned. Drinks mainly consisted of Soma & Sura, milk, honey and water mixed with fruit juice. Reference to various professional fishermen indicates the inclusion of fish as an item of food. During this period, beef was probably not regarded as an agreeable food-item and the cow-killing was probably not sanctioned. Cow has been mentioned as an animal which should not be killed.

Utensils and tools of various types were used for domestic and sacrificial purposes.

Practice of medicine was a well-established profession. Various types of diseases are enumerated. Physicians were well versed in the science of toxicology, embryology, anatomy and osteology.

Agriculture and cattle rearing were regarded as important sources of income. The Vaiśva class was generally engaged in trade and commerce. Sea going vessels existed and maritime trade was known.

Book II deals with political aspect. As a general rule, monarchy was the system of government prevailing in this age. Theory of the divinity of king was not upheld, on the other hand, Yajurvedic texts clearly illustrate one of the fundamental characteristics of Vedic state, namely, human origin of king. Kingship was hereditary in character. In the invocation formulas as cited in the imperialistic and monarchical sacrifices termed Vājapeya and Rājasūya, the king is referred to as the son (or descendant) of such a man and such a woman and so forth.

Kingship of different types are mentioned by such terms as—Svarāṭ, Satrarāṭ, Janarāṭ and Sarvarāṭ meaning self-ruler, ruler for a long period, ruler of the people and ruler of all respectively. These different grades of monarchy were connected with different types of sacrifices viz. Rājasūya, Vājapeya, Aśvamedha, Puruṣamedha and Sarvamedha which had political and spiritual significance. Kingship or kingdom, monarchy or state were identified with each other as they were used in the sense of Rāṣṭra. Kings were benevolent and they kept ever wakeful vigilance over the state.

Though administration was run by the monarch, two popular assemblies—Sabhā & Samiti were in existence. It was urged that the members of the assembly (Sabhā) should be impartial in discharging the judicial & other functions.

The existence of Sabhā as a public assembly indicates the prevalence of democratic spirit behind the monarchical type of administration.

The reference to various government officials in the S. Yv. indicates the gradual development of the administrative organisation of that period. The king's cabinet was formed by persons technically known as Ratnins (Jewels). It included the chief queen (Mahiṣī), the chief priest (Purohita), the ministers (Mantrins), the Senānī, the Suta, the Grāmaṇi, the Kṣatṛ, the Saṃgrāhitṛ and the Bhāgadugha. For discharging various administrative functions, the king had to depend on these officials.

Book III deals with Religio-philosophical aspect. Theology, monotheistic tendency, origin of Bhakti cult, emergence of popular religious cults, Eschatology and Cosmogony etc. form the major topics of discussion in this book. Theological chapter contains discussion on different deities—their names, number and functions.

Behind the pluralistic Vedic pantheon, a monotheistic tendency gradually grew up. All personal gods were regarded as the manifestations of Impersonal Absolute Godhead. The Yajurvedic seers knew that the Godhead is Supreme and Absolute and therefore, uncomparable.

The Bhakti cult which is well developed in the age of Purāṇas had its root in the Yajurvedic period. A tendency is seen in different Bhakti cults to chant the prayer of a personal God enumerating as many names of his as possible. Such a tendency is met with in the eulogy of Rudra in the Śatarudrīya chapter of the S. Yv.

Book IV : It comprises miscellaneous topics such as flora an fauna, calendar, language and literature, treatment of metre etc. which have no logical connection with each other. As these topics are not homogenous in nature, these have been classified as miscellaneous. The chapter on flora and fauna attempts a detailed accont of wild life. The Sanskrit names of plants have been given with their botanical nomenclature. The chapter on Calendar is devoted to a clear discussion of the then Aryan calendar comprising the seasons, months, days of the year, intercalary months etc. The chapter on 'language and literature' and 'treatment of metre' forms an interesting and illuminating study. The literature of the S. Yv. bespeaks the transition from the literature of early

Saṃhitās to the Upaniṣadic literature through the Brahmanical literature.

Let us hope, it will not be too extravagant a claim to assert the thesis is an original one from the view point of its presentation and analysis. So far my knowledge goes, no such work presenting an analytical picture of the Aryan civilisation of the Śukla Yajurvedic era has yet been compiled. So I have undertaken this work wherein I have tried my level best to draw a penpicture of the then Aryan civilisation in all its diverse aspects.

REFERENCES

1. 'Mantra brāhmaṇātmaka śabdarāśir-vedaḥ'—Sāyaṇa on Ṛgveda bhāṣyo-pakramanikā.
2. 'Mantra-brāhmaṇayor vedanāmadheyam'—A.S. S. 24-1.31
3. 'Mantrāśca brāhmaṇāśca vedaḥ'—Śabarasvāmin on Pūrva-mīmāṃsā—2.1.33
4. 'Vedohakhilo dharmamūlam'
5. 'Ādityādimāni Śuklāni yajuṃsi Vājasaneyena Yājñavalkenkhyāyante' —B. U. 6-5-3
6. In Books VI-IX of the S. B. Yājñabalkya is not mentioned at all instead of him another sage Śāṇḍilya is quoted as an authority.
7. Yājñabalkya Smṛti-110 sloka (Prāyaścitta Ch. Jātidharma Prakaraṇa)
8. Bhāgavat Purāṇa : IX.22.38
9. B. U. III.1-9
10. 'Sohaṃ bhagavate videhān dadāmi māncāpi saha dāsyāyeti'—B. U. IV.4
11. A. A. Macdonell—A History of Sanskrit Literature...pp. 149-150
12. Winternitz—Indian Literature, Vol. I, p, 163

BOOK I

THE SOCIAL AND ECONOMIC ASPECT

CHAPTER I

GEOGRAPHICAL AND HISTORICAL BACKGROUND

In order to ascertain the extent of the Aryan settlement in the period of the Śukla Yajurveda we should consider the references to mountains, rivers, localities, countries, tribes and kingdoms made in the hymns. Reference to mountains and rivers is, however, scanty. No mountain is here directly mentioned except a mountaineous tribe known as Mūjavant who dwelt probably on a mountain-peak of the north Himālaya. As regards rivers, we get in the S.Yv. only the reference to the Sarasvatī and the Saptasindhu.

Rivers on the bank of which the Aryan civilisation developed were esteemed as deities from the Ṛg Veda onwards. Such a reference was due to the immense benefit they derived from the rivers. Sarasvatī, the holy river of the vedic age, is frequently mentioned in the R.V. and in later saṃhitās. She is invoked as the greatest among rivers (Nadītame), the greatest among mothers (Ambitame) and the greatest of goddesses (Devītame) in the R.V.[1]

This river is said to go to the ocean[2] and is referred to as a large river on the banks of which many kings[3] and indeed five tribes lived[4] and many vedic sacrifices were performed. In later vedic texts, specially in the Brāhmaṇas[5] this river lost its prominence as it disappeared under the sands of Vinaśana (Patiala district) and reappeared at Plākṣa prasravaṇa at a distance of fortyfour days' journey from Vinaśana. But this was not the case during the period of the S.Yv. as is evident from the hymn (S.Yv. XXXIV.11) wherein five rivers—all of them mighty and over-flowing—were said to merge into the Sarasvatī. From this, it can be assumed that this river did not lose her existence till the period of the S.Yv. According to Uvaṭa and Mahīdhara, the five rivers that joined the Sarasvatī were Dṛṣadvatī, Śatadrū, Chandrabhāgā, Vipāśā and Irābatī.[6] The names of these five tributories of the Sarasvatī as given by these two illustrious commentators uphold the opinion of Roth that the Sarasvatī was the Sindhu (Indus). The Sarasvatī was regarded as the holy river in the vedic age. It was on the banks of the Sarasvatī that great sacrifices used to be performed and the Aryans composed most of their hymns. In praise of the Sarasvatī, the following beautiful verses are met with :

‘May Sarasvatī, the purifier, the giver of food, the bestower of wealth in the shape of sacrificial fruits seek viands of our sacrificial rite’. (S. Yv.XX.84 ; R.V. 1.3.10)

‘Sarasvatī, the inspirer of truthful words, the intructress of the right minded, has accepted our sacrifice’. (S.Yv. XX.85 ; R.V. 1.3. 11)

‘Sarasvatī makes manifest by her deeds huge river and generates all knowledge’ (S.Yv. XX.86 ; R.V. 1.3.12)

These verses are an unimpeachable testimony to the grateful acknowledgement by the ancient Aryans of the facility that the Sarasvatī afforded them to perform their sacrifices and compose vedic mantras. In some other passages of the S.Yv.,[7] the Sarasvatī is mentioned as a deity, the wife of twin Aśvins. In the details of Aśvamedha sacrifice in the ch. XXII of the S.Yv.,[8] the Sarasvatī is invoked as the goddess of speech, purity and greatness.

In many verses of the R.V., seven rivers are meant by the term Saptasindhava.[9] Similarly in the Taittirīya Saṃhitā[10] and in the S.Yv.[11] seven rivers are designated by this word. The constant flow of Saptasindhava (the seven rivers) is alluded to in the S.Yv. in connection with the acceptance of curd for Indra. According to Maxmuller, the seven streams are the five rivers of the Pāñjāb along with the Indus and the Sarasvatī. Ludwig, Lassen and Whitney substitute Kubhā for the Sarasvatī and think that origi-nally the Oxus also must have been one of the seven rivers. A. D. Pusalkar[12], however, accepts the view of Maxmuller to be a reasonable one in defining the seven rivers. References to Sapta-sindhava are met with in the S.Yv. XXXIV.24 and XXXVIII.26 where seven oceans are meant by Uvaṭa and Mahīdhara. The Zend Avesta also refers to the seven rivers as ‘Haptahindu’.

It is curious enough to note that the river Gaṅgā is mentioned only once in the Xth mandala of the R.V. in connection with the 'praise of rivers' (nadīstuti)[13] ; but the name of this does not occur in the S.Yv. In the sixth Mandala of the R.V. occurs the term 'Gāṅgya' which is interpreted by Sāyaṇa as something located on the banks of the Ganges.[14]

TRIBES

The status, formation and nomenclature of the various tribes mentioned in the R.V., underwent considerable changes during the period of the S.Yv. saṃhitā. Some of the old tribes placed into insignificance, some disappeared wholly and many new tribes emerged and attained prominence. The five premier tribes of the Pāñjāb—the Purus, Anus, Druhyas, Yadus and Turvasas are no longer heard of in this saṃhitā. The Kurus along with Pāñcālas, Vaśas and Uśīnaras cccupied the Madhyadeśa or middle country. The R.V. does not mention the Kurus as a tribe but a king named 'Kuruśravaṇa' is mentioned therein.

The names of the two states Kuru and Pāñcāla always occur jointly as if the two formed a composite tribe. The Vājasaneyī Saṃhitā or the S. Yv. expressly refers to these two states as the unity of a united tribe.[15] In the same passage which is chanted in the Rājasūya sacrifice, Kuru-Pāñcālas are said to have had one king. Their kings Kraivya and Soṇa Satrasāha are spoken of as having performed the Aśvamedha sacrifice and another king Durmukha is said to have conquered the whole earth. In one passage of the S. Yv. saṃhitā,[16] the epithet Kāmpila-Vāsinī is applied to a woman, perhaps the King's Mahiṣī or the chief wife, whose duty was to sleep beside the slaughtered animal at the Horse-sacrifice (Aśvamedha).

The Sṛñjayas were closely allied with the Triṣṭus in the Ṛgvedic age. The Yajurveda Saṃhitā refers to the Sṛñjayas as having suffered some serious loss due to some ritualistic error, though what calamity exactly befell them, is not mentioned.

R. V. does not mention the Magadhas who make their appearance in the Yajurveda and Atharva Veda. From this, it may be assumed that the Aryans at the time of the Y. V. proceeded towards the east. The Y. V.[17] includes Magadha in the list of victims at the Puruṣamedha (Human-sacrifice). Zimmer regards Magadha referred to in the Y. V. and A. V. as a member of the mixed caste born of a Vaiśya man and a Kṣatriya woman. By the term Magadha, according to Mahīdhara,[18] is meant either the resident of Magadha country or the mixed caste born of Pratiloma marriage.

The Mūjavants have been mentioned in the A.V. along with Mahāvṛṣas, the Gāndhāras and the Balhikas as dwelling away. Similarly in the S.Yv., the Mūjavants are referred to as a type of distant folk, beyond whose habitat Rudra with his bow is entreated to depart. The Indian commentators[19] agree with Yāska in taking Mūjavant as the name of a mountain. As this mountain is described as the residence of Rudra, it may be in the Himalayas. If the people took their name from the mount Mūjavant, they were a hill tribe of the Himalayas.

The Niṣāda mentioned in later Saṃhitās and Brāhmaṇas[20], appears to be not the name of any particular tribe, but the generic term for Non-Aryan tribes, who were not under Aryan control. Niṣādas have been distinguished from other four varnas. Weber considers the Niṣādas to be the settled aborigines while the commentator Mahīdhara thinks that Niṣādas were Bhillas—the inhabitants of mountaineous tracts.

That the Aryan culture during the age of the S.Yv. did spread to the far eastern region is evident from the reference to Magadha. This place not mentioned in the R.V. corresponds to Southern Bihar. The A.V.[21] describes the Angas and Magadhas as the eastern people. In the Vrātya hymn of the same samhitā,[22] the Magadhas are associated with the Vrātyas.

Like the Magadha, the Vrātya is also included in the list of victims at the Puruṣamedha in the S. Yv.[23] where, however, no further explanation of the term is given. According to the A. V. the Pañcaviṃśa Brāhmaṇa and the Sūtras, the Vrātyas may be regarded as outcaste.

Fish was not included as an item of food and no fishing profession was known during the period of the R. V. The S. Yv., on the other hand, refers to a number of fishing tribes such as Dhaivara, Mainala, Kaivarta, Puñjistha etc. This suggests the extent of Aryandom in the East during the period of S. Yv. because unlike the rivers of the North-Western regions of India, where fish is rarely available, the rivers of the Eastern regions of India are abundant in fish still today.

From the foregoing discussion, it appears that the vedic civilisation during the Śukla Yajurvedic period spread further to the east and the geographical area referred to in the S. Yv. was akin to that mentioned in other Saṃhitās and Brāhmaṇas, differing only from what is referred to in the R. V. The geographical data of the S. Yv. refer to the territory in the middle of the Northern India, occupied by the neighbouring people of the Kurus and Pāñcālas.

REFERENCES

1. R.V. 2.41.16
2. R.V. VI.61, 2.8 VII 96.2
3. R.V. VIII.21.18
4. R.V. VI.61.12
5. P.B. XXV.10.1.S.B.1.4.1.14
6. 'Pañcanadyaḥ dṛsadvatī, śatadrū ścandrabhāge rāvatītyādikāḥ'—Uvaṭa on S. Yv. XXXIV.11
   'dṛsadva tyādyāḥ, pañca nadyaḥ sarasvatīmapiyanti gacchanti'—Mahidhara on S. Yv. XXXIV 11.
7. S. Y. XIX. 93-94
8. S. Yv. XXII.20
9. R.V. I. 32. 12 ; 34.8.35.8.71.7 ; 102. 2. IV. 28. 1. VII. 76. 1. etc.
10. T. S. IV. 3. 6. 1
11. S. Yv. XXXVIII. 26
12. The History & Culture of the Indian People, Vol. I, p. 244
13. R. V. X. 75. 5
14. R. V. VI. 45.31
15. S. Yv. XI. 3.3 (Kāṇva recension)
16. S. Yv. XXIII.18

17. S. Yv. XXX.5.22,T.S.III.4.1.1
18. 'Māgadham magadhadeśajam Kṣatriyāyāṃ Vaiśya puṃse jātaṃ vā—Mahī,
      dhara on S. Yv. XXX.5
19. Mahīdhara & Uvaṭa on S. Yv. III.61 ; Sāyana on R.V. 1.161.8
20. T.S. IV 5.4.2 ; K.S. XVII.13 ; M.S.II.9.5 ; S. Yv.XVI.27 ; A.B. VIII.11
21. A. V. V. 22.14
22. A. V. XV. 2. 1-4
23. S. Yv. XXX.8

CHAPTER II

THE CASTE-SYSTEM

The four castes—Brāhmaṇa, Rājanya, Vaiśya and Śūdra are mentioned only once in a passage of the Puruṣa-Sūkta of the R. V. (X. 90). Though all the four castes are not mentioned in other Maṇḍals of this Veda, yet the upper three castes—Brāhmaṇa, Kṣatriya and Vaiśya are clearly mentioned in the fourth Maṇḍala[1] and eighth Maṇḍala.[2] The caste-system was not rigid and no detailed account of this system is available in that Veda. During the Yajurvedic period which was contemporary to the Brahmanical period, the caste-system developed in various directions. Not only the four castes but also many sub-castes originated at this period. There are many reasons behind the caste-development and ramification. Guilds of workers tended to crystallize into castes, as occupation became more or less hereditary. As for example, carpenter (Takṣā), chariotwright (Rathakāra), potter (Kulāla), smith (Karmāra) etc. are instances in point. The peculiar family constitution which prescribes that a man should normally marry a woman of equal birth i.e. within the same caste, stood as contrary to the development of complications in the caste system at this period.

The names of four castes occur in the S.Yv. in connection with Purusamedha[3] (Human-sacrifice) where God is urged to create a Brahmin for propagating the knowledge of the Veda, a Kṣatriya for the safety of the kingdom, a Vaiśya for rearing cattle, a Śūdra for hard labour and service.

Many other variants are found as Brāhman, Kṣatra, Śūdrāryau[4] where 'arya' stands for Vaiśya. Again, in another passage,[5] Brāhmaṇa, Rājā, Viśya and Śūdra are mentioned. Rājā and Viśya as mentioned there, are equivalent to Kṣatriya and Vaiśya respectively and Agni is being praised for bestowing the same lustre

2

to the sacrifice as is given to these four castes. In one more passage,[6] the salutary speech is addressed to render benefit to four castes. Often only the three upper classes are mentioned as : Brāhman, Kṣatram and Viś (S.Yv. X 10-12,XXXVIII.14) where Brāhman is mentioned along with the eastern region, Gāyatrī metre, Rathantara Sāma, tṛvṛt stoma, and spring season ; Viś with western region, Jagati metre, Vairupa Sāme, Saptadaśa stoma and rainy season ; Kṣatra with southern region, Tṛṣtup metre, Vṛhat Sāma, fifteen stoma and summer season.

There are castes among gods, vegetable and animal world as well. Among gods, Indra, Varuṇa, Soma and Rudra are regarded as Kṣatriya[7]. The Soma creeper, so essential for sacrifice, belongs to Kṣatriya class and this kingly soma had to be purchased in exchange of a cow. Hence the cow is regarded as Kṣatriya.[8]

We get the reference to the origin of four castes in a verse of the S.Yv. ch. XXXI which is but a mere repetition of the famous Puruṣa Sūkta of the R.V. (R.V.X.90). The verse states that the Brāhmaṇa emanated from the mouth of the Primeval Being, the Kṣatriya from His arms, the Vaiśya from His thighs and the Śūdra from his feet.[9] Thus in God's creation, the Brāhmaṇa in body politic is the head in the body, a Kṣatriya is like arms, a Vaiśya is like thighs and a Śūdra is considered as feet. For the proper functioning of a human body, all the limbs like mouth, thighs, arms and feet are essential. The loss of any one of them makes the body defective. Similarly for the smooth progress of the society, four classes should be taken together in order to make up the organic whole of the social structure ; every varṇa or class is necessary for the proper functioning of the social body. Thus the Brāhmaṇas were the spiritual heads, well versed in Vedas, the Kṣatriyas or the military class were next to Brāhmaṇa in the hierarchy of castes. The Kings belonged to the Kṣatriya class. Their function was to protect the country and people and to enforce law and order in the state. The Vaiśyas were entrusted with the duty of manning agriculture, trade and commerce. They were the chief supports of the society because the growth of national income largely depended on their co-operation. Śūdras were labour class on whose toil and industry, all prosperity ultimately depended. A verse in the S.Yv.[10] narrates how Prajāpati after taking the shape of different metres, created the four castes. Commenting on this verse Devichānd advances a clear picture of the function of different castes.[11]

The Brāhmaṇa is the foremost, in the society like the head in the body. His importance lies in his ability to protect humanity through knowledge, religion and austerity. The Kṣatriya is a member of the ruling class ; his power lies in his ability to provide happiness to humanity through justice, humility and strength. The Vaiśya belongs to another class which amasses food-stuffs. His strength lies in becoming the lord of riches. The artisan, Śūdra, is a member of a fourth class whose strength lies in doing hard work.

The status of the Śūdra was not yet so degraded as it was during the Brahmanical period. While narrating the origin of castes, most of the Brāhmaṇa texts do not mention the Śūdra caste. As for example, the Śatapatha Brāhmaṇa[12] excludes the Śūdra from the list of the original castes and mentions only three upper castes such as—Brāhmaṇa, Kṣatriya and Vaiśya. Again, the Taittirīya Brāhmaṇa[13] states that the Śūdra originated from the demons or Asuras while the Brāhmaṇa sprang from the God. This sort of a humiliating attitude towards the Śūdra community was not maintained in the period of the S.Yv. Thus the S.Yv. utters in an equal tone with the R. V. that the Śūdra originated along with other three castes from the same body of Puruṣa, the lord of creation. The Śūdra is the feet—the organ of motion Just as the body becomes motionless without feet, similarly a society can not proceed even a step forward without the dignified existence of the Śūdra community whose hard labour tends to the steady progress of the body-politic. Many Brāhmaṇa texts amply testify to the deplorable condition of the Śūdras. They were debarred from milking cows for sacrificial purpose ; moreover, they were prohibited from entering the sacrificial campus. The prohibition of Śūdra's participation in the vedic sacrifice does not find a mention in the Vājasaneyī and Taittirīya collection of the Yajus ; it, however, occurs only in the supplementary portion of the Maitrāyanī and Kapisthala collections and also in Brahmanical works. For instance, a rite connected with the building of the fire altar (agnicayana), without which there can be no sacrifice, is explained as a means for removing Agni from the Śūdra caste.[14] The Śūdra is expressly prohibited from milking the cow for the milk required at the Agni-hotra sacrifice[15] because he is supposed to be born of untruth.[16] In the S.Yv. we get quite a different picture. In general, there was no hatred towards the Śūdras at this period. In many passages of the S. Yv.[17] we find Śūdras mentioned along with the Arya i.e. the Vaiśya caste.

'God has created the day and night for work and the Śūdra and Arya' (S. Yv. XIV. 30).

From this passage, we can infer how important a part the Śūdra played for the proper functioning of the social machinery. They formed a composite and complementary part of the Aryan society, just as the night is composite and complementary part of the day.

The united effort of the Vaiśya and Śūdra was acclaimed as an inevitable necessity for any progressive work in the society. Any feeling of hatred towards the Śūdra and Vaiśya communities was regarded as a crime, for which there could be no other expiation except God's mercy.[18] In the following verse, the Almighty is invoked for bestowing love and lustre to all the four castes without any discrimination.

'O God, grant love to our holy priests ; instil love in our ruling chiefs ; grant love to the Vaiśyas and Śūdras ; give out of Thy unbounded store of love unto me.'[19]

Matrimonial relationship between a Vaiśya and a Śūdra was not however welcomed.[20] In one of the supplementary formulae of the S. Yv. relating to various seasonal and domestic sacrifices, a desire is expressed for talking 'Kalyaṇīvāk' to the members of all the Varnas (castes).[21] It is contended that this refers to the equal right of all classes to the study of the Veda. But according to Uvata and Mahīdhara, this word is used in the sense of kind and courteous speech.[22] It implied that friendly words were to be used in talking to the members of all castes.

The Śūdras seem to have played a correspondingly important part in the political life of the period. It is striking that they found position in the exalted body of about a dozen 'high functionaries of the state'[23] called 'ratnins' (Jewel-holders). The Ratnins were so important that on the occasion of the Rājasūya sacrifice the king had to repair to their houses to perform ceremonies of offering jewels to various gods. The list of Ratnins shows that they included the representatives of all the Varnas[24]. Two of the ratnins, the rathakāra and the takṣan, mentioned in several texts[25], belonged to the artisan section of the Śūdra Varṇa. The Śūdras' participation in the political life of the period is further evident from the ritual of the game of dice, which is prescribed as a rite in the Rājasūya sacrifice and presented to us in two versions. In the earlier version which occurs in the Krishṇa Yajus texts, the Brāhmaṇa, the Rājanya, the Vaiśya and the Śūdra are described as participating in a game of dice for the ownership of a cow which is won finally by the King.[26] In the later version, which occurs in the Śukla Yajurveda texts, the Vaiśya and Śūdra are eleminated from the list of candidates competing for the cow, which is staked by the Kinsman (Swajāta) of the King and won for him by the officiating priest (adhvaryu).[27] The Śūdra was possibly connected with another ceremony of the Rājasūya sacrifice, in which the newly consecrated king was called on to ascend the four quarters of the sky, when 'Brahma' in the east, Kṣatra' in the south, 'Viś' in the west and 'Phala varcas' and 'Puṣṭam' in the north were asked to protect him.[28] Dr. Jayaswal says that 'Phala' is evidently a substitute for Śūdra.[29] This is, however, not accepted by Dr. Ghosal who takes the ceremony as symbolising the influence of three higher castes in the vedic policy.

According to a passage of both the schools of the Yajurveda[31], the King on the occasion of the Rājasūya-sacrifice used to pray to God for the expiation of the sin, if any committed against the 'arya' and the Śūdra. Relying on Pāṇini, the commentators Uvaṭa and Mahīdhara[32] take word 'arya' in the sense of Vaiśya. This shows that not even the King in the Yajurvedic period was free to oppress the members of the two lower varnas. The situation was entirely different in the Brahmanical period. For instance, in the Aitareya Brāhmaṇa[33] the Vaiśya appears as one to be oppressed and the Śūdra as one to be beaten at the pleasure of the King.

The Kṣatriya or Rājanya community stood as a definite member of the social body, distinct from the period, the subject people and the labourers. His origin from the arms of the creator indicated that his essential qualities were power and strength required for the protection of the kingdom. The essential qualities of powerful deities like Soma, Agni, Sūrya and Indra were suppo- sed to be Kṣatriyas.[34] On the occasion of the Rājasūya sacrifice, the officiating priest expresses his desire to install the King with qualities of different deities.

'O King, I shall install thee with brilliance like the moon, lustre like the fire, splendour of knowledge like the Sun and the strength of mind like the lightning. Be thou lord of Princes. Guard cons- tantly all acts conducive to knowledge and piety........'(S.Yv. X.17).

Manu Saṃhitā ch. VII, while discussing the origin and duties of the king repeats the same idea.

In the Yajurvedic period, the Kṣatriya class came in close contact with the Brāhmaṇa class in power and prestige—the two together being, as it were, the moral and essential factors of the society Both these Varnas are described as prosperity with long life, knowledge and offspring.[35] The Soma is directed to overflow the Brāhmaṇa and the Kṣatriya races with joy [36] The sin or death being discarded, the Brāhmaṇa and the Kṣatriya would attain to supremacy.[37] The Soma with its healing properties is asked to make the Brāhmaṇa and Kṣatriya vigorous and mighty.[38] The verse XXXVIII-14 of the S.Yv. longs for the proper growth of the two castes. The real strength and progress of the society depended on the concerted functioning of these two important Varnas. They together maintain the balance of power in the socio-political sphere. It is expressly stated that the country in which these two forces work together harmoniously, is considered to be an ideal[39] one. Again we find the prayer for the birth of Brāhmaṇa and

Kṣatriya, possessing their requisite qualifications :

'O God, let there be born in our country the Brāhmaṇa, illustrious for the knowledge of the Vedas ; let there be born the prince, heroic skilled archer piercing the foe with shafts, mighty warrior......,(S. Yv. XXII. 22).

The priestly class by virtue of their wisdom and knowledge attained supremacy over all castes, just as the head—the upper limb, being the seat of intelligence is regarded superior to other limbs of human organism. The aim of the priest was to obtain pre-eminence through sacred knowledge and power (brahma-varcas).[40] The Brāhmaṇa acted as the spiritual guide, the house-hold priest or chaplain and as the prime minister of the king. The royal line of which he held the position of a household priest attained victory and power.[41] With the strength of his spiritual power and lore vedas, the Brāhmaṇa priest superseded wicked persons in strength and might and thereby lifted his friends to a high position. (S.Yv. XI.82). The sun, which stands first and foremost at the centre of all heavenly bodies is regarded as the priest of gods.

The learned Brāhmaṇa who knows the true character of the Sun, their representative priest in the heaven, can control even the god through the power of supreme knowledge...(S.Yv.XXXI.20.21). These verses amply testify to the high and honourable status of the Brāhmaṇas among men, their counterpart in priesthood being the Aditya among gods.

The term brahma-hatyā in the sense of 'Killing of Brāhmaṇa' is referred to,[42] but there is no clear mention regarding the nature of punishment to be meted out to the person committing this henious crime. The Śatapatha Brāhmaṇa, the single Brāhmaṇa of the S.Yv., however, makes a categorical statement in this regard, 'Whosoever kills a human Brāhmaṇa is deemed guilty.'[43]

CASTES OTHER THAN THE FOUR CASTES :

Besides these four main castes, some lower castes and some castes of inferior types are mentioned in the Vājasaneyī Saṃhitā. The commentator Uvaṭa on S.Yv. I. 13 observes the Rākṣasas as impure castes while Mahīdhara treats the Takṣas (the craftsmen) of lower origin as belonging to impure castes.[44]

The Śatarudrīya hymn (S.Yv. XVI) and the chapter XXX of the S.Yv. mention multifarious professions viz. Takṣā (Craftsmen), Rathakāra (Chariotwright), Kulāla (Potter), Karmāra (Smith), Maṇikāra (Jeweller) etc. Every profession was meant for a particular caste in the period of the Yv. onwards. Many castes emerged during this period as a result of intermixture of castes of every conceivable description. Besides these castes connected with particular occupations, some outcastes and semi-Aryan tribes are also mentioned in the S.Yv. XVI & XXX as well as in the T.S. IV. 5.4.2. They are—the Niṣādas, the Baindas (wild tribesmen like Niṣādas), the Karivartas (fishermen), the Mārgāra (sons of huntsmen), the Kirātas, the Jambhakas (fish-eating tribe), the Paulkasas (sons born of Niṣāda fathers and Kṣatriya mothers), the Chaṇḍālas, the Mṛgayus (hunters), the Mainālas and Dhivaras (fishermen). The Paulkasa, according to Macdonell[45] is 'a despised race—may be a son of a Niṣāda or a Śūdra by a Kṣatriya woman.' The varieties of caste names having hereditary character and occupational stamp were quite unknown in the Ṛgveda. Thus, we find in the S.Yv. not only the four castes firmly established as the main divisions of Indian society but also many of the mixed castes.

A passage of the S.Yv. (XII.23) explicitly mentions the existence of five castes—Pañcajanaḥ.

Explaining the passage, Uvaṭa, Mahīdhara,[46] and other commentators[47] opine that the term pañcajana signifies—the four wellknown castes—Brāhmaṇa, Kṣatriya, Vaiśya & Śūdra along with a fifth one termed as Niṣāda. And these five castes are enjoined to worship the fire god. From this, it may be assumed that not only the upper three castes but even the lower castes like Śūdra and Niṣāda had access to the fire sacrifice. Mahīdhara and Devicānd,[48] however, find out some alternative meanings of the term—pañcajana. Again in another verse of the S.Yv. (XXVI.9) these five castes are alluded to and the sacrificial deity Agni is invoked as the benefector of these five castes (pañcajanyaḥ). While explaining this verse Mahīdhara and Uvaṭa[49] declare in clear and unambiguous language that these five castes had right to observe sacrificial ceremonies.

REFERENCES

1. R. V. IV. 50.8
2. R. V. VIII.35.16.17.18
3. S. Yv. XXX.5
4. S. Yv. XIV.28.30
5. S. Yv. XVIII.48
6. S. Yv. XXVI.2
7. '......deveṣu kṣatrajātyabhimanī somaḥ'—Mahīdhara on S.Yv. IV. 19
8. '......he gauḥ tvam......Kṣatriyāsi somakraya sādhanatvena'—Mahīdhara on S. Yv. IV. 19.
9. 'Brāhmaṇohasya mukhamāsīt vāhu rājanyaḥ kṛtaḥ
   Uru tadasya yadvaisyaḥ padbhyāṃ śūdrohajāyata'—R.V.X. 90.12, S.Yv. XXXI.11
10. S. Yv. XIV.9
11. The Yajurveda—Devichand, p. 207
12. S. B. 2-1-4-12
13. T. B. 1-2-6-7
14. S. B. VI. 4.4.9
15. T. B. III.2.3.9.10 ; Kap.S. XLVII.2. M.S.IV.13
16. Ap. Sr. S. VI.3.12......'asato va eṣa sambhūte yacchudraḥ'
17. S. Yv. XIV. 30 ; XX.17
18. S. Yv. XX.17......
19. S. Yv. XVIII.48......'rūcaṃ no dhehi Brāhmaṇeṣu rūcaṃ Vaiśyeṣu Śūdreṣu'
20. S. Yv. XXIII.30-31
21. S. Yv. XXVI.2.
22. Uvaṭa & Mahīdhara on S. Yv. XXVI.2
23. Jayaswal—Hindu Polity, II.20
24. Dr. U. N. Ghosal—Historiography & other essays, p. 253
25. M.S. II. 6.5.Ap. Sr.S. XVIII.10.17
26. M.S. IV. 6.Ap. Sr.S. XVIII.19.2-3
27. S. Yv. X.29., S.B. V. 4.4.19-3, Ka. Sr. S.XV.7.7.11-20
28. Phala & varcas in S. Yv. X.10-13, bala & varcas in T.S.I.8.13, puṣṭam & phalam in M.S. II.6.10, puṣṭam & varcas in K.S. XV.7
29. Jayaswal—Hindu Polity-II. 29.fn.2

3

30. Dr. U. N. Ghosal—Historiography & other essays, p. 264
31. S. Yv. XX.17., T.S.I. 8.3.1., K.S. XXXVIII.5
32. Panini, III.1.103, Uvata & Mahidhara on S. Yv. XX.17
33. A. B. VII.29
34. S. Yv. XXX.5, IV.19,X.4
35. S. Yv. V.27
36. S. Yv. VII.21......'Somaḥ pavate asmai kṣatrāya......'
37. S. Yv. XIV.24
38. S. Yv. XIX.5
39. S. Yv. XX.25......
40. S. Yv. XXII.22 ; XXVII.22
41. S. Yv. XI.81
42. S. Yv. XXXIX.3
43. S. B. 3.9.4.17...... 'Yo nu evemaṃ mānuṣam brāhmaṇaṃ hanti taṃ nveva paricakṣate, atha etaṃ devo hi Soma ghanti va enam'
44. '......aśuddhaḥ-rakṣapravṛtaya'......Uvaṭa ; 'a-śuddhaḥ—nicajātaya stakṣādayaḥ'......Mahīdhara.
45. Vedic Index, Vol. II, p. 27
46. Uvaṭa on S. Yv. XII.23......
     Mahīdhara on S. Yv. XII.23
47. Devichand—Yajurveda p. 180...
     Jaydev Vidyālaṇkara—Yajurveda Saṃhitā, Vol. 1.332
48. Mahīdhara......'Yadvā catvāro mahartvijo Yajāmanaśca......'
     Devichand......'Pañcajana—Brāhmaṇa, Kṣatriya, Vaiśya, Śūdra & Niṣāda. It may also mean the four Ṛtvijas—Hotā, Adhvaryu, Udgatā, Brahma and five Yajamana, sacrificer. It may also mean five pranas.
49. 'Viprādaya ścatvāro varṇa nisādaśceti pañcajanāsteṣāṃ Yajñādhikarat.'—Mahidhara.
     'Pañcajanyaḥ—pañcajanebhyo hitaḥ. Catvāro varṇa nisādaśca pañcamaḥ. pañcajanaḥ. Teṣāṃ hi yajñe adhikāroasti'—Uvaṭa.

CHAPTER III

MARRIAGE AND POSITION OF WOMEN

The institution of marriage was well-established in the Vedic age and was regarded as a social and religious duty and necessity.[1] In the Ṛgveda[2], the marriage was regarded as the unfolder of a new chapter of holy life which was to be led on the altar of truth and duty. This continued to be the view in the Yajurveda as well as in the Brāhmaṇa texts. Emphasising the necessity of marriage, the T.B. and the S.B.[3] declare in the same strain that a person who is unmarried is not worthy of performing sacrifice. Without the accompaniment of a wife, the household remains incomplete and therefore, he has no right to participate in sacraments.

Marriage system during the period of the S.Yv. was almost the same as that mentioned in R.V. After puberty, two young persons of the two different sexes generally were united in marriage. As regards the restriction of marriage, it was banned within the circle of agnates and cognates ; but the Brāhmaṇa[4] of this Veda, allows marriage within the third or fourth degree on either the paternal or maternal side. Marriage within the same caste was highly laudable.

But intercaste marriage was also prevalent. In such a marriage the male of a higher caste was allowed to marry a girl of a lower caste. Thus a Brahmin could marry women of any lower caste, a Kṣatriya could marry girls of next two lower castes—Vaiśya and Śūdra, and a Vaiśya male could marry a Śūdra female. The Smṛti texts designate this type of marriage i.e. marriage of a man of a higher caste with a woman of lower caste as 'anuloma' marriage. The three wives of a King—Mahiṣī,. Vāvātā and Parivṛktā belonged to the three castes—Kṣatriya, Vaiśya and Śūdra respectively. Besides lawful anuloma marriages, the S.Yv. refers to illicit unions of Śūdras and Aryas (Vaiśyas) both male and female, but such illegitimate wedlock was stated to be the cause of the degeneration of family life.

'A Śūdra lady who has got illicit connection with her master— the Vaiśya male, does not desire the progress of her family, just as a deer who destroys the barley field, cannot see his people thrive'[5].

The men of higher castes could have relationship with women of lower castes only for enjoyment and not for fulfilment of any higher purpose. The children who were born of the union between a man of a higher caste and a woman of a lower caste, were called 'anulomajas'.

These 'anulomajas' had inferior status in the society and certain names were assigned to them. They later formed certain sub-castes. As for example, the Niṣāda, born out of a Brāhmaṇa male and a Śūdra female was treated as the sub-caste or fifth-caste.

Pre-puberty or child-marriage was probably not sanctioned in the Vedic society. A perusal of the marriage hymn of the R.V. shows that the bride was fully mature and quite grown up at the time of marriage.[6] She is expressly described as blooming, with youth and pinning for a husband. A hope is expressed that the bride would forthwith take over the reins of the household from the parents-in-law.[7] This would have been possible only in the case of grown-up brides. The S. Yv. agreeing with the R. V. expresses the desire that a young maiden after the attainment of puberty should join her husband just as the flow of ghee would proceed to the sacrificial fire uninterruptedly.[8]

There was a general custom that the younger brothers and sisters should not enter into wedlock before their elders got married. The younger brother who entered into wedlock before his elder brother was termed 'Pari-vividāna' and till then un-married elder brother was termed 'Parivitta'. The husband of a younger sister whose elder sister remained unmarried was termed 'edidhisu-Pati'. The mention of these terms shows that the order of priority in the matrimonial alliance was broken at times but such precedence of younger in wedlock was censured as the said terms occur in the list of sinful persons who were victims at the puruṣamedha of the S. Yv.[9]

Polygamy undoubtedly prevailed at this period. A passage of the Taittirīya school of Kṛṣṇa Yajus states that polygamy was well-established in certain sections of the society.[10] Yājñavalkya, the seer of the S. Yv. had two wives. 'One man may have many wives'—declares the Śatapatha Brāhmaṇa.[11] The system of polygamy was fairly common in the rich and ruling sections of the society. Every king could legally marry four wives such as—Mahiṣī, Vāvātā, Parivṛktā and Pālāgalī. Though these four names are not directly mentioned in the S.Yv., we can infer their existence from the commentary of Uvaṭa and Mahīdhara on the S. Yv., ch XXIII. The first three wives were entrusted with the duties of anointing the sacrificial horse with butter, uttering the verse. The fore part, the middle and the hind part of the horse were anointed by Mahiṣī, Vāvātā and Parivṛktā respectively.[12] On the occasion of the most famous horse sacrifice, there occurred some interesting dialogues between Brahmā (the superintending priest) and Mahiṣī (the chief queen)[13] between Udgatā and Vāvātā (the most favourite queen)[14] between Hotṛ (the Ṛgvedic priest) and Parivṛktā (the barren and hence neglected queen)[15] and lastly between Kṣattā and Pālāgalī (daughter of some courtier).[16] Though polygamy was the rule of the day, polyandry was neither prevalent nor countenanced in the society. There is no passage in the S.Yv. containing any clear reference to such a custom. It should be borne in mind in this context that the polygamous form of marriage was not the general custom. It was practised by kings and nobles who held high position in the society. There are references to illicit love. Jāra—a person having illicit connection with a domestic woman, Upapati—a paramour who cohabits with another's wife, Smarakarī—a lustful woman bent on arousing passion—are mentioned in the Puruṣamedha chapter of the S.Yv. In the same chapter are mentioned women of immoral character viz. Atitvari (characterless courtesan) and Atiṣkadvari (procuress of abortion). The son of a maiden (Kumari putra) is also spoken of.[17] All these references, however, may be looked upon as exceptions that go to prove the high standard of ordinary sexual morality.

The primary duty of a woman or a wife was to look after the household affairs. She had to serve the husband and other elders of the family as also to perform duties like cooking, sewing, knitting etc. The onerous responsibility of rearing up children and such other jobs befitting her position devolved on her. There are numerous passages in the S.Yv.[18] referring to ladies' motherly affection towards their children.

The earth rears up the creatures living on it with all the existing means—air, water, fruits and flowers etc. Similarly the the mother rears up her children with all possible affectionate means. The mother is, therefore, compared to the mother earth.[19] Household duties and sacrifices had to be performed by the householder accompanied by his wife. It was believed that the duties rendered jointly would proceed for hundred years without any interruption just like the movement of a cart dragged by two bullocks with joint effort.[20] A cart drawn by a single ox is called 'Sthuri'. It cannot work well. Just as the cart drawn by two bullocks goes smoothly, so should the household affairs be performed though the joint deliberation of both the husband and the wife and not singly and independently by either.

A person after the successful completion of a life of celibacy (brahmacarya) was to be married to a girl of auspicious character. The entrants into the married life were advised to stick to truth and to honour the solemn promise taken at the time of marriage.[21] The following passage illustrates the way of life to be followed by the married couple :-

'O good tempered, lovely woman, retain carefully dearly loved and well nurtured child in the womb. O nice, dignified husband, this is thy domestic life ; made it resplendent with pleasure and instruction and guard it every possible way'. (S.Yv. VIII. 26).

In a home where the married couple fulfils honestly the duties of married life, a sinless and enterprising son is born. A child is generally born after attaining the age of ten months in the womb of its mother. A painless and easy delivery is prayed for in the following passage.

'Let the still unborn, the ten month old child move with

secundines. Just as the wind moves, as the ocean moves, uninterruptedly, so may this ten-month child come forth together with the secundines………'(S. Yv. VIII. 28).

A passage of the S. Yv. requests the praiseworthy husband and forbearing wife to perform the domestic Yajña (duties of married life) jointly.

'Just as mothers lovingly feed the children, so the wives are expected to discharge the highly pleasant and joyful duties of the domestic life'…(S. Yv. VIII. 32).

The sweet and holy relation between the husband and the wife is enjoined in many passages of the S. Yv.   The husband and the wife should always remain together and never be separated even in the battle field.   The grand ideal of cordial relationship between the married couple is described in the following verse.[22]

'O wives, be pure and sweet like water and full of happiness. Stick to us steadfastly for energy and valour even in highly memorable battle fields' (S. Yv. XI. 50).

The indissoluble relation between the two in a married couple is described in a excellent manner in the S. B. 12.8.26.

'Truth is male, faith is female, mind is husband, speech is wife, whereever the husband is there is the wife too'.[23] The above references are enough to prove that divorce was not in vogue during this period.

The widow-remarriage was not a common custom. There is not even a single reference to a widow who had been reunited with another person. That the widow could inherit the property of her departed husband, is evident in the following passage :-

'O woman, protect the valuable ancestral property of the husband' (S. Yv. XI. 62).[24]

REFERENCES

1.   Dr. A. S. Altekar—The position of women in Hindu Civilisation, p. 31
2.   R. V. X.85.24……'ṛtasya yonau Sukṛtasya lokhaḥ.
3.   T. B. II. 2.2.6, S. B. V.1.6.10…… 'ayajñiyo vā eṣa yohapatnīkaḥ'

4. S. B. 1.8.3.6......'samanādeva puruṣādatta cādyaśca jāyate idaṃ hi caturthe paruṣe tṛitīye saṃgacchāmaha iti'
5. S. Yv. XXIII.30.31
6. R. V. X. 85.22......'anyāmiccha prafavaryā samjāyāṃ patyā sṛja'.
7. R. V. X. 85.46   'Samrājñī śvaśure bhava samrājñī śvaśrvaṃ bhava.
8. S. Yv. XVII.97. ; Rv. IV.58.9. 'Kanyā iva vahutametavā U......
9. S. Yv. XXX.9
10. T. S. VI. 6.4.3...'Yodekasmin yupe dve rasane. tasmāt eko dve bhārye......'
11. S. B. 9.4.1.6...'Ekasya pumso vahubhyo jāyā bhavanti'
12. Uvaṭa on XXIII.8., Mahīdhara on XXIII.8
13. S. Yv. XXIII.24.25
14. S. Yv. XXIII.26.27
15. X. Yv. XXIII.28.29
16. S. Yv. XXIII 30.31
17. S. Yv. XXX.6
18. S. Yv. XI.51......'Gaśatoriva mātaraḥ'
    S. Yv. XI.57.XII 35.39.61
19. S. Yv. II.10......Pṛthivī mātopa...
20. S. Yv. II. 27
21. S. Yv. VIII.5
22. S. Yv. XI.50......'Apo hi sthā mayobhūva stā na ūrje dadhātana.   Mahe raṇāya cakṣase'
23. S. B. 12.8.26......'Vṛṣā satyam, yoṣā śradhhā, vṛṣa mano yeṣā vāk yatraiva patistatra jāyā.'
24. Devichand—Yajurveda, p. 161

CHAPTER IV

EDUCATION

The Śukla Yajurvedic age marked the progress of Indian culture, literature and science : thus the Indians had started their progress in the different departments of knowledge. People of this period had a keen desire to achieve progress in the realm of knowledge. Every householder of this age, therefore, naturally regarded the education of his children as a sacred duty. Great emphasis was laid on the proper development of body, mind and spiritual power. The educational system of this age was successful in forming character, developing integrated personality, promoting progress of the different branches of knowledge and achieving social efficiency and happiness.

SPIRITUAL REGENERATION OF THE STUDENT :

Education for higher three castes was compulsory. After the initiation ceremony, the students belonging to these castes went to the preceptor's house for all round training and efficiency in different branches of learning. Spiritually the teacher used to impregnate, as it were, the disciple in his womb and gave birth to a new man full of knowledge and illumination.[1] The Śatapatha Brāhmaṇa[2] gives a clear picture of this custom. The teacher who had accepted the student as his disciple, developed him physically, morally, intellectually and spiritually by his teaching and sure-footed guidance.

In the preceptor's sylvan academy, the student had to observe the vow of celibacy and there he attained 'dvijatva' or spiritual regeneration through initiation or consecration. The importance of consecration is borne out by the following verse of the S.Yv.[3]

'From consecration, wealth and treasure were attained, and from wealth and treasure was attained faith, the highest quality in

4

life and lastly the knowledge of Truth was attained from the observance of faith'. (S. Yv. XIX.30).

After the attainment of 'dvijatva' or second birth, the student had to recite the the famous Gāyatrī mantra or Sāvitrī verse regularly. This mantra of the R. V. finds place in different chapters of the S. Yv.[4] The repeated allusion to this verse drives home its great importance. Even to-day this deeply significant Sāvitrī verse is recited by a large section of Brahmins all over India. The verse reads thus :—

'O creator of the Universe, O holy and worthy of adoration, may we mediate on thy adorable self. May thou guide our understanding'.

The sacrificial paraphernalia played a prominent part in that age. Many sacrificial priests were necessary for various types of sacrifices. Among the Ṛtviks, the Hotṛ had to be well-versed in the Ṛgveda, the Udgātṛ in the Sāmaveda, the Adhvaryu in the Yajurveda and the Brahmā in all the three Vedas.

The study of Veda was, therefore, essential for the priests. The sphere of vedic study was, however, extended to the students belonging to other castes also. The knowledge of Veda among the students belonging to different social status has been highly eulogised in a verse of the S. Yv. (XXVI. 2).

COURSE OF STUDY :

Various subjects were included in the course of study prescribed for students of that period. The four Vedas—Ṛg, Sāman, Yajus and Atharva—were regarded as the chief subjects of instruction and therefore, these were learnt most reverentially. In the verse of the S.Yv. Agni, the god of power, is addressed to protect the teacher and the student with Ṛgveda, with Ṛgveda and Yajus, with Ṛg, Yajus and Sāman and with the four—Ṛg, Sāman, Yajus and Atharva.[5] Besides the knowledge of the four Vedas, the knowledge of yoga-śāstra, astronomy, geography, geology, hydrostatics, medicines and aviation were also included in the syllabus. The following verse of the S.Yv.[6] according to Devichand, lends support to this assertion.......

'O disciple, a student in the science of Government, sail in the ocean in steamers, fly in the air in aeroplanes. Know God, the creator, through vedas, control thy breath through yoga, through astronomy know the functions of day and night. Know all the vedas—Ṛg. Yajur, Sāma and Atharva by their constituent parts. Through astronomy, geography and geology, go thou to all the different countries of the world.'[7]

The vedic knowledge imparted to students is referred to as of various types ranging from one footed to eight footed.[8] By the term 'one footed' is meant the teaching of the significance of "Om" alone.

Two footed : that tells of the pleasure of this world and the next world.

Three footed : that preaches the delights of speech, and body.

Four footed : that tells of the four desiderata of human life, viz.—Dharma (religion), Artha (worldly prosperity), Kāma (desire) and Makṣa (salvation).

Eight footed : that dilates on four Āśramas and four Varṇas.

On the discussion of the Vājapeya sacrifice this Veda presents through some verse, a detailed account of metrical science and various courses of learning. The subdivisions of the seven principal metres as recorded in these verses are as follows :

Penta-syllabic	metre......meaning,	Daivī paṅkti	Chanda.
Six-Syllabic	„ ...... „	Daivī Triṣṭubh	„
Hepta-Syllabic	„ ...... „	Daivī Jagatī	„
Octo-Syllabic	„ ...... „	Yajuṣi Anuṣṭubh	„
Nine-Syllabic	„ ...... „	„ Bṛhatī	„
Deca-Syllabic	„ ...... „	„ Paṅkti	„
Hendeca-Syllabic	„ ...... „	Āsurī „	„
Do-deca-Syllabic	„ ...... „	Sāmni-Gāyatrī	„
Thirteen-Syllabic	„ ...... „	Āsurī Anuṣṭup	„
Fourteen	„ „ ...... „	Sāmni Uṣnik	„
Fifteen	„ „ ...... „	Āsurī Gāyatrī	„
Sixteen	„ „ ...... „	Sāmni Anuṣṭup	„

In these verses (S.Yv.IX.32-34), the desire is expressed that one may gather different types of knowledge with the help of these different metres. As for example, he would learn fifteen-fold objects by means of fifteen syllabic metre and so on. The fifteen fold objects of learning may be classified as follows :—four vedas, four upavedas (Āyurveda, Dharmaveda, Gāndharva-veda, Artha-veda), six aṅgas...Śikṣā (phonetics), Kalpa (ritualistic science), Vyākaraṇa (grammar), Nirukta (etymology), Chanda (Prosody), Jyotiṣa (astronomy) & beauty in action.

SCIENCE OF ARITHMATIC :

In the days of such hoary antiquity, the vedic aryans were well-versed in the science of Arithmatic. A verse of the S.Yv. (XVII.2) describes that millions and billions of bricks were used for the construction of the great fire altar. This verse preaches the science of Arithmatical digits which are named variously and can be multiplied ad infinitum. [9]

They are : $1 \times 10 = 10$ (daśa) ; $10 \times 10 = 100$ (Śata) ; $100 \times 10 = 1000$ (sahasram) ; $1000 \times 10 = 10,000$ (ayutam), $10,000 \times 10 =$ 100,000 (niyutam) ;

$100,000 \times 10 = 1000,000$ (prayutam) ;

$1000000 \times 10 = 10000,000$ (koti-crores) ; $1,0000000 \times 10 = 100000000$ (arbudam), $100000000 \times 10 = 1000000000$ (nyarbudam), $1000000000 \times 10 = 10000000000$ (kharva) ; $10000000000 \times 10 = 100000000000$ (nikharva), $100000000000 \times 10 = 1000000000000$ (mahāpadma), $1000000000000 \times 10 = 10000000000000$ (śaṅkha) ;

$10000000000000 \times 10 = 100000000000000$ (Samudra, ten times of hundred thousand crores) ; $100000000000000 \times 10 = 1000000000000000$ (madhyan ; ten times of samudra) ; $1000000000000000 \times 10 = 10000000000000000$ (anta) ; $10000000000000000 \times 10 = 100000000000000000$ (parārdha).

From the sight of the above arithmatical table, it can be imagined how progressive was the Arithmatical science and its culture in that remote past. No other country of the world can name the figure beyond crores, but here in the S. Yv. ; we find the Aryan Arithmaticians were able to enumerate the digits upto ten thousand times of hundred thousand crores by the figurative name 'Parārdha'. There are two other passages in the S. Yv. (XVIII. 24-25.) in which Arithmatical progression is well-illustrated. In the former, the odd digits of Arithmatic have been enumerated.[10]

$1+2=3$; $3+2=5$; $5+2=7$ and so on ; again,
$33-2=31$; $31-2=29$; $29-2=27$ etc.

This verse, thus, illustrates the addition and subtraction, of Arithmatic from which are deduced multiplication, division, square, cube, square root, cube root and reduction of fraction to a common denominator. This verse also refers to Arithmatical progression with a common difference of 2 (two).

In the later verse the even numbers are enumerated.[11] This verse refers to the Arithmatical progression with a common difference of 4 (four) viz. $4+4=8$; $8+4=12$; $12+4=16$; $16+4=20$ etc & $48-4=44$; $44-4=40$; $40-4=36$; $36-4=32$ etc.

SCIENCE OF GRAMMAR :

That a well developed science of grammer existed in those days of remote past is evident from one of the different interpretations given by Mahīdhara on verse No. 91 of the S. Yv. Ch. XVIII. The science of grammar is personified as 'Vṛsabha' and is said to be composed of four horns, three feet, two heads, seven hands and triple bonds.[12]

Four horns are : nāma (noun) ; ākhyāta (verb), upasarga (preposition) and nipāta (indeclinables).

Three feet are : past, present and future or 1st person, [2nd person & 3rd person.

Two heads are : nitya & kārya (effect)

Seven hands are : seven cases.

Triple bonds are : three numbers—singular, dual and plural. This verse has been cited by the later grammarian Patanjali in his immortal grammatical treatise—Mahābhāṣya.

DEBATES AND DISCOURSE :

Some intellectual discourses between Hotṛ priest and Brahman, the superintending priest, occur in the Aśvamedhika chapter of the S.Yv.[13] These discourses may be counted as the germ of Brahmodya' or debates of ancient times. This came to be termed as 'Vidyā-vicāra' or 'Vidyā-vivāda' in the later classical literature.

While engaged in the performance of the Aśvamedha sacrifice the Brahman puts the following questions to the Hotṛ priest :-

"Who moves singly and alone ? Who is brought forth to life again ? What is the remedy for cold ? What is the vast field for production ?:" (S.Yv.XXIII.9).

The answers from the Hotṛ priest are as follows :-

'The sun moves singly and alone. The moon is brought to life again. Fire is the remedy for cold. The earth is the vast field for production' (S.Yv. XXIII.10). The Hotṛ then puts a series of cross-questions to the Brahman in the following manner :—

'What is the primary thought ? What is the bird of mighty size ? What is the majestic beautiful thing ? What absorbs light ?' (S.Yv. XXIII.11). To these, the fitting reply comes from the Brahman :

'Rain is the primary thought. The Aśvamedha is like the mighty bird. The earth is the majestic beautiful object that nourishes us with corn. Night absorbs light' : (S.Yv. XXIII.12).

The above-mentioned discourses and debates are examples of the earliest intellectual expositions.

'The terms 'praśnin'—questioner and 'abhi-praśnin'-cross questioner occur in the Puruṣamedha chapter of the S.Yv.[14] and in the Taittirīya Brāhmaṇa.[15] The commentators—Sāyaṇa and Mahīdhara interpret these terms as some sort of persons of inquisitive nature. 'But there can be little doubt', holds Macdonell[16]—'that these terms must have had a legal reference of some sort perhaps indicating the plaintiff & defendant—the two opposite parties in a civil case who placed arguments and counter arguments against each other.

TEACHER-STUDENT RELATIONSHIP :

The teacher-student relationship was very cordial. The teacher aimed at the proper development of the student and the student tried to acquire all the good qualities of his teacher by his utmost devotion, diligence and sincerity. The teacher to be an ideal one, was expected to possess various fine qualities as indicated in the S.Yv. XI.37. He was asked to assume the role of a teacher since he was pure and attractive and possessed noble qualities. In the following passage, we see how the student addresses his teacher with a view to be endowed with knowledge.

'O learned teacher, thou art the guardian of my vow. Let thy vast knowledge be mine. Let my learning be subordinate to thee. Let my wisdom depend upon thee. O Lord of vows, let our vows of noble conduct be accompanied amicably. O Lord of initiation, teach me truth. O Lord of austerity, teach me to lead an austere life (S.Yv.V.40).'

This passage stresses the necessity of the students' humble nature, faithfulness, attitude of self-surrender and the mutual understanding between the student and the teacher ; these were the essential criteria for the proper acquisition of knowledge.

In another verse[17] of this Veda, we find how the teacher addresses the student advising him to keep all the organs of his body and mind pure, healthy and free from evil devices. The following is the English rendering of that beautiful verse.

'(O disciple) through various sermons, I enjoin upon thee, to purify thy voice, thy breath, thy eye, thy navel, thy generative organ and all thy dealings.'

TYPES OF BRAHMACĀRĪ :

Commenting on different passages of the S.Yv. Devichand tries to classify the Brahmacarins (celibates) into three classes. They are according to him :-

Āditya Brahmacārī—One who has observed 48 years of celibate life and gathered first class knowledge.

Brahmacārī of Rudra type—One who observes celibacy for 36 years and possesses good knowledge.

Brahmacārī of Vasu type—One who observes celibacy for 24 years and possesses ordinary knowledge.

Three sorts of Vedic speech—Bhāratī, Sarasvatī and Idā are ascribed to them respectively.[18]

The Veteran Vedic scholar Devichand, in his English rendering
of the verse 32 of S.Yv. ch. XXIX takes the word 'Karu' to mean
two persons who are competent in fine arts and handicrafts. Students were to learn these subjects from experts.

TWO TYPES OF TEACHER :

Teaching (both religious and secular) was normally imparted
to the student in the residential institutions by teachers who were
either celibate or married. Besides them, there was another kind
of teachers who used to move from place to place carrying the
torch of knowledge. These wandering teachers known as 'Carakas'
are referred to in the Puruṣamedha chapter of the S.Yv.[19]

The mobile schools run by these carakas were highly necessary
for mass education and they became an important landmark in
the social advancement.

Vedic people of that glorious age of the S.Yv. had a deep
aspiration for knowledge and wisdom. The following verses are
evidence in point.

'That wisdom which the sages and scholars long for, with
that wisdom, O God, with Thy truthful speech, make me wise
today.'[20]

'May the God Varuṇa, grant me wisdom. May Agni and
Prajāpati, Indra and Vāyu grant me wisdom. Similarly may the
creator of the Universe grant wisdom'.[21]

FEMALE EDUCATION :

Unlike the Upaniṣads, the Yajurveda and Brāhmaṇas are
lacking in depicting an explicit picture of female education. The
R.V. mentions several female seers like Ghosā, Viśvavārā, Romaśā,
Lopāmudrā, Apālā etc. In the Upaniṣada highly intellectual
and learned female savants like Gārgī, Maitreyee etc. are referred
to. Though there are no such references to female savants in the
S.Yv., it makes, however, the mention of the goddesses of learning
by such names as :—Idā, Bhāratī and Sarasvatī.[22]

From this it can be guessed that females were not debarred from intellecutual training. Before entering wedlock, the women-folk had to observe some period of celibate life. They were specially trained for looking after the domestic life nicely and for cooking well. At the same time, other sorts of educational training were imparted to them. For this task, female teachers were generally engaged. This fact is supported by a verse of the S.Yv.[23] which indicates that a female teacher was asked to impart to her pupil the art of cooking and the knowledge of different branches of learning. Another verse[24] of this Saṃhitā illustrates that a student girl was advised to lead a life of celibacy and gather knowledge from different learned ladies.

REFERENCES

1. S. Yv. II.33—'Ādhatta pitaro garbha Kumāraṃ puṣkarasrajam.'
2. S. B. II. 5-4-12.
3. S. Yv. XIX.3......'Vratena dikṣāmāpnoti dikṣāmāpnoti dakṣiṇām dakṣiṇā śraddhāmāpnoti śraddhayā satyamāpyate'.
4. S. Yv. XXII.9 ; III.35 ; XXX.2 ; XXXVI.3
5. ,Pahi nohagne ekayā pāhyuta dvitīyayā
   Pāhi girbhi stisṛbhirūrjāpate pāhi catarsṛhirvaso' S. Yv. XXVII.43
6. S. Yv. VI.21
7. Devichand—Yajurveda P. 88
8. S. Yv. VIII.30
9. Mahīdhara on S. Yv. XVII.2
10. Mahīdhara on S. Yv.XVIII.24......' ayujastomān juhoti'
11. Uvata on S. Yv. XVIII.25......'Yugmate' juhoti'.
12. Mahīdhara on S. Yv. XVII.91......'Catvāri śṛṅgāni nāmakhyātopasarga nipātaḥ trayaḥ pādāḥ prathama puruṣo madhyamapuruṣottama puruṣaḥ trayaḥ kālāḥ vā ; dve śirṣe kāryatāvyaṅgatve, sapta hastaḥ......vibhaktirūpāḥ tridhā vaddhaḥ, ekavacana dvivacana vahuvanair vaddhaḥ'
13. S. Yv. XXIII.9.12
14. S. Yv. XXX.10
15. T.B. III.4.6.1

16. Vedic Index Vol. I & II P. 28 & 42
17. S. Yv. VI.14
18. S. Yv. XXIX.8
19. S. Yv. XXX.18
20. S. Yv. XXXII.14
21. S. Yv. XXII.15
22. S. Yv. XXVII.19. ; XXI.19
23. S. Yv. XI.59
24. S. Yv. XI.61

CHAPTER V.

(a) MUSIC AND DANCE.

Music both vocal and instrumental was widely practised. The existence of several professional musicians and varieties of instrumental music can be inferred from the references to various types of musicians viz,—lute players (vīṇā-Vādam), flute-players (tuna-Vedhma), conch blowers (śaṅkha-dhvam), drummers (dundubhya), hand clappers (tālavam) etc. The respective function of these professional musicians are mentioned in the puruṣamedha chapter of the S.Yv.[2] Thus the lute-player was associated with great festivals, the flute-player was engaged for making a distant signal, the conch blower for calling neighbouring and distant people and the drammers for announcements and encouragement in public function or in military expedition. Among musical instruments there are references to vīṇā (lute or string instrument), Vāṇa or tuna (flute), drums (dundubhiḥ). These instruments are still used but some other insturments are not familar at present viz, āhananam[3] (some sort of musical instruments made or sticks) etc. were also in vogue. Both dundubhiḥ and āhananam were the favourite musical insturments to Lord Rudra. He is saluted and eulogised as the player of these instruments.

Dancing was practised publicly both by male and female artistes. The term Śailūṣa that occurs in the list of victims of Puruṣamedha, probably meant public dancer or actor. In the same list the suta or bard is said to be associated with dancing.[4]

It is interesting to note that—Vaṁśa-nartin'—pole-dancer or 'acrobat' is mentioned in the Puruṣamedha chapter.[5] This sort of bamboo-dancing is still prevalent among some tribal sects of India as also among circus parties.

(b) GAMES AND SPORTS

Horse racing and chariot-racing were regarded as the most popular items of amusement. The wide popularity and at the same time the importance of these sports are inferred from their connection with sacrificial rituals. Thus in the Vājapeya sacrifice, the chariot race used to play an essential part. In that ceremony, the sacrificer, i.e. the emperor designate, was generally made to win the race as a symbol to his victory at all stages of life. In the Rājasūya sacrifice also a formal race was regarded as a normal feature.

Dicing was another favourate pastime. We get frequent references to this game in the samhitā texts but no clear account of the method of this game is available.

As the dice were marked with eye-like dots, they were termed Akṣa (i.e. eye). The commentators, Uvaṭa and Mahīdhara say that the number of dice throw was five.[6] According to Uvaṭa, these throws were named as—Kṛta, Tretā, Dvāpara, Kali and Ramana. Mahīdhara differs in naming the throws. According to him the four dice were called Kṛta and the fifth was Kali. After throwing them in the dice-board, if all the dice took the same turn i.e. with dotted sides either upwards on downwards, then the throw was treated as a winning one i.e. Kali. The dice were normally made of Vibhidaka nuts ; but Mahīdhara opines that they were made of golden chowries. The common name for a gamblor or dice player was Kitava, but some other names equivalent to Kitava occur in the S.Yv. These were Ādinava-darśa, Kalpin, Adhi-Kalpin and Sabhā-sthānu. All of them are included in the Puruṣamedha chapter[7] where they are referred to as associated with different dice-indicating objects. Thus, Kitava is said to be assocsated with Akṣarāja, the Ādi-navadarśa with the Kṛta, the Kalpin with the Tretā, the Adhi-Kalpin with the Dvāpara and the Sabhā-sthānu with the Āskanda. The Akṣa-rāja, perhaps was equivalent to Akṣa-vāpa, the superintendent of dice-play, and his function was to supervise the dice house (the place of gambling) and to realise royal revenue therefrom. Just like that of the chariot-racing, the importance of the game of dice is indicated by its being an indispensible part of the famous Rājasūya sacrifice where the game was played by the consecrated king himself.

(c) DRESSES AND DECORATIONS

Vedic Aryans of this period generally put on three varieties of garments—an undergarment called Nīvi, an overgarment called Adhivāsa and a garment proper called vāsas. Mekhalā, a very soft type of cloth made of Śana and Muñjā grasses, was often used as undergarment or Nīvi[8] The garments worn by the people were made of wool, cotton or silk.

The clothes made of cotton were known as vāsas. In the sacrifice known as pitryajña, fathers are requested to accept the cotton clothes as their garments.[9] Urṇā refers to sheep's wool as sheep is called urṇāvatī (woolly) in a verse of the Ṛgveda. Woollen clothes were in common use. This is evident from the frequent reference to Urṇa and Urṇa-Sūtra (woollen thread) in the S.Yv.[10] and in other saṃhitās. Urṇāyu[11] meaning blankets were used for protecting oneself against cold. A very fashionable and costly garment known as peśas was generally worn by the well to do persons. These were nicely decorated and embroidered with golden thread. A certain section of the women folk engaged in such embroidery works was known as peśaskarī.[12] It is alluded to in some passages[13] that white and dark coloured pesas were used by Aśvins and other gods.

The skin of black antelope (Kṛṣṇājina) was sometimes used as garment. Agni is asked to wear this type of garment of variegated colour. Generally, this dress was meant for Brahmacārins.

Turban or Uṣṇīṣa was put on the head both by men and women. It is mentioned that Indra's wife put on Uṣṇīṣa on her head.[14]

Aryans of this period were very fond of using ornaments and various hair decorations Niṣka an ornament made of gold, was the most popular item of decoration. Mahīdhara mentions that such an ornament was to be placed on the neck of the sacrificer by the Adhvaryu priest at the beginning of the Horse-sacrifice.[15] The use of another kind of gold ornament called Dākṣāyana is also referred to.[16] Maṇi, a kind of jewel was used as an amulet. Setting the jewels and making ornaments were profession of a section of people known as Maṇikāra.[17]

In different passages of the S.Yv. various patterns of hair-dressing are alluded to. Various styles of hair dressing such as, Opaś, Kurīra and Kumba are referred to as being used occasionally by men and usually by women. Opaś[18] was such a kind of hair dressing in which the hair remained in circular formation with a knot at the end. Kurīra-type[19] of hair dressing was usually undertaken by the bride at the nuptial ceremony. Kurīra, according to Mahīdhara, means a kind of love-inducing hair-do used by women. The words kapardin, Kaparda (braid & wearing braids) refer to the vedic custom of wearing the hair in braids or plaits. Thus, in the Vājasaneyi Saṃhita,[20] the goddess Sinīvālī is described as wearing hair braids (Sukaparda).

This sort of hair braiding was popular amongst men even. So in a number of verses of the Śatarudrīya chapter, Lord Rudra is described as the wearer of braids or long locks.[21]

As regards footwear, there is, however, no mention of leather-shoes in the S.Yv. but from the reference to the professonal artisans on leather (Chrmamnas) found in the Puruṣamedha Ch. of the S.Yv.[22] it will not be worng to form an idea that the leather-made articles such as shoes etc. were in vogue. The use of wooden-footwear is also referred to. As these pādukās were made of wood, they were fitly called ‘drupada’.[23]

(d) FOOD AND DRINK.

The staple food of the Aryans during the period of the Yajur-veda was wheat and rice just like that of the Indians of modern age. It is to be noted that Rice (Vrīhi) which is not referred to in the R.V. is referred to in the S.Yv., A.V. and other Saṃhitās. It is also noteworthy that wheat (godhuma) which is another principal food of Indians, is not mentioned anywhere in the R.V. It is refered to for the first time in the S.Yv. and its relevant Brāhmaṇa. The Aryans of this period were acquainted with various kinds of pulses and cereals (Viz-Mudga), Māṣa and Masura and other articles of consumption such as Yava (barley), Tila (sesamum), Khalva (grams), priyaṅgava (millet), anu (beans) etc.[24] Paddy was of two types—śyāmāka, produced in the villages by farmers, and Nivāra, or wild rice, produced by ascetics in the forest. Not only rice but its different products, viz. lāja, dhāna, karambha, and saktu, were also used as items of food. Laja[25] is the roasted or parched rice. Dhāna[26] means both roasted rice and roasted barley. The powdered dhāna, again, fried in butter was called Karambha.[27] Śaspāni (malted rice) and Tokmāni (malted barley) are also mentioned as food.[28] The following passage of the S.Yv. gives a list of the edibles.

'Roasted grains, gruel, barley meal, grains of roasted rice, milk, and curd mingled milk, whey and honey—are the materials of soma sacrifice.[29]

From this passage, it appears that milk and its various products were also regarded as favourite items of food. Āmikṣā (Curdled milk) unknown to the Ṛgvedic people was a new discovery of this period. Ghee was used as food as well as a main item of sacrificial offering. Honey (madhu) was generally used for sweetening the food. Milk products were the most delicious items of food.

In a verse of the S.Yv. (III. 20) various milk-products such as kṣīra (condensed milk), Ājya (ghee) etc. are said to be obtained through the grace of the cow which is regarded as the source of these food products. In that verse, the term 'andha' is used to denote Kṣīra and Ājya and the term 'Maha' signinfes, according to Mahīdara, ten varieties of milk and milk products. These are : fresh milk (pratidhuk) boiled milk (Sṛtam), thickened surface of the milk (Sara), curd (Dadhi), butter milk (mastu), thickened curd (ātañcana), crudled milk (āmikṣā) and whey (vājina).[30] These delicious milk products were regarded as health promoting diets.

FRUITS :

Reference to various kinds of fruits indicate that the vedic people were fond of taking fruits. It is, however, not clear whether these fruits were grown by the householders or these were indigenous. Among fruits, the jujube fruits (Karkandhu) were in common use. The name of this fruit occurs in a number of verses of of the S.Yv.[31] The frequent reference to Badara (berry)[32] and Kuvalaya[33] (soft berry) indicate the extensive use of these fruits.

DRINKS :

Drinks mainly consisted of soma and Surā, milk, honey and water mixed with fruit juice. Soma was regarded as holy, hieratic and healthy drink. It was one of the most essential items of sacrifice, specially of Soma sacrifice. It was prepared from a rare creeper, grown in inaccessible mountains of northern or north-western regions of India. In the Yajurveda it is mentioned that the Soma-plants had been ceremonially purchased before the juice was pressed for sacrificial purpose. The drinking of soma was appreciated while that of Surā was denounced. Surā, an intexcating spirituous liquor was generally treated as an ordinary drink and was often condemned as its excessive use caused mental derangement and led men to degradation. The Sautrāmani sacrifice, described in the S.Yv. Ch XIX-XXI, was celebrated for an expiation or penace for indulgence in Surā. There is an allusion that Indra lost his vigour due to excessive drinking of Surā and thereafter he was healed by the divine physicians Aśvins and Sarasvatī with the help of Sautrāmani.[34] Soma being superior to Surā, was to be kept in a separate vessel and not to be mixed with Surā. Surā with its intoxicating effects makes one restless and crazy whereas Soma is famous for its calm and strength-infusing qualities.[35] Macdonell,[36] opines that the use of Surā must have been common, for, by the time of Vājasaneyi Saṃhitā, the occupation of a maker of Surā (Surākāra)[37] or distiller has become a profession.

The S. Yv. records the names of two other drinks, viz. 'Pariś-rut'[38] and Māsara[39]—which were distinct from Soma and Surā and were used as household beverage. Pariśrut was the immature form of surā or wine. Surā was prepared by fermenting grains and herbs fully, whereas pariśrut was made by the half-fermentation of these articles. The beverage 'māsara' was a mixture of rice and millet (Śyāmāka) with malted rice, malted barley and powdered grains of roasted rice.[40]

Kīlāla, a kind of sweet drink not mentioned in the R.V. was known in the S. Yv.[41] and other Saṁhitās.

The relative merits of different articles of food have been stated in the following verse of the S. Yv. XIX.23.

'Barley grains are the symbol of milk, ripe jujube fruits are the symbol of curd. The essence of corn is the symbol of soma. The juice of soma plants is like the mixture of milk and curd.'

Just as milk strengthens the body, so do the barley grains, just as curd produces semen, so does the jujube fruit produce strength, just as soma-juice makes the body vigorous, similarly does the mingled milk and so on.

MEAT :-

Meat was generally eaten on ceremonial occasions. After offering the animals like goat, sheep etc. to the sacrifices, their meat was taken as food. It is a controversial point whether the flesh of the cow was taken as food or not during this period.

COW-KILLING :-

Special reverence to the cow is attached in a number of mantras of the S. Yv. and the cow has been mentioned as such an animal which should not be killed.[42] The word 'aghnyā' is used as a synonymn of the cow. The intrinsic meaning of this synonymn of the cow itself proclaims that the cow should never be slaughtered. The same meaning is the basis of a stanza in the Mahābhārata which declares—The very name of the cow is 'aghnyā' that is the cow is not to be slaughtered. Then, who can slay them ? Those who kill a cow or a bull, commit the most heinous crime.[43]

6

The following Śukla-Yajurvedic passages proclaim in an unequivocal strain the prohibition of cow-slaughter :

'The cow is illustrious and inviolable, therefore do not slay her.'[44]

'The cow is inviolable and she yeilds ghee for the people, therefore donot slay the cow.'[45]—These are clear injunctions against cow killing.

The synonymn for cow as 'aghnyā' (not to be killed) has been repeatedly referred to in other Saṁhitās as well. A Ṛgvedic passage asserts that the inviolable cow should prosper.

'May this inviolable cow yield milk for both the Aśvins and may she prosper for our great good future.'[46]

The following mantra of the A.V. is also noteworthy in this respect.

'All the herbs that inviolable cows feed on and all those on which goats and sheep feed, may all of them increase your well-being.'[47] Dr. Griffith has translated the word 'aghnyā' as "whom none may slaughter". Moreover, the cow is described in the S. Yv. as the highly adorable creature.[48] This Veda enjoins that for every thing else there is a comparison, but the cow is beyond comparison.

'The effulgence of knowledge can be compared to the sun, the Heaven can be compared to the sea, the earth is very vast, yet Indra is vaster than her, but the cow cannot be compared to any thing.[49]

This passage indicates the loftiness of the cow at this period of S. Yv. It is, therefore, absurd to think that flesh of such a reverential animal could be taken as food.

Though there is a prescription in the Śatapatha Brāhmaṇa (3-4-1-2) regarding the killing of a great ox or goat in honour of a guest, the custom of cow-killing or beef eating was generally disfavoured in the S. Yv. That the cow killing was highly condemned is evident from a verse of the S.Yv.[50] where it is stated that the cow-killer must suffer the punishment in the way of begging alms. Even now-a-days in the Hindu society, a man has to go for expiation, if he commits a sin by killing a cow even unintentionally.

FISH-EATING :

It is sure that the Aryans belonging to this period were accustomed to fish-eating. We find reference to several professional fishermen such as—Dhaivara, Mainala, Kaivarta, Puñjistha etc. which amply prove this fact.

QUALITY OF FOOD :

Regarding the quality of food, the Śukla-Yajurvedic text states that it should not be injurious to health and should be free from poison or any sort of adulteration. In a verse,[51] Agni is praised for keeping watch so that the meal may not be poisonous or adulterated. In this verse, the words 'adma' and 'pitu' are used in the sense of food.[52]

(E) UTENSILS AND TOOLS

Utensils and tools of various types were used for domestic and sacrificial purpose. The importance of Soma-juice as a hieratic drink and sacrificial oblation has already been discussed. Two 'Adhiṣavanas' were used for pressing out the juice from the Soma-creeper. Adhiṣavanas usually consisted of two boards. By the pressure of these boards, soma was pressed. Pressing stones (grāvāṇa), various types of ladles such as—Juhu, Dhruva or Śruk, Soma-containers viz. Camasa, Vāyabya, Putabhṛt, Drona-Kalaśa (great wooden-jar, a reservoir of Soma) etc, are mentioned in the S. Yv. XVIII.21. The tool necessary for digging the earth for sacrificial purpose was known as 'Abhṛ'[53] which was made of bamboo or wood tipped with metal blade.

The cooking pot for sacrificial purpose called Ukhā was usually made of clay.[54] The cooking-pot for domestic use was known as Sthāli.[55] Surādhānī (the pitcher for containing surā or liquor), Karotara (a fitter or sieve necessary for purifying the surā or liquor)—are mentioned. A large earthen pot named 'Mahāvīra' is also referred to.[56] This pot was usually placed on fire at the initial Soma ceremony called pravargya. In that ritualistic era of the S. Yv. 'Yupa'[57] played an important part. It was a post to which sacrificial victims were tied. Kumbhī (wooden vessel), Āsandī (wooden chair) etc. are mentioned in the S. Yv. Ch. XIX.16. Āsandī was indispensible in the Rājasūya sacrifices for making a throne-like seat for the consecrated king. Rasanā i.e. cord or rope was necessary for fastening the sacrificial horses and other animals. In the Aśvamedha sacrifice, needles (Sūci) were used. According to the commentator Mahīdhara, these needles numbering 101 were made of copper, silver and gold and were used by the queens for piercing the skin of the horse.

Although certain utensils and tools viz. Ulukhala musala, Śūrpa, Kapāla etc. are not mentioned in this saṃhitā explicitely, but their application for different purposes can be assumed from the commentaries of Uvaṭa and Mahīdhara[58] on some verses of this Saṃhitā. For the preparation of sacrificial cakes (purodāśa) rice was grinded by the mortar and pestles (ulukhala-musala).

The grains being grinded into small particles were to be well winnowed by a flat basket called Śūrpa. The ulukhala-musalas though made of wood were as hard as stone. The Śūrpas were designated as 'Varṣa-Vṛddham' as these were made of bamboo-strings—for the growth of which rainfall was necessary. Kapālas were used for baking the sacrificial cakes.

(F) MEDICINE AND DISEASES

In several verses of the Vājasaneyi Saṃhitā, the term 'Bhiṣak' is used in the sense of physician.[59] The inclusion of a physician in the list of other professional persons in the Puruṣamedha chapter[60] shows that the practice of medicine was an ancient and well established profession. The physicians of this period were endowed with scientific knowledge of medicines and the treatment depended on proper diagnosis of diseases. In a passage in the S. Yv.[61] the physician is thus invoked :—

'O physician, the dispeller of ailments, chief amongst the learned, the teacher of the first class science of medicine, the remover of diseases by diagnosing them, the banisher of diseases deadly like serpents with efficacious medicines, preach unto us the law of health.'

The twin Aśvins were the physicians of deities. Goddess

Sarasvatī joined them as a lady doctor. Once Indra lost his vigour as he drank adulterated soma. Aśvins having mastery over Āyurveda and Sarasvatī having proficiency in the vedic lore, stood to his aid as his physicians and cured him.[62]

In this period Aryans were acquainted with the technique of curing the diseases with the help of natural elements like water, air, heat and earth. The healing power of water is repeatedly mentioned. In water lies the healing medicine, proclaims a verse of the S. Yv.[63] In another verse[64] water is described as the cause of digestion, healer of consumption and other diseases. Fire or heat in the belly digests the food and keeps one's body fit.

Soma was regarded as the king of all medicinal plants and waters. This is indicated by the following line :-

'May the Soma, produced on earth, or grown in water be highly efficacious for us' (S. Yv. IX.23)

A verse[65] directs the woman to use medicinal plants laden with bloom and godly fruit so that their conception experienced at the time of menstruation may stay in the womb in its proper place. Water and medicinal herbs are often described as good friends.[66] To them, special healing power was ascribed.

The science of texicology was well known. With a view that the food might not be poisonous or adulterated proper attention was paid to ascertain that the food was wholesome. In a verse, Agni is urged to keep a watch in this regard.[67]

EMBRYOLOGY

Observations on the growth of the foetus in the womb are also met with in a verse of the S. Yv.[68] It says that the foetus becoming fully developed in the tenth month, moves with the secundines (Jarāyu). In a poetic style this verse observes :—

'Just as the wind moves, as the ocean moves uninterruptedly so may this ten month child (foetus) come forth together with the secundines'.

ANATOMY :

That the Vedic Indians of this period possessed a sound knowledge of anatomy is proved beyond doubt from the detailed account of different organs of the sacrificial horse displayed in the XXVth Ch. of the S. Yv. in connection with the Horse-sacrifice. Names of different external limbs and internal organism are mentioned therein including the liver, omentum, spleen, pancreas, kidneys and the like.[69] Again the anatomical knowledge of the Aryans of that period can be well proved by illustrating the enumerations of different parts of the body that occur in the XXXIXth Chapter of the S. Yv.[70] They include the hair (lomāni), skin (tvac), flesh (māmsa) bone (asthi), marrow (majjā) liver (yakṛt), lungs (kloman), kidneys (matasne) gall (pitta), entrails (antrāni), spleen (plīhān) navel (nābhi), belly (udara) rectum (vaniṣṭhu), womb (yoni), penis (plāśi & śepa), face (mukha), head (śiras), tongue (jihvā), mouth (āsan), rump (pāyu), leech (vāla)—etc. The description of bones, specially that of the thirteen ribs of the right side of the chest and thirteen of the left side[71] points out their accurate knowledge in the branch of Osteology.

DISEASES :

Vājasaneyi Saṃhitā enumerates quite a large list of diseases.[72] A few of them may be mentioned such as—yakṣmā (tuberculosis), 'arśa' (piles), 'pākāru' (ulcer of the stomach), 'kilāsa' (white leprosy)[73] 'dūṣīkā' (disease of the eyes)[74], 'viṣucikā' (violent diarrhoea or cholera).[75]

In the R. V. and A. V. 'Yakṣmā' is described as such an illness that renders the body of the patient emaciated. In the S. Yv. a hundred kinds of yakṣmā are referred to. For the treatment of this disease, medicines are prepared from certain herbs and plants. In the śatarudrīya hymn, Lord Rudra, the powerful one is invoked for healing the creatures suffering from yakṣmā.

The following passage describes how a patient suffering from tuberculosis, may be cured.

'O physicians, try to extirpate tuberculosis through well regulated nourishing diet, through control of breath and through medicines, which fully relieve the patient of its pain.[76]

By the disease 'Kilāsa', white leprosy in meant in the A. V.

and the S. Yv. It resulted in the appearance of grey (palita) and white spot (śukla śveta) all over the skin. The disease 'viṣucikā, originated from non-assimilation of food in the stomach and for its cure soma or Surā juice was prescribed.

The great utility of certain medicinal herbs is brought out in the following passages of the S. Yv. and the physicians are asked to know herbs for curing ailment of the people.

'O men go to place, where there are herbs, just as kings go to the battle fields.[77]

'When I, obtaining them beforehand, hold these medicinal herbs within my hands, the root of life-killing diseases like tuberculosis disappears.[78]

'May I know for the health of the patient, all medicines effacacious in nature, full of juice, rich in nourishments and possessing strength-giving power. May they all give me ease'.[79]

'O medicines, when ye creep into a patient part by part, joint by joint, ye destroy his pulmonary disease, as a strong man destroys the delicate bodily parts of the foe.[80]

From the above discussion, it appears that the Aryans of this period were conversant with different types of diseases and different branches of medical science. The science of healing or Āyurveda, according to Devichand, was regarded as a kind of holy sacrifice and the physicians, therefore, engaged themselves in learning this subject properly.

REFERENCES

1. S. Yv. XVI. 35......'Namo dundubhyāya'.
2. S. Yv. XXX. 19. 20
3. Mahīdhara on S. Yv. XVI.35......'āhananaṃ vādyasādhanam daṇḍādi'
4. S. Yv. XXX.6......'nṛttāya sūtam'
5. S. Yv. XXX.21
6. S. Yv. X.28...'Pañcakṣān sauvarṇakapardān'—Mahīdhara
7. S. Yv. XXX.18

8. 'he mekhale tvaṃ somasya nivīrasi...śanamuñjamayī mekhalā' Mahīdhara on S. Yv. IV.10

9. S. Yv. II. 32. 'Pitara vāsa ādhatta' (he pitara. Yusmabhyametad vāsaḥ sūtrameva paridhānamastu'—Mahīdhasa)

10. S. Yv. IV.10. XIX.80

11. S. Yv. XIII.50 ('manusyāḥ śītavivṛtyai kamvalam dadhate—Mahīdhara).

12. S. Yv. XXX.9

13. S. Yv. XIX.82-89 ; XX.40

14. '...Indrānyā uṣṇiṣaḥ'—S. Yv. XXXVIII.3

15. Mahidhara. on S. Yv. XXII.1

16. ...'dākṣāyanaṃ hiraṇyam...dākṣāyanaṃ iti alamkāraviśeṣaḥ'—Uvaṭa on S. Yv. XXXIV.51

17. S. Yv. XXX.7

18. S. Yv. XI.50

19. S. Yv. XI.56

20. S. Yv. XI.56

21. S. Yv. XVI.10.29.43.48.59

22. S. Yv. XXX.15

23. S. Yv. XX.20 (drumamaya pada drupada pādukā ucyante)—Uvata

24. 'Vrīhayaśca me yavāśca me māṣāśca me tilāśca me mudgāśca me khalvāśca me priyangavaśca me anavaśca me śyāmākaśca me nivārāśca me godhumāśca me masurāśca me yajñena kalpantām'...(S. Yv. XVIII.12)

25. S. Yv. XIX.13.81 ; XXI 42. etc.

26. S. Yv. XIX.22

27. S. Yv. XIX.22

28. S. Yv. XXI.42 ; XIX.13

29. S. Yv. XIX.21......'Dhānāḥ karambhaḥ saktavaḥ parivāpaḥ payodadhi, somasya rūpaṃ haviṣa āmikṣā vājinaṃ madhu.'

30. 'He gāvaḥ ..yasmād-samvandhi andhaḥ kṣīrājyādirūpamannamahaṃ bhakṣīya seveya. Yadvā mahaḥ śabdena daśa. Tāni yathā...gaurvai pratidhuk, tasyai śṛtam, tasyai sarastasyai dadhi, tasyai mastu, tasya ātañcanaṃ, tasyai navanitaṃ tasyai ghraṃ, tasya āmikṣā, tasyai vājinamiti śrutyuktāni'— Mahīdhara on S. Yv. III.20

31. S. Yv. XIX.23.91 ; XXI.32 ; XXIV.2

32. S. Yv. XIX.20.90 ; XXI.30

33. S. Yv. XIX.22.89 ; XXI.29

34. Uvaṭa and Mahīdhara on the S. Yv. XIX.12

35. Uvaṭa on S. Yv. XIX.7

36. A History of Sanskrit Lit., p. 139

37. S. Yv. XXX.11......'Kīlālaya Surākāram'

38. S. Yv. XIX.15 ; XX.59 ; XXI.29

39. S. Yv. XIX.14.82 ; XX.68

40. 'Vrīhiśyāmākaudanācāmayoḥ Śaṣpatokamlājanagnacūrnaiḥ saṃsarge māsa-
ram'—Mahīdhara on S. Yv. XIX.14
41. S. Yv. XXX.11
42. S. Yv. VI.22......'Yadāhuraghnyā ā iti'.
43. 'Aghnyā iti gavāṃ nāma ka etā hantumarhati.
Mahaccakārākuśalam vṛṣam gā vā ā labhet tu yaḥ' —Mahābhārata-Śānti-
parvan. 26.2.47
44. S. Yv. XIII.42
45. S. Yv. XIII.49
46. R. V. 1. 164. 27
47. A. V. 8. 7. 25
48. S. Yv. 20...('he gāvaḥ ..yūyaṃ mahastha pujyasthā stha'.—Mahīdhara)
49. 'Brahma sūryasamaṃ jyotirdyauḥ samudrasamaṃ saraḥ.
Indra pṛthivyai varṣīyān gostu mātrā na vidyate' (S. Yv. XXIII.48)
50. 'Mṛtyave go-vyacchamantakāya go-ghātam kṣudhe
Yó gāṃ vikṛntantaṃ bhikṣamāna upatiṣṭhati' (S. Yv. XXX.18)—'a cow
killer for gallows ; one who cuts a cow will suffer the pangs of hunger and
will be bound to resort to begging to other'—Devichand on Yajurveda.
51. 'Pāhi duradmanya aviṣam naḥ pitu kṛṇu'. (S. Yv. II.20)
52. 'Adma iti anna nāma. Pāhi durbhojanāt...Piturityannanāma.
Viṣarahitamannamasmākam kuru'.—Uvaṭa on S. Yv. II. 20
53. S. Yv. XI. 10
54. S. Yv. XI. 59...Sā mahīmukhāṃ mṛnmayīm
55. S. Yv. XIX.27
56. S. Yv. XIX.14
57. S. Yv. XIX.17
58. 'He ulukhala tvaṃ yadyapi vānaspatyaḥ dārūmayastathāpi dṛḍatvāt
adrirasi paṣāṇohasi'. Mahīdhara on 3, Yv. 1.14
59. S. Yv. XVI.5.45 ; XIX.12.88 ; XXX.10
60. S. Yv. XXX.10...'Pavitrāya bhiṣajam'.
61. S. Yv. XVI.5
62. S. Yv. XIX.12 (...'tatrāśvinau sarasvatī ca bhiṣajaḥ sautrāmaṇi tvauṣa-
dham.'—Mahīdhara).
63. S. Yv. IX.6...Apsvantaramṛtam apsu bheṣajam.
64. S. Yv. IV.12
65. S. Yv. XI.48
66. S. Yv. VI.22.... 'Sumitriyā āpaḥ oṣadhayaḥ santu'
67. S. Yv. II.20
68. S. Yv. VIII.28...'ejatu daśamāsya garbho jarāyuṇā saha
yathāyaṃ vāyurejati yathāsamudra ejati.
Ebāyaṃ daśamāsyo asrajjarāyuṇā saha'

7

69. S. Yv. XXV.1-9
70. S. Yv. XXV.4-5
71. S. Yv. XXXIX.8-10
72. S. Yv. XIX.97...'Nāśayitrī valāsasyarśasa upacitamasi.
            Atha śatasya yakṣmānām pākārohasi nāśam'
73. S. Yv. XXX.21...('Kilāsam sidmarogavantam'—Mahīdhara)
74. S. Yv. XXV.9
75. S. Yv. XIX.10
76. 'Sākam yakṣmā pra pata cāṣena kikidīvina
     Sākam vātasya dhrājyā sākam naśya nihākayā' (S. Yv. XII.87)
77. 'Yatrauṣadhīḥ samagmata rājānaḥ samitāviva'...(S. Yv. XII.80)
78. S. Yv. XII.85
79. S. Yv. XII.81
80. S. Yv. XII.86

CHAPTER VI

(A) AGRICULTURE AND CATTLE-REARING

The term Kṛṣi, used in the sense of Agriculture or cultivation of land, is derived from the root Kṛṣ—meaning to draw or make furrow or to plough.   Its occurrence is frequent in the S. Yv.

‘Kṛṣantu’ (XII.69) ; Kṛṣiḥ (XIV.19 ; XVIII.9)

‘Kṛṣiḥ (IV.10) ; Kṛṣṭāpacyāḥ (XVIII.14).

India was an agricultural country from the very ancient period of the R.V. and the Vedic Aryans took to agriculture as their main profession.   They devised various ways and means to improve their methods of cultivation.   Ideal process of cultivation viz. irrigation or watering to the soil, application of fertilizers and ploughs etc. were known to them.   In the Yajurvedic period also, we find the same picture.

Great importance was attached to agriculture as it was regarded as the best source of material prosperity.   A verse of the S. Yv. declares that ploughing brings prosperity[1] and wealth in the form of cattle and conveyances.   A verse of the Akṣa-Sūkta of the R.V. urges the people to cultivate their lands in order to achieve wealth and hapiness.[2] ‘Agriculture is verily food’—says the S. B.[3]

In the Rājasūya sacrifice, described in the S. Yv., it is seen that the priest reminds the consecrated king of his duty to pay much attention to the development of agriculture.

“The intelligent play the ploughs, the wise through desire of bliss from gods, carry the yokes in different directions”[4]

“O people, use various implements for cultivating the earth. Employ ploughs and yokes.   Sow seed in a well-prepared field. With the knowledge of the science of agriculture, be quick to sustain and nourish yourselves.   May we get the corn fully grown and ripened in the near fields.”[5]

“Happily let the ploughshares turn-up the plough land, happily

go the ploughers with oxen. Śunā and Sīrā pleased with our oblation, cause ye our plants to bear abundant fruitage."[6]

One of the above-mentioned verses (S. Yv. XII.68) outlines
the different processes of cultivation as—yoking the plough, sowing
seed in the line of furrow, mow the ripe crop with sickle. The same
processes are mentioned also in the S.B.[7] In the Akṣa-Sūkta of
R.V. people are enjoined to take to agriculture which is source of
all material prosperity ; they are asked to shun gambling which is
the cause of all distress.

Aryans as ideal agriculturists were aware of the fact that the
chief necessities for good cultivation were air, sunshine, fertile
soil and water. The first two factors are always abundant but the
scarcity of the last factor i.e. water may arise for the time being.
Much attention was paid, therefore, towards watering or irrigation of lands. Timely rainfall in sufficient quantity was always
prayed for bumper crop.[8] There were artificial reservoirs also for
watering the land that did not get sufficient water from rainfall.
For this purpose, a section of people called 'Khanitṛ'[9] (a digger
or delver) was engaged. They used to dig the earth with spade
(Abhriḥ).[10] The essentiality of air, sunshine and water for good
cultivation has been evinced in a passage of the S. Yv.[11] Where
Vāyu (the god of air) and Āditya (the Sun god), designated as
Śunāsīrau are invoked for making the land highly planted being
associated with water (haviṣā).

For tillage, plough which was known as lāṅgala[12] or Sīra
was in common use. It was drawn by oxen and was 'lanceplanted'
(pavīravat) and iron-edged (Suphalā).

There is mention of two categories of land, fertile (Urvara)[13]
and non-fertile or barren (iriṇa)[14] of which the first type of land
was usually selected for productive cultivation. Cow-dung was
used as manure for increasing fertility of the soil.

AGRICULTURAL PRODUCTION :

The special name for the ploughman or cultivator of the soil
was Kīnāśa'. The rich agriculturist or one whose field is full of
barley was known as 'Yavamantam'.[15] The agricultural products

commonly in use, were as follows :[16]

Vrīhi (rice), Tila (seasamum), Priyaṅgu (millet), Yava (barley), Mudga (Kidney-beans, Anuḥ (panicum milliaceum), Māsa (beans), Khalva (Vetches), Śyāmāka (panicum furmenta-ceum), Nivāra (wild rice), Godhūma (wheat) Maṣūra (lentil) etc.

In the S. Yv. Horticultural and Agricultural products have been described under four heads viz[17] :-

i) Vīrūdha ii) Oṣadhi iii) Kṛṣṭapacyā iv) Akṛṣṭapacyā,

CATTLE REARING :

Next to agriculture, cattle rearing was regarded as an impor-tant source of income. The wealth of the people was known in terms of cattle, heroes and good sons. The chief cattle ware cows and bullocks. The importance of these cattle in the agriculture-based Aryan society is easily conceivable. Naturally, cows and oxen were regarded as the most valued possession. Oxen were generally employed in cultivation in the process of drawing the ploughs and the cows were milked thrice a day—in the early morning (prātardoha), in the fore-noon (saṃgava) and in the evening (sāyaṃdoha).[18] The milk of the cow was either drunk fresh or made into butter, curds or mixed with Soma. Milk and its products were necessary for sacrificial offering and specially for daily Agnihotra sacrifice, the milk of the cow was essential. This most useful animal was, therefore, reared by almost all the Vedic Aryans with care and respect. The Soma creeper, the juice of which was primarily needed for the Soma sacrifice, had to be purchased in exchange of a cow only. Hence the cow was treated as Kṣatriyā.[19] Sometimes the cow was offered as the sacrificial fee (dākṣiṇā) to the priests. This cattle due to its immense useful-ness and sacrificial attachment came to be regarded as the most sacred animal. Special reverence was ascribed to it in a number of verses of the S. Yv.

As regards the sanctity of the cow, it will suffice to cite the reference from the S. Yv. wherein the cow has been described as an animal that should not be killed[21] and a cow-killer is said to be punishable with death.[22] The Śukla-Yajurvedic seers have expressed their gratitude to this beneficial animal by deifying it as Aditi—the mother goddess. Cows were regarded as the treasure and wealth (revati) hence they were chosen out for meeting sacrificial expenses. A verse of the S. Yv. in connection with the Sautrāmaṇi sacrifice, prescribed the employment of a hundred and thousand cows for meeting the expenses of that sacrifice. The most adorable cow is described in a verse as the source of various healthy food-products, strength and treasure.[24] She is again eulogised as being attached to the sacrifice by producing sacrificial oblation like milk etc. and the cow-possessor (gopati) is told to be nourished with milk and milk products.[25]

The importance ascribed to the possession of cattle is shown in many passages. Lord Rudra is urged to protect the cattle from diseases.[26] The house that possessed a good number of cattle in good condition, was regarded as the most resourceful one.[27] The cattle was the medium of barter.

The pasture-land for the cow was known as goṣṭha.[28]

The following passage of the S. Yv. (Ch. XVIII.26) shows how cow and bulls of different ages were marked with different terms.

"May my eighteen months bull and cow (tryavī), my two years bull & cow (dityavāt and dityauhī), may thirty months bull and cow (pañcābi & pañcābī), may three years bull and cow (trivatsa and trivatsā), may four years bull and cow (turyavat & turyauhī) prosper through the science (sacrifice) of rearing cattle".

"The milch cow (dhenu) is contrasted with the bull (anadvān). Cow in various stages of growth and motherhood are narrated in the S. Yv. (Ch. XVIII.27).

Animals in general were classified in two classes—domestic (grāmya) and wild beasts (āraṇya) of which the domestic animals such as cows, goats, sheep, horses etc. were reared by the householders.

Horses come next in value to cows. To people so frequently engaged in battle, the horse was of essential value in drawing the war-chariot, it was also indispensable in the chariot-race which was favourable amusement of vedic Indians. The horse sacrifice, moreover, was regarded as the most important and efficacious of animal sacrifices. The term 'Aśvapati' (possessor of horses) is used as an epithet of Lord Rudra.[29]

(B) OCCUPATIONS AND INDUSTRIES

The principal occupations and professions and the various arts and crafts were distributed among and assigned to the various groups of people in accordance with the scheme of class system which had by now struck root in the vedic society. For example, the Brāhmaṇas or the priestly class dedicated themselves to the highly specialised occupations or professions of officiating at the sacrifices and preserving the sacred hymnology of the Aryans by conducting Vedic classes. The Kṣatriya or Rājanya class had taken to the fighting profession and was entrusted with the administration of the kingdom, maintenance of law and order and protection of the people. Agricultural and pastoral pursuits were mainly the professions of the Vaiśya class. The Śūdra community was mainly engaged in the service of the three upper communities. In the period of the S. Yv. many new occupations unheard in the Ṛgvedic period came into existence to provide the mixed castes with profession.

The XXXth chapter of the S. Yv. dealing with the enumeration of the victims at the puruṣamedha sacrifice gives a comprehensive and exhaustive list of professions, occupations, arts, crafts and industries of this period. There is the mention of fiftyeight varieties of professions of which six were earmarked for women.

These are as follows :

Minstrel (magadha), actor (śailuṣa), herald or panegyrist (sūta), counsellor (sabhākāra), chariotwright (rathakāra), carpenter (takṣa), potter (kulāla), black smith (karmāra), jeweller (maṇikāra), barber or sower (vapa), arrow-smith (iṣukāra), bow-maker (dhanuṣ-kāra), maker of the bow-string (Jyākāra), rope-maker (rajju-sarja), hunter (mṛgayu), dog-keeper (śvanin), bird-catcher or fishermen (puñji-ṣṭha), Physician (bhiṣaja), astronomer (nakṣatra-darśa), elephant-keeper (hastipa), horse-keeper or groom (aśvapa), cow-heard (gopāla), shepherd (avi-pāla), goat-herd (aja-pāla), cultivator

(kināśa), distiller of liquor (surākāra), housekeeper (grhapa), charioteer (kṣattā), assistant charioteer (anukṣatta), fuel-fetcher or wood
-gatherer (dāvāhāra), image-maker (paṣitā), spy or informer (piśuna)
door keeper (kṣattā), Assistant door-keeper (anu-kṣattā), horseman
(aśva-sada), tax-collector (bhāga-dugha), furrier (ajina-sandha),
tanner (carmāra), fisherman (dhīvara, maināla, kaivarta, dāśa),
dealer of dried fish (śauṣkala), gold-smith (hiraṇya-kāra), merchant
(vaṇija), keeper of forests (vanapa), extinguisher of bonfire (davapa),
lute-player (vīṇāvāda), flute-player (tūnavadhma), conch-blower
(śaṅkhadhma), acrobat or pole-dancer (vaṃśa-nartin), headman
of village (grāmaṇī), astrologer (gaṇaka), the herald or announcer
(abhikrośaka) etc.

The occupations earmarked for women are as follows :—

Female cane worker or basket maker (vidalakārī), female worker in thorns (kaṇṭakīkārī), female expert in embroidery (peśaskārī),
washerwomen (vāsa palpulī), female-dyer (rajayitrī), a female
expert in preparing unguents and cosmetics (añjani-kārī), female
scabbard maker (koṣa-kārī). Women belonging to certain castes
used to take these occupations as means of their livelihood.

Again, from some of the epithets ascribed to Rudra in the
Śatarudrīya hymn of the S. Yv. we may trace the following occupations as held by some professional persons. The hymn concerned thus alludes to :

House-builder (sthapati), forester (vanaspati or aranyapati)
takṣā (carpenter), Kulāla (potter), Karmāra (black smith), kṣatṛ
(door-keeper), saṃgāhitṛ (treasurer), rathakāra (chariot-maker),
niṣāda & Mṛgayu (huntsmen), iṣukṛt, dhanuṣkṛt (arrow-maker,
bowmaker), puñjiṣṭha (fisherman[30] or bird catcher),[31] bhiṣaj
(physician).

Besides these, we meet with some other professions as cook
(samitṛ)[32] preventor of diseases[33] or mediator in a dispute
(madhyamaśi), and sorcerer or magician (Yātudhāna)[34]—in some
other chapters of the S. Yv.

From the above discussion, it is evident that so many varieties
of occupations were prevalent in such a hoary antiquity of the
S. Yv. and many of them are similar even to some occupations of

our present day. It can further be assumed that both heavy
industries and small-scale industries such as weaving, knitting,
sewing, embroidery etc. were widely practised by the womenfolk.
Large-scale industries such as-chariot-building, carpenting, tanning,
manufacturing of missiles & weapons etc. were usually run by men.

(C) HOUSE BUILDING

Aryans of this period were well acquainted with the art of
house-building. In a passage of the S. Yv., Agni is invoked as
one having three metallic formations of iron, silver and gold.
According to Mahīdhara, Agni received these metallic formations
after he had burnt down three mansions made of iron, silver and
gold which were built by Asuras in three regions.[35] House building
and other wooden works became the professions of a certain section of people. This is evident from some passages of the S. Yv.
where the professional house builder (sthapati),[36] carpenter
(takṣā)[37] and expert house contractor (vāstavya)[38]—are mentioned.

A verse of this Veda refers to the necessity for the construction
of a house for the dwelling of a householder.[39] Duroṇa[40] refers
to the sacrificial house and house in general are denoted by the
term 'Durya'.[41] Pastyā (dwelling or house) in a wider sense means
'dwellers of the house or subjects.'[42] Doors (dvāra) of the houses
are suggested in a passage to be of different colours and to hold
the capacity of easy access to the rooms.[43] The term 'ātā' occurring
in that passage, denotes the framework of the door and the term
'chadih'[44]—the thatch or roof of a house.

(D) TRADE AND COMMERCE

The Vaiśya class was generally engaged in trade and commerce The wealth acquired by them through agricultural pursuits
was invested in trade and commerce. The merchant was meant by
the term vaṇik or Śreṣṭhin. The profession of the merchant was
often hereditary, as the term 'Vāṇija' (son of a vaṇija) in the sense
of merchant occurs in the S. Yv. (XXX.17). Gold, rice or food-
grains, cloth and cattle, cows in particular constituted the medium
for barter. The purchase of soma in exchange of cow or gold is
8

referred to.[45]

The Aryans of the S. Yv. were acquainted with sea or ocean. Ocean or Samudra has been mentioned several times in the S. Yv.[46] and also in other Saṃhitās and Brāhmaṇas. 'The ocean swells round the earth'...says the S.B.[47] Referring to the saline water of the sea, the T.B.[48]—remarks...'hence men do not drink the water of the sea'. The A.B.[49] mentions 'inexhaustible sea' and 'the sea as encircling the earth'. It is beyond doubt, therefore, that Vedic Aryans were endowed with the sound knowledge of the ocean. It was also known to them as to how to sail across the vast ocean as expert navigators. Sea-going large vessels existed and the maritime trade was known.[50] The S. Yv.[51] just like the R.V.[52] speaks of a vessel of hundred oars (Satāritra).

(E) MEANS OF TRANSPORT.

Along with the progress in different spheres of life, the system of communication and transport developed at this period to an astonishing degree. References to such conveyances as chariots (ratha), bullock-carts (śakaṭa), ships, boats (aritra, nāva) and vimāna, which means probably the aeroplane, go to prove that transport was developed in three regions—road, water and even on air.

Chariots used to play a prominent part in the transport system. Chariots were also used in warefare, sports and hunting. The extensive use of chariots tended to the growth and progress of chariot-making industry. A particular class of people known as Kṣattās or Śutas (charioteers) used to undertake to chariot-driving as their profession. Horses were generally chosen for drawing the chariots. Mules were also used for this purpose. In a passage of the S. Yv., the bounding and strong bodied horse has been termed 'Ratha-vāhana' i.e that drags the chariot.[53] In a verse,[54] god Vāyu is asked to reach the sacrifice speedily being carried by his thousand chariots drawn by a number of horses.

Apart from chariots, carts (Śakaṭa) pulled by oxen are referred to as a means of transport. These were also used specially for carrying soma plants to any sacrificial ground.[55]

Ships and boats playing on rivers and seas were treated as a popular mode of transport. The word 'nāva' occurring in the S.Yv. (X. 19) is explained by Macdonell[56] and others as boats and ships that navigate in great rivers or the sea. Mahīdhara and Uvaṭa,[57] however, interpret the term as the great navigable rivers like the Ganges etc. Anyway, it proves the existence of navigation as one of the systems of communication. Large sea-going strong-built vessels propelled by hundred oars (śatāritra) are mentioned.[58] For welfare, it is adivsed to embark on such a ship that should be free from leakage and defect.

There is, however, no explicit reference to Air-flight as a means of transport, but from the mention of the word 'VIMĀNA' used as an epithet of Sūrya in the S. Yv.,[59] we might have an idea about the existence of some sort of air flight. Devichand holds that the word 'Vimāna' is used here to mean aeroplane and that the sun is likened to an aeroplane because both the Sun and aeroplane appear beautiful and wondrous when soaring and shinning high in the sky. Mahīdhara and Uvaṭa, however, interpret it in a different way.

(F) METALS AND MEASUREMENTS.

Four stages or periods of human progress are enumerated as- (i) the Bone and the Stone age (ii) the Copper and the Bronze age (iii) the age of Iron and (iv) the age of Gold. Achievement of the people of this period in metals indicate the advanced stage of their culture and civilisation.

Different metals are enumerated in the Śukla-Yajurvedic text. Among these, the most important are the following six :-[60] Viz. Hiraṇya (gold), Ayas, Śyāma (iron), Loha (copper), Śisā (lead) and Trapu (tin),

According to Macdonell, Śyāma (swarthy) and Loha (red) must mean 'iron' and 'copper' respectively and 'ayas' would mean 'bronze'. Mahīdhara views 'Ayas', to mean 'iron'. A heater of 'ayas' (iron) is spoken of in the S. Yv. as 'ayastāpa'[61] Gold was looked upon as a mark of nobility whereas iron as a mark of the common people.

A gold-made ornament called 'Niṣka' had to be put on the

neck of the king at the Rājasūya sacrifice. The tips of arrows (śalya) were made of iron.[62] Silver was quite familiar. Rajata, the popular word for silver, appears to be termed as 'Rajas' in the S. Yv. where in a passage Agni is addressed as a deity whose force or power lies in silver (Rajahśayā), gold (Harihśayā) and in iron (Ayahśayā)[63].

With the development of trade and commerce, there arose the necessity of weighing or measuring the commodities—sold or purchased. It is to be noted that the Aryan businessmen in that remote past were acquainted with the use of scales (Tulā)[64] for weighing commodities. That very process still now prevails in our modern business societies.

REFERENCES

1. 'Kṛṣisamṛddhyāveva gavādikam Yajamānasya sulabham iti.' —Mahīdhara on S. Yv. XII.71
2. R. V. X. 34.13...'Kṛṣimit Kṛṣasva...vitte ramasva vahumanyamānah'
3. S. B. 7-2-2-6...'Annam vai Kṛṣih'
4. S. Yv. XII.67...'Śira Yuñjanti kavayo yugā vitanvate pṛthakdhirā deveṣu sumnayā'
5. S. Yv. XII.68...'Yuṅkta sīrā viyugā tanudhvam kṛte yonau vapateha vījam girā ca śruṣṭih savarā asanno medīya(itsṛnya pakvameyāt'
6. S. Yv. XII.69 Śunam suphalā vikṛṣantu bhūmim śunam kināśā abhiyantu vāhaih.
   Śunāsirā haviṣā tosamānā supipplā oṣadhih kartanāsmai
7. S. B. 1.6.1.3
8. S. Yv.XXII.22...'Nikāme nikāme nah parjanyo varṣatu phalavatyo na oṣadhaya pacyantām...'
9. S. Yv. XII.100
10. S. Yv. XI.10
11. ...Śuno vāyuh sīra ādityah, Kidṛśau sunāsīrau...Jalena teṣamāna...jalena bhūmim siñcantau santāvoṣadhaīh saphalāh Kurutāmiti bhāvah—Mahīdhara on S. Yv. XII.69
12. S. Yv. XII.71...'Iāngalam pavīravat...'
13. S. Yv. XVI.33
14. S. Yv. XVI.43

15. S. Yv. X. 32
16. S. Yv. XVIII.12...'Vṛhayaśca me yavāśca me māsaśca me tilaśca me
        mudgaśca me khalvaśca me priyaṅgavaśca me anavaśca
        me śyāmākaśca me nīvāraśca me godhūmāśca me masu-
        rāśca me Yajñena kalpantām'
17. '...Vīrūdhaḥ gulmāḥ ḥ Oṣadhaya phalapākānta...Bhūmikarṣana-Vīja-vāpā-
        dikaramaniṣpādyā Kṛṣṭapacyā.   Tadviparītā akṛṣṭapacyā svayamevot-
        padyamāna nīvāragavedhukādayaḥ...Mahīdhara on S. Yv. XVIII.14
18. T. S. VII.5.3.1
19. S. Yv. IV.19...('he gau tvam...Kṣatriyāsi somakrayasādhanatvena')—Mahī-
        dhara)
20. S. Yv. III.20 ; IV.20-22 ; VIII.42-43
21. S. Yv. VI.22 '...Yadāhuraghnyā iti...'
    S. Yv. VIII.43...'Aghnye'
22. S. Yv. XXX.18...'...Antakāya goghātam...'
23. S. Yv. VIII.43
24. S. Yv. III.20
25. S. Yv. III.22
26. S. Yv. III.59
27. S. Yv. VII.45
28. S. Yv. III.21
29. S. Yv. XVI.24
30. Macdonell on Vedic Index
31. Mahīdhara on S. Yv. XVI.27
32. S. Yv. XVII.57, XXIII.39
33. According to Mahīdhara (vide : S. Yv. XII.86)
34. According to Macdonell (vide : Vedic Index, Vol. II)
35. Mahīdhara on S. Yv. V.8
36. S. Yv. XVI.19
37. S. Yv. XVI.27 ; XXX.6
38. S. Yv. XVI.39
39. S. Yv. XIX.18 'Patnīśālaṃ gārhapatyaḥ'
40. S. Yv. XXXIII.72 (...Duroṇe Yajñagṛhe—Mahīdhara & Uvaṭa)
41. S. Yv. I.11...('Duryāh gṛhaḥ'—Mahīdhara & Uvaṭa)
42. S. Yv. X.7.27
43. S. Yv. XXIX.5 'Sumbhamānā dvāro devīḥ suprāyanā bhavantu'
44. S. Yv. V. 28 (Vide Macdonell—Vedic Index, Vol. I)
45. S. Yv. IV.19-21, 26
46. S. Yv. XVII.4.7 ; T. S. II. 4.8.2 ; VII.5.1.2
47. S. B. 7-4-1-9...'Samudro hīmamabhitaḥ pinvate'
48. T. B. 2.2.9.2
49. A. B. V.16.7.,VII.25.1

50. R. V. VI.55.6.,VII.88.3

51. S. Yv. XXI.7

52. R. V. I. 116.5

53. S. Yv. XII.71 ('Rathavāhanaṃ rathavāhakamaśvādikam'—Mahīdhara)

54. S. Yv. XXVII.32

55. S. Yv. IV.33 ; VIII.56 ('Śakaṭādāgatohavarūḍaḥ soma-nāmako bhavati'—
      Mahīdhara on S. Yv. VIII.56

56. Macdonell—Vedic Index, Vol· I, Devichand-Yajurveda, p. 142

57. 'Nāvā tāryā mahānadyaḥ'—Uvaṭa on S. Yv. X.19
      'Nāvo nau tāryā mahānadyo Gangādyāḥ'—Mahīdhara on S. Yv. 19

58. R. V. I. 116.5, S. Yv. XXI.7...'Sunāvamāruheyamasravantīmanāgataṃ
      śatāritra svastaye'

59. Devichand—'Yajurveda'—P. 261

60. S. Yv. XVIII.13

61. S. Yv. XXX.14...Manyave ayastāpam ('Ayastāpaṃ lohatāpakam'—Mahi-
      dhara)

62. S. Yv. XVI.10...('Bānāgragata lohabhāga śalyam'—Mahīdhara)

63. S. Yv. V.8

64. S. Yv. XX.17...'Tulāyai vaṇijam'

BOOK II

THE POLITICAL & MILITARY ASPECT

BOOK II

CHAPTER I

POLITICAL THEORY

(A) THEORY OF THE DIVINITY OF KING

Unlike the post-Vedic Smṛti texts,[1] the theory of the full-fledged divinity of king was admitted in some of the Vedic texts as well. In the vedic hymns of creation, there is not a single passage where the king is described to be created by God. On the otherhand, some Yajurvedic texts clearly illustrate one of the fundamental characteristics of Vedic state namely the human origin of kings. In the invocation formula as cited in the imperialistic and monarchical sacrifices termed Vājapeya or Rājasūya, the king is referred to as 'the son (or descendant) of such a man and such a woman',[2] and so forth. From this, it can be held that kingship was purely of human origin and no divine heredity was acsribed to it. According to Dr. U. N. Ghosal— 'The king is here described simply by the names of his parents, and not the slightest attempt is made on such a solemn occasion to trace back his ancestry to the gods'.[3]

There is, however, in the Vedic texts reference to some of the gods namely, Soma, Indra, Varuṇa etc. as the kings in the divine realm i.e. kings of gods. The earthly kings were sometimes identified with these divine kings and their priests and advisers were identified with the divine priest and minister Bṛhaspati. Just as in the coronation ceremony the celestial kings were besprinkled by Bṛhaspati with sacred water, similarly, the earthly king is described to be besprinkled with holy water. The following verse of the S.Yv. may be cited as the illustration in point.

'I am sprinkling you with the same water of sweet, stṛenght infusing, refreshing and sovereignty bestowing character with which the heavenly kings like Mitra, Varuṇa and Indra were consecrated.'[4]

Divine epithets and attributes were ascribed to the earthly

9

king in the Veda. In the performance of the Rājasūya sacrifice, the gods were invoked for granting special powers to the king designate. The following Śukla Yajurvedic verse is worth-quoting in this respect :—

'(O King) May Savitā quicken thee for ruling, Agni for house-holders, Soma for trees, Bṛhaspati for speech, Indra for lordship, Rudra for cattle, Mitra for truth and Varuṇa for the lord of the law'.[5]

Again, in another Verse,[6] the king, is desired to be installed with the brilliance of the Soma deity, lustre of Agni (fire-god), splendour of knowledge like the Sun and prosperity like Indra. Being endowed with these divine qualities the king is asked to reign over other kings and subjugate his subjects properly. The attempts for acquisition of divine qualities, however, may not stand as proof of divinity of the king. "The acquisition of divinity consequent upon the performance of the sacrifice, had to be individually acquired and would not be transmitted by inheritance."[7] According to Altekar also 'the doctrine of the divinity of the kings which became so popular in India in the first millenium of the Christian era, was unknown during the Vedic period'.[8] V.D. Mahazan[9] is of opinion that the idea of the divinity of king was not developed in the Saṃhitā period but began to grow by slow degrees in the age of Brāhmaṇas.

(B) ORIGIN OF KINGSHIP

As regards the origin of kingship in the Vedic age, different theories have been propagated by different scholars. Dr. Narayan Chandra Bandyopadhyaya[10] referring to Vedic traditions relating to Manu and Pṛthu, argues that the kingship evolved out of Military chieftain. Dr. Beniprasada,[11] after quoting the stories of the creation of Divine Kingship from the A.B.I. 14 and the T.B. 1.59 suggests that warfare tended somehow to originate or strengthen the Vedic kingship. Dr. Jayaswal in his Hindu Polity[12] suggests that the Indo-Aryans then living in a tribal stage borrowed their institution of kingship from the Dravidians. Dr. A. S. Altekar[13] following Dr. Zimmer holds the theory that kingship arose out of the patriarchal atmosphere prevailing in society. According to Dr. V. M. Apte[14] monarchy was the real form of Government in the early Vedic age ; because of the patriarchal organisation of Aryan society and of the constant warfare between the Vedic Aryans and their neighbours.

After analysing all these above views, Dr. U.N. Ghosal[15] holds that neither the Vedic evidence nor the historical analogy justifies the conclusion that kingship arose among the Vedic Aryans exclusively under the stress of war with their Dravidian and other enemies. Equally unwarranted is the conclusion that it was developed out of patriarchal organisation of the Vedic society. 'The true origin of Vedic kingship', according to him, 'should probably be sought in military and other necessities of the people in the pre-vedic times.'

Kingship of different types is mentioned in a passage of the S. Yv. (V.24). These are—Svarāṭ, Satrarāṭ, Janarāṭ and Sarvarāṭ meaning self-ruler, ruler for a long period of time, ruler of the people and ruler of all, respectively. According to Mahīdhara and Uvaṭa, the term 'Satra' is equivalent to a long standing sacrifice and hence Satrarāṭ signifies a ruler who reigns over great sacrifices. Eggeling, however, commenting on this verse quoted in the S.B. (3-5-4-15) takes the term 'Satra' to mean 'a long passage of time'. The forth category of kingship mentioned here is Sarvarāṭ or ruler of all which according to Dr. Jogiraj Basu[16] corresponds to Sārvabhauma and Ekarāṭ meaning the paramount sovereign who rules or holds sway till the end of the country touching the ocean without any rival sovereign'. Kings in general are termed 'Rājan' while the terms Samrāṭ or Virāṭ are used to indicate as sovereign who is more powerful than a king or Rājan. A sovereign holding over the Sāmrājya or Vairājya type of sway over the people was designated as Samrāṭ or Virāṭ respectively. According to the Gopatha Brāhmaṇa, a ruler became Rājā by performing the Rājasūya sacrifice.

The Vājapeya sacrifice was to be performed by the Samrāṭ, the Aśvamedha by the Svarāṭ, the Puruṣamedha by Virāṭ and the Sarvamedha by Sarvarāṭ. The ideal set before the king was to win all victories, find all wolds, attain superiority, preeminence and supremacy over all kings and achieve overlordship, paramount rule, self-rule, sovereignty, supreme authority, kingship, great kingship and ruler of all territories, the sole single sovereign of the earth upto its limit in the ocean.

The characteristic and ideal political institution of Vedic Aryans was kingship. The kings ruled over either one or several Rāṣṭras or states. The Rāṣṭra was formed, according to Dr. V. P. Verma, 'by the integration of the Kulas (families), Viśaḥ (the people or the tribe) and the Janaḥ or the clan.'[17] These three terms—the families, the people and the clan would indicate the population structure of the Vedic state or Rāṣṭra while Gramas or villages would indicate its territorial structure. Though the Vedic Rāṣṭra was not an exactly defined political term, we can use it in the sense of a cognizable political unit with an acknowledged head. Kingship or kingdom, manarchy or state were identified with each other as they were used in the same sense of Rāṣṭra.

In several passages of the S.Yv. the term Rāṣṭra is met with.[18] In the Rājasūya chapter of this Veda, it is repeatedly stated that kingdom or Rāṣṭra should be bestowed on him who is most deserving candidate for kingship.[19] A benevolent king pledges to keep a wakeful vigilance over his state.[20] The state—its ruler and subjects—their mutual relationship and interdependence have been stated in verse of the S.Yv. where the strong back of well-bodied person is compared to a well-governed state and other limbs of the body to the subjects residing in that state. Just as the different limbs of the body are sustained by a strong back, similarly the subjects are nourished by a well governed state and the ruler of that state with happy and prosperous subjects reigns majestically just as a well-bodied person with a strong back and healthy organs stays undauntedly.[21] The king takes oath to stand in the midst of his subjects with even handed justice and to rule with full fame.[22]

REFERENCES

1. Manu Saṃhitā Ch. VII
2. S. Yv. IX 40 ; X.18 ; M.S. II.6.6

3. Dr. U. N. Ghosal—Studies of Indian History and Culture, p. 310
4. S. Yv. X.1
5. S. Yv. IX.39
6. S. Yv. X.17
7. V. P. Verma—Hindu Political Thought, p. 224
8. Altekar—State & Government in Ancient India—P. 84
9. V. D. Mahazan—Ancient India (Ancient Indian Polity, Ch. XVI—P. 183)
10. 'Development of Hindu Polity & Political Theories', Part I, pp. 83-87
11. The State in Ancient India—P. 26
12. K. P. Jayaswal—Hindu Polity—P. 84
13. A. S. Altekar—States and Governments in Ancient India—P. 26
14. V. M. Apte—The Vedic Age—P. 352
15. Dr. U. N. Ghosal—'Studies in Indian History & Culture, P. 348
16. Dr. Jogiraj Basu—India at the Age of Brāhmaṇas, p. 89
17. Hindu Political Thought—P. 8
18. S. Yv. IX.23 ; XX.8.10
19. S. Yv. X.2-4
20. S. Yv. IX.23 'Vayaṃ rāṣṭre jāgryāmaḥ'
21. S. Yv. XX.8 'Pṛsthirme rāstraṃ...viśo me-haṅgāni sarvataḥ'
22. S. Yv. XX.10 'Dharmohasmi viśi rājā pratiṣṭhitaḥ'

CHAPTER II

MONARCHAL AND IMPERIALISTIC SACRIFICES AND THEIR POLITICAL AND SPIRITUAL SIGNIFICANCE

There are references to various kinds of sacrifices in the S.Yv. of which the following are of political and spiritual significance viz.—the Vājapeya, the Rājasūya, the Aśvamedha, the Puruṣamedha and the Sarvamedha. These sacrifices connected with kingship and paramount sovereignty are known as Monarchal and Imperialistic sacrifices. The Rājasūya was celebrated by a king for the attainment of kingship or Rājya ; the Vājapeya by a monarch for sovereignty or sāmrājya ; the Aśvamedha by a svarāt or paramount sovereignty for self-rule ; the Puruṣamedha by one known as Virāt for the achievement of suzerainty and lastly, the Sarvamedha by one known as sarvarāt or ruler of all territories.

The S.Yv. (Ch. IX. 1-34) deals with the Vājapeya sacrifice. The description of the Rājasūya is contained in Ch. IX 35-44 and Ch X. 1-30. The four chapters from XXII to XXV comprise the prayers for Aśvamedha sacrifice. The prayers for Puruṣamedha are found in the two chapters (Ch. XXX to XXXI). The prayers of Ch. XXXII to XXXIII, 1-54 are connected with Sarvamedha performance.

(A) THE VĀJAPEYA SACRIFICE

The Vājapeya literally means 'drink of strength'. The S. B. interprets the term Vājapeya as Annapeya—food and drink ; the term Vāja stands for food, one who performs Vājapeya, wins food.[1] By Vājapeya, one becomes a samrāṭ or emperor whereas kingship was attained by the celebration of Rājasūya and an emperer is obviously superior to a king. One who had become an emperer never wanted to be a king while a king always used to hanker after the attainment of emperorship.[2] Due to its relative priority, the Vājapeya had to be performed prior to Rājasūya. Rājasūya was specially meant for the Kṣatriya or warrior class whereas the Vājapeya though specially meant for the Brāhmaṇas could also be performed by Kṣatriyas. Thus, the S.B[3] justifies the eligibility of the Brāhmaṇa and the Rājanya to Vājapeya at the outset by saying that it was performed by Brahaspati and Indra representing the Brāhmin and Rājanya class respectively. By the celebration of Vājapeya, Bṛhaspati and Indra, the two gods representing Brāhmaṇa and Kṣatriya respectively are instructed in the S.Yv.[4] to win over food.

The Vājapeya starts with the following mantra[5]—O illustrious Savitā, inspire the sacrificer (king) towards the preformance of Vājapeya sacrifice. Through your instruction let Vācaspati or Bṛhaspati be gracious to him so that he may be able to achieve the result of that sacrifice in the form of 'food'.

Here with a view to perform the Vājapeya successfully, the sacrificer king seeks inspiration from Savitā who inspired Bṛhaspati also for a similar performance.

The Vājapeya is the one-day Soma sacrifice. With utterance of certain mantras five Vājapeya grahas (ladles connected to Vājapeya sacrifice) are taken of. These mantras are met with in the S.Yv. (IX.2-4). These mantras point out certain qualities which a person should possess in order to be elected as a King. Thus it is said that he should be accepted as a king who is well-versed in knowledge, yoga-practices and full of humility, leader of leaders, expert in science and full of affection.

A rite called assocation and dissociation of two ladles containing soma and surā, is connected with the Vājapeya sacrifice. Firstly, the soma ladles are placed above the axle (akṣa) by the Advaryu priest and the surā ladles beneath the axle by the Neṣṭā priest with the desire that the king should be united with bliss and then the ladles are disunited with the desire that the king should be free from sins and evil motives.

Thereafter, three component rites of Vājapeya sacrifice bearing social and constitutional significance commence. These are firstly, a chariot-race, which is won by the sacrificer in a contest with sixteen other competitors ; secondly, mounting the sacrificial post by the sacrificer and his wife ; thirdly and lastly, besprinkling by the priest of the sacrificer who is seated on a 'āsandī', a seat made of udumvara wood which is covered with the skin of black antelope.

In the most celebrated chariot-race, the sacrificer mounts a well built chariot drawn by four speedy horses and sixteen other competitors on sixteen other chariots of equal status. The race starts with the beating of seventeen drums (dundubhi) placed on the sacrificial altar. The sixteen drums are beaten silently by the priest while the remaining one is beaten with the utterence of the following mantra :—

'Let the drums cause Bṛhaspati and Indra to win over food and speech.[6]

Some passages describe in a picturesque way as to how the first galloping horses bound by the neck and at the flanks and in the mouth, ever accelerating their speed, pass by the way with full force like a high soaring bird and reach the goal of the race.[7]

Many western Vedic scholars try to lay stress on the importance of this chariot race, comparing it to the age-old national Olympic games.[8] Weber, on the otherhand, asserts that the whole aim of the rite was the feast of victory of the winner in the chariot race ('Vāja'—strength, 'pā'—to protect).

Coming to the second ceremony, we have to state that the sacrificer and his wife, while mounting the sacrificial post at the end of the chariot race, declare in a formula which is common to both the schools of the Yajurveda that they have become Prajā-pati's children and have become immortal.[9] The notion of king's divinity due to its connection with sacrifice may be inferred from this Yajus text. Observes Dr. U. N. Ghosal—'This passage, by connecting the sacrificer and his wife with Prajāpati, marks the climax of the Brāhmaṇa doctrine of the King's divinity by means of sacrifice'.[10]

After mounting the sacrificial altar, the sacrificer looks over the quarters with a view to attain the different properties befitting his kingly profession. Then he looks downward to the earth and pays homage to her like a son to his mother.

In this rite, the cordial relation between the king and the kingdom or earth over which he reigns is emphasised. Just as a son cannot be harmful to his mother and the mother to her son, similarly, the benevolent king should not be injurious to his subjects living on the mother earth ; in that case, there will be no possibility of his dethornment by the people living in his kingdom.

After the king designate's descending from the sacrificial post, the sacrificer is seated on a throne, made of udumvara wood and covered with the skin of black antelope. Then royal power is conferred to him with a remarkable prayer[11] by the priest or group of priests which according to the authoritative version of Eggeling on S.B. (V. 2. 1. 25) runs thus :

'This is thy kingship'—whereby he endows him with royal power. He then makes him sit down with— 'Thou art the ruler, the ruling lord.'—whereby he makes him the ruler ruling over those subjects of his. 'Thou art firm and steadfast in this world'.—'Thee for the telling—Thee for peaceful dwelling—Thee for wealth—Thee for thrift'—whereby he means to say (here I seat) —Thee for the welfare (of the people).

Interpreting the opening of the above passage in a different sense, Dr. Jayaswal[12] concludes that Hindu kingship depended upon the sacred act of delivering the trust, and not on any other principle such as that of succession or inheritance.

In the final ceremony of the Vājapeya sacrifice, the sacrificer is besprinkled by the priest with water mixed with milk and seventeen other substances and said to be consecrated to the supreme lordship (Sāmrājya) of Bṛhaspati.[13] Explaining this rite, the S.B. observes that the priest thereby makes him attain to the fellowship of Bṛhaspati and co-existence in this world.[14] This festival closes with seventeen 'Ujjitis' (benedictions—described in last four mantras)[15] by which the priest acclaims the sacrificer as 'All ruler' and commends him to the protection of gods of whom he has become one. The sacrificer here pledges to win over or control the seventeenfold objects namely—five life breaths, bipeds, the three worlds, four-footed animals etc. following the process by which the different deities—Agni, Aśvins, Viṣṇu, Soma, Pūṣan,

10

Savitā and Maruts etc. elevated the different objects. According to Devichand, the duties of the king and subjects are described in these mantras.[16]

    The following table contains the list of the names of deities and the objects gained by them through different means.

No.	Name of deities	The process by which the objects are won	The objects	The nature of the objects elevated
1.	Agni	Monosylabic 'Om'	Prāṇa	five life breaths
2.	Aśvins.	Two syllabic metre	Bipeds	Human beings.
3.	Viṣṇu	Three ,, ,,	Three worlds	Earth, atmosphere & Sun.
4.	Soma	Quadri ,, ,,	Four footed animal	
5.	Puṣan	Penta ,, ,,	Five regions—East, West, North etc.	
6.	Savitā	Six ,, ,,	Six seasons—Spring, Summer etc.	
7.	Maruts	Hepta ,, ,,	Seven domestic animals—Cow, Horse, Buffalo, Camel, Goat, Sheep, and Ass	
8.	Bṛhaspati	Octo ,, ,,	Gāyatrī	Self-preserving policy.
9.	Mitra	Nine ,, ,,	Tṛbṛtstoma	Knowledge of God
10.	Varuṇa	Deca ,, ,,	Vairājam	Knowledge of kindly affairs.
11.	Indra	Hendeca ,, ,,	Triṣṭuvam.	
12.	Viśvedevā	Dodeca ,, ,,	Jagati	Knowlege of worldly affairs.
13.	Vasus	Thirteen ,, ,,	Thirteenth stoma	10 Prāṇas, soul, mana and primordial matter.

No.	Name of deties	The process by which the objects are won		The objects	The nature of the objects elevated
14.	Rudras	Fourteen Syllabic metre		Fourteenth stoma	10 organs, mind, intellect, discerment, egotism.
15.	Adityas	fifteen ,,	,,	fifteenth stoma	4 Vedas, 4 Upavedas, 6 aṅgas, beauty and action.
16.	Aditi	Sixteen ,,	,,	Sexteenth stoma	(i) Pramāna (testimony) (ii) Prameya (iii) Samśaya (doubt) (iv) Prayojana (v) Dṛṣṭānta (vi) Siddhānta (principle) (vii) Avayava (Syllogism) (viii) Tarka (logic) (ix) Nirnaya (x) Veda (discussion) (xi) Jalpa (xii) Vitaṇḍā (Wrangling) (xiii) Hetvābhāsa (fallacy) (xiv) Chanda (Semblance) (xv) Jāti (futile answer) (xvi) Nigrhasthana (flow of an argument by which a disputant is brought low).
17.	Prajāpati	Seventeen ,,	,,	Seventeenth stoma	4. Varnas ; 4 āśramas ; (ix) Śravana ; (x) Manana (cognition) (xi) Nidhidhyāsana (Mediation) (xii) Desire for the non-obtained. (xiii) Retention of the obtained.

No.	Name of deities	The process by which the objects are won	The objects	The nature of the objects elevated
(17. Contd.)				(xiv) Development of the retained. (xv) Proper use of the Developed. (xvi) Desire and (xvii) Endeavour for salvation.

(B) RĀJASŪYA SACRIFICE

We shall now discuss Rājasūya, a sacrifice that bears political and constitutional significance of immense degree. This sacrifice is best known as the consecration ceremony of kings. This royal consecration ceremony is a Soma sacrifice having the usual Dīkṣā and Upasad days and is preceded by a long series of preparatory rites.

The main ceremony connected with the Rājsūya is the Abhisecanīya or the besprinkling the king with the sacred waters collected from seventeen sources. The ceremony starts with the offerings to eight deties called Devasus or divine instigators, divine quickeners. The name of the deities are : Savitā, Agni, Soma, Bṛhaspati, Indra, Rudra, Mitra and Varuṇa. These divinities being dignified with appropriate epithets are invoked to quicken the sacrificer for the various kinds of royal authority. Thus Savitā is invoked for instigating the sacrificer as a righteous promulgator of law and order; Agni for quickening him as the master of houses, soma for giving him the power of protection over the forests and agriculture ; Bṛhaspati (Vāk) for power of speech ; Indra, the most excellent one for leading him to jyeṣṭhatva or lordship or eminence ; Rudra as Paśupati for the protection of cattle ; Mitra as Satya for truth and finally the offering to Varuṇa—Dharmapati, the lord of law and morality for upholding of law and justice.[17]

Commenting on the term 'Dharmapati' Dr. R K. Mukherjee observes—'The Hindu theory of Dharma or law, as the real sovereign, and the king as Daṇḍa or the executive to support and enforce Dharma'.[18]   After the offering of the oblations the priest utters the following hymn.[19]

'Quicken him, O gods, to be unrivalled, for great kingship, for great lordship, for great man-rule and for self-controlling power'. Here in this hymn, the word 'Janarājya' stands for 'lordship over all people.' Dr. U.N. Ghosal suggests that by this term the rule over the whole folk as distinguished from the rule over a single tribe, is to be meant.   In the same invocation formula, the king is referred to as the son (or descendant) of such a man and the son of such a woman.[20] The king is here described simply by his parents and no attempt is made to relate him with any divine being. From this Dr. U.N. Ghosal infers the human origin of Vedic kingship. In the concluding stage of the devāsu offerings, the priest declares in presence of the assembled folk the words :—

'(Oh people), this person is your king, soma is the king of us— the Brāhmaṇas'. The same formula is repeated with or without variant forms in S. Yv. X.18 ; T.S. 18.10 ; K.S. XV. 5-8 ; M.S. II.66.27 ; T.B. I.74 at the besprinkling of the sacrificer and again, with slight variations in T.S.1.8.12 ; M.S. II.6.9. at the preparation of sacred waters.

This assertion, according to Dr. U.N. Ghosal emphasises the Brāhmaṇa's independence in the political sphere. Differing from Dr. Ghosal, Dr. Jayaswal interprets this declaration in the follow- ing way—(This man, O Ye people, is your king : he is Soma, the king of us Brāhmaṇas)—'Here the king consecrated as the king of the whole people including the Brāhmaṇas, and the priest expresses this by calling him Soma.'[21]

After the Devāsu oblations, the Abhiṣeka or sprinkling cere- mony starts. Holy waters collected from seventeen different sources consisting of rivers, pools, wells, dew-drops, floods, rain water, seas etc. are collected and mixed in a wooden udumvara vessel.[22] These waters are significantly called the bestowers of kingdom and they are ardently prayed for granting sovereignty to the person conscerated. Explaining the significance of the different kinds of water, the S.B.[23] says that the king is hereby made the lord as well as the offspring of the people.   He absorbs not only the people of his own kingdom but also the people belonging to some other kingdoms. In that Vedic age the Sarasvatī was regarded as the most holy river and therefore, it is prescribed that the first water to be collected should be that of the river Sarasvatī.[24] The water of different sources embodies the different qualities of the king. Thus Sarasvatī symbolises sweet nature, strength infusing and refreshing power, the flowing river symbolises vigour ; flood stands for plenty, sea for monarchy.

After the collection of the sacred waters, the priest offers oblations to twelve deities viz. Agni, Soma, Savitā, Sarasvatī, Puṣan, Brhaspati, Indra, Ghoṣa (the lord of sound), Sloka (the lord of hymns), Aṅśa (the lord who discriminates the virtue and vice), Bhaga, Aryaman (the deity that pervades). These twelve oblations known as Pārtha-libations of which the first six beginning with the mantra—'Agnaye svāhā' are offered before the consecration and the remaining six libations beginning with the mantra—'Indrāya svāhā' are invoked to the deities concerned after the consecration ceremony. While explaining this formula, the S.B. indentifies Brhaspati and Soma with Brahma and Kṣatra respectively and it says that the priest thereby sprinkles the sacrificer with Brahma and Kṣatra respectively.......At first all the holy waters are mixed together in a vessel made of udumvara wood. Then that mixed consecrating water is distributed into the four smaller vessels made of wood of Palāśa, Udumvara, Nyagrodha (ficus Indica) and Aśvattha (ficus religiosa) trees respectively.[25]

After the Pārtha oblations just mentioned the sacrificer puts on various garments symbolising the development of an embryo till it reaches maturity. He is to put on new garments—an under-garment called Tārpya, a blanket made of red-wool (Pāṇḍva), a mantle or cloak (Adhivāsa) and a head band (Uṣṇīṣa). This ceremony of wearing new garments is regarded as a new birth of the sacrificer and as such the garments symbolise the different parts of an embryo. Thus the Tārpya stands for amnion (Ulva), Pāṇḍva for uterus or chorion (Jarāyu), Adhivāsa for womb (Yoni) and Uṣṇīṣa or head-band for the navel or umbilicus. The priest, then, strings a bow for the king and hands over the same to him with three arrows. The bow stands as a symbol of king's strength and power and it is desired that the king will subdue all his enemies with this bow as is done by Mitra, Varuṇa and by Indra who defeated Vṛtra with his bow. It is also desired that the arrows fixed on the bow will protect the king from all quarters.[26]

The above ceremnoy is followed by a series of seven formulas. Of these, the first one is the announcement of the sacrificer to mortals or sacrificial priests. By other formulas the king is announced to gods like Agni (the lord of house), Indra (the lord of riches or fame), Mitra and Varuṇa (the upholders of pious deeds), Puṣan (the all-knower), Sky and Earth (that sanctions happiness to all) and lastly to Aditi (the repositor of all). The significance of these 'āvid' formulas lies in the fact that the sacrificer king with a view to become a dignified monarch, aims at the attainment of these godly qualities.[27]

At the close of the above ceremony the king figuratively mounts the four quarters and the zenith to symbolise his assumption of universal sovereignty.

In the accompanying formula which is common to both the Yaju Schools, the appropriate metres, chants, stomas, seasons along with Brahma, Kṣatra, Viśa and Dyads of objects (for attributes) are invoked successively to protect the sacrificer. These last are stated to be 'Phala' and 'Varcas' in the S.Yv., 'Bala' and 'Varcas' in the T. S. Interpreting the term 'Phala' as 'Śūdra' as opposed to Brahma, Kṣatra and Vis., Dr. Jayaswal finds out 'the greater constitutional import' namely that 'the king is to be protected by the four estates of the realm'.

After the mounting of quarters, the king is made to stop on a tiger's skin prior to the besprinkling ceremony. A small gold plate is placed below the king's feet and another gold plate having nine or hundred holes is placed on his head. Gold symbolises immortality, vigour and strength. With this rite, it is, therefore, expected that the king should be immortal, strong and vigorous.[28]

With gold under his feet placed on a tiger-skin and a gold fillet over his head, the sacrificer-king is sprinkled with holy water by four distinct persons, representing the whole kingdom. Four wooden vessels made of Palāśa, Udumvara, Nyagrodha and Aśvattha containing the holy water are placed there.

The Adhvaryū priest standing in front annoints the king for the first time with the water of Palāśa vessel. The remaining three sorts of people viz. Sva (king's kinsman or brother), Mitra-rājanya (friendly kings) and Vaiśya sprinkle over the king from his back-side with water from the three vessels of Udumvara, Nyagrodha and Aśvattha respectively. The mantra uttered by the Adhvaryu-priest in this annointing ceremony is as follows :—

'O King, I install thee with brilliance like the moon. Being annointed thus, be lord of princes. Guard constantly all of us from the arrows of the enemy.'[29]

Thereafter, the priest declares the kingship on the sacrificer before the subjects, royal kinsmen and friendly kings present there. The declaration runs thus :—

'This is your king and Soma is the king of us, the Brāhmaṇas. This person who is now endowed with kingship should be made foeless, for adorable warrior-class, for mighty lordship, for mighty domination over princes and for enhancing the wealth of the wealthly.'[30]

To begin with the Śukla-Yaju ritual, the S. B.[31] explaining the result (or the cause) of the besprinkling by the Brāhmaṇa, one of the king's own kinsmen and the friendly Rājanya respectively, states that the sacrificer is thereby sprinkled (endowed) successively with priestly dignity, with the sustenance and with support.

Following the besprinkling ceremony, the king is made to mount a chariot, pulled by four horses. The chariot moves round all the directions of the sacrificial campus, suggesting the king's victory of all the quarters.

Just before his descending from the chariot, the king looks down on the earth and invokes the earth as his mother and pledges to be non-injurious to each other. After the king has descended from the chariot he is ceremonially seated on a wooden throne known as 'Āsandī'. The priest touches him on the chest with a formula stating thus :—

'(As he has sat down on the throne) similarly he is well-placed (among his) subject like Varuṇa, the upholder of law and moral order, he the most intelligent one is thus endowed with sovereignty'.   (S.Yv. X. 17).

Commenting on the above verse of the S.Yv. (X. 17), the S.B. (V. 4.4.5) transferring the epithet 'Dhṛtavrata' to the king and to the Śrotrīya or the learned Brāhmaṇa, attaches the high moral and righteous status of these two classes of people.   The king is surely the upholder of law among the people, therefore, he should speak only what is right and do what is right.   This passage, observes Dr. U. N. Ghosal—'by attaching the notion of unrivalled moral greatness to the king along with the learned Brāhmaṇa, marks a distinct phase in the evolution of Vedic Kingship.   The Vedic king, according to this view, is the embodiment of the moral law, being matched only by the learned Brāhmaṇa'.[32]   This indicates how severe moral restraint the king should possess in order to maintain the status of his imperial dignity.

While the king remains seated on the throne, five dices made of gold are given to him with the expectation that he should win over the five regions.   Thereafter, an interesting dialogue takes place for five times between the king and the assembled priest. The king addresses the Brahman priest as— 'O Brahman'.   The latter replies as many times with words beginning with—'O Brahman', and followed in turn by the phrases—'Thou art Savitṛ of true impulsion'; 'Thou art Varuṇa, of true power'; 'Thou art Indra, mighty through the people'. 'Thou art Rudra, the most kindly'. Bringing out the significance of this dialogue, Dr. Jayswal[33] holds that—'the Brahmin may not now be addressed by his privileged designation of superiority which is given to the king by the whole nation including the Brahmin'.   Thus 'the sovereign and the popular representative character of the king is pointed out.'   The above mentioned dialogue (S.Yv. X.28) certainly bespeaks the superior status of the king to that of the Brāhmaṇa and the foremost social status of the king in the Vedic age is implied therein.

The next rite is the placing of gold on the dice-board.[34]   At this stage, Agni is urged to flood the sacrificer king with the beams

11

of the Sun so that he might acquire sovereignty.[35]

Lastly, twelve divine beings viz. Savitā, Sarasvatī, Tvaṣṭā etc. are invoked with a desire to instigate the king with certain qualities.

At the end of this important ceremony the sacrificial priests and other persons present there express their heartfelt well wishes for the all-round betterment of the newly consecrated king.

'O wealthy and adorable king, with the foremost wisdom, enjoy the gladdening rule of thine, may a learned and devoted wife serve thee. O speaker of the Assembly and commander of Army, protect the state, as father and mother protect their child'.[36]

(C) THE AŚVAMEDHA (HORSE SACRIFICE)

Now our discussion will start regarding another political sacrifice known as Aśvamedha or Horse sacrifice—the sacrifice that attained high importance and dignity in Royal circles of ancient India. It can only be performed by a powerful king, a mighty conqueror or one desiring paramount sovereignty.

The four chapters from XXII to XXV of the S. Yv. discuss this great sacrifice in detail. The monarch desiring to gain paramount sovereignty or to attain supremacy over all, used to perform this sacrifice on the eighth day of phālguna.[37] The purpose of the Horse sacrifice is expressed very beautifully in the following prayer of the S. Yv.[38]

'O Brahman, let there be born in this kingdom the Brāhmaṇa for the knowledge of the Vedas ; let there be born prince who is heroic, skilled archer piercing the foe with shafts, mighty warrior, let there be born the cow giving abundant milk ; the ox, good at carrying burden, the swift horse ; the good housewife. May the sacrifices he blessed with sons conquering, a mighty chariot fighter eloquent in the assembly, young and heroic. May cloud send rain according to our desire. May our fruit-bearing trees ripen. May acquisition and preservation of property be secured to us'.

The effect of this great sacrifice is thus eulogised in the S.B. thus :—

'One who performs the Aśvamedha conquers all the quarters, conquers the world, the priest makes him a ruler and upholder'.[39]

He acquires all kingdoms, all people, all the Vedas, all the gods and all created beings.[40]

In the initial day of the sacrifice, the mass of rice is cooked for the priests, and the sacrificer king, his four wives and their four hundred maidens of different ranks assemble. In the next morning the horse selected for the sacrifice is bound with a rope in front of the sacrificial fire and is sprinkled with waters by the Adhvaryu priest for five times invoking the deities like Prajāpati, Indra, Agni, Vāyu, and Viśvedevah etc., with a view to make the horse poweful, strong, steadfast and non-injurious. Then a man, born either of Śūdra and Vaiśya caste, being directed by the Adhvarya priest, kills a four eyed dog with a club of khadira wood. By this rite it is desired that if anybody kills the horse, he will be punished by Varuṇa and such a person of low character will be subdued like a dog.[41] The horse is then led to the sacrificial fire and offerings are made to ten principal gods viz. Agni, Soma, Savitā, Vāyu, Viṣṇu etc. The elaborate description of 49 activities of the horse then follows. After that the special offering to Lord Savitā for three days starts with the famous Gāyatrī verse[42] :—

'We meditate upon that adorable effulgence of the resplendent vivifier, Savitā, may He stimulate our intellects'. (R.V.III.62.10 ; S. Yv. XXII. 9).

The horse is then set free to wander at its sweetwill with a hundred old horses and guarded by four hundred youths. They are armed with armour, with swords, arrows or sticks according to their rank, as princes, warriors, sons of heralds and headmen and sons of attendants and charioteers. They must guard the horse anointed for sacrifice from any danger including bathing and intercourse with mares. These protectors of the horse are designated as 'Aśvapālas' in the Śukla-Yajurvedic text.[43] The description of the attendants of the horse as given in the commentary of Mahīdhara, bespeaks that the people belonging to the rank of both the nobility and the common people are picked up to form the complete battalion to guard and protect the horse. Their main duty is to guard the horse by all means and take it back safely after the completion of its course. If the horse is seized by any other contemporary king challenging the paramount supremacy of the sacrificer king, he must be defeated by attendants of the horse, otherwise the sacrificer will have to be stopped.

When the horse returns safely, it is anointed by the three queens of the king. The chief queen called Mahiṣī anoints the forepart of the horse's body, the favourite queen termed Vāvātā anoints middle part and the third and neglected wife known as Parivṛktā anoints the hind part. This bespeaks the relative grade ahd position of the wives in the royal family. Then, 101 gold pieces are placed by these wives in the mane and tail of the horse. The three queens along with the fourth one named pālāgalī caress the horse and lie down by its side and perform various rites connected with the sacrifice. From this, it is clear that the wives of the king play an important part in the performance of this great sacrifice.

In the midst of this long sacrifice, some debates in the form of curious riddles known as 'Brāhmodyas' take place between the Brahman and the Hotṛ, between Hotṛ, and Adhvaryu, between Brāhmaṇ and Udgātṛ and also between sacrificer (Yajamāna) and Adhvaryu. The necessity of these riddles is not only to break the monotony of the lengthy sacrificial performance but also to bring out the solution of certain important problems relating to sacrifice and religion.

Then, a huge number of animals both wild and domestic are bound to the posts. The horse is covered with a garment and then it is slain ; the chief queen goes near the horse ; both of them are covered with garment and the queen unites herself with the horse. Meanwhile the priests and other queens indulge in ribald dialogue.[44] Then the horse and other animals are sacrificed.

REFERENCES

1. Ś.B. 5.1.6-25...'Annapeyaṃ ha vai nāmaitad-yadvājapeyaṃ...annaṃ va eṣa ujjayati yo vajapeyena yajate'

2. S. B. 51.1.13 'Rājā vai rājasūyeneṣṭvā bhavati, Samrāṭ vājapeyena avaraṃ hi rājyaṃ paraṃ sāmrājyam.

3. S. B. 5.1.1.11-12

4. S. Yv. IX.11. 'Bṛhaspate vājam jaya...Indra vājam jaya'

5. S. Yv. IX.1

6. S. Yv. IX.11

7. S. Yv. IX.14.15

8. Hillenbrandt—Vedische Mythologie I.247

9. S. Yv. IX.21

10. Studies in Indian History & Culture, Ch. IX. p. 333

11. S. Yv. IX.22

12. Hindu Polity, p. 207

13. S. Yv. IX.30

14. S. B. V. 2.2.14

15. S. Yv. IX.31-34

16. Devichand—'Yajurvedea'...p. 134 fn.

17. S. Yv. IX.39

18. Hindu Civilisation, Ch. V. under conditions & coronations.

19. S. Yv. IX.40...'Imaṃ devā asapatnaṃ ..indriyāya'

20. S. Yv. IX.40

21. Dr. Jayswal—Hindu Polity, pp. 204-205

22. Enā Sārasvat ādyā apa udumvara kāṣṭha-pātre ekikaroti—Mahīdhara on S. Yv. X.4

23. S. B. V. 3.4.5

24. Sarasvatī-nadīsambandhinīrapa ādau gṛhnāti—Mahīdhara on S. Yv. X.1

25. 'Utpūtā abhiṣekārthā āpohabhiṣekārtheṣu palāśaudumvaravāṭaśvattheṣu pā-treṣu pūrvasāditeṣu caturdhā vibhajya ninayati'—Mahīdhara on S. Yv. X.7

26. S. Yv. X.8

27. S. Yv. X.9

28. 'He suvarṇa mṛtyoh sakāśānmāṃ pāhi pālaya...Navacchidraṃ śatacchidraṃ vā sauvarṇamaṇḍalam yajamāna śirasi kuryāt. He hiraṇya, tvamojohasi...śarīraṃ valaṃ sahastadrūpamasi...Amṛtam Vināśarahitaṃ tvamasi'—Mahī-dhara on S. Yv. X.15

29. S. Yv. X.17

30. S. Yv. X.18

31. S. B. V. 3-5, 11-14

32. Dr. U. N. Ghosal—Studies in Indian History & Culture, p. 318

33. Dr. Jayaswal—Hindu Polity—p. 209

34. S. Yv. X.29

35. S. Yv. X.30

36. S. Yv. X.34

37. …'Sarvakāmasya rājñohaśvamedhaḥ tasya phālgunaśuklaṣṭhamyāmāra-
     mbhaḥ'—Mahīdhara on S. Yv. XXII.1
38. S. Yv. XXII.22
39. S. B. 13.1.2.3…'Aśvamedhayājī sarvā diśohabhi jayati bhūvanaṃ jayati—
     yantāramevainam dhartāraṃ karoti…'
40. S. B. 13.4.3.15…'Sarvāni rājyānyācaṣṭe sarvā diśaḥ sarvān vedān sarvān
     devān sarvāni bhūtāni…aśnute'
41. S. Yv. XXII.5 'Yo arvantam jighānsati tamabhyasīti varuṇaḥ, Paro martah
     parah śvā'. (…Śvarūpenaśvahanteva parakṛtaḥ ityarthaḥ—Mahīdhara)
42. S. Yv. XXII.9…'Tat savıturvareṇyam bhargo devasya dhīmahi. Dhiyo yo
     naḥ pracodayāt'.
43. …'Devā āśāpālā etaṃ devebhyohaśvam medhāya prokṣitaṃ rakṣata. Iha
     rantiriha ramatāṃ iha dṛtiriha svadhṛtiḥ svāhā'
     (Vide : Mahīdhara's commentary on this verse)
44. S. Yv. XXIII.22-31.

CHAPTER III

THE CABINET & THE ADMINISTRATIVE ORGANISATION

(A) THE POPULAR ASSEMBLIES

The popular control in the affairs of the states was exercised
in the Ṛgvedic and Atharva-Vedic age by two popular assemblies
known as 'Sabhā' and 'Samiti'. There was, however, slight distinc-
tion between the functions of these two assemblies. The discussion
and decision of policies of all kinds as well as legislation constituted the main function of the Samiti which was a larger body.   The
Sabhā, a more select body, had the power to discharge the judicial
work and had also the right to discuss political matters. According
to Dr. R. K. Mukherjee—'The Sabhā functioned as a parliament
for the disposal of public business by debates and discussions.'[1]
According to Dr. Keith and Dr. Macdonell—'Sabhā is the name
of an assembly of Vedic Indians as well as the hall where they met
in assembly.'[2]   According to Ludwig, the Sabhā was an assembly
not of all the people but of the Brāhmaṇas and rich people, while
the Samiti included the common people as well.   In Zimmer's
opinion, the Sabhā was the village assembly.   Macdonell does not
accept these opinions and agrees with Hillenbrandt in holding that
the Sabhā and Samiti cannot be distinguished.

Dayananda, Jayaswal and some other writers, however, consider them as two distinct institutions and this fact is borne out by
the Vedic texts.

Sabhā is mentioned in some passages of the S.Yv.[3] It is
urged that the member of the assembly (Sabhā) should be impartial in discharging the judicial and other functions.   He should
not commit sin in the form of partiality while he remains seated
in the assembly.[4]   If such a sin is committed, the mercy of God
may alone absolve him. In another passage'[5] Lord Rudra him-

self is identified with Sabhā, perhaps with a desire that He may cast his ever vigilant eyes at the performance of the assembly so that the decisions might be impartial and fruitful. In the same passage, the term Sabhā-pati (Lord of the house or speaker of the assembly) occurs as an epithet of Rudra.

The word 'Sabheya' in the sense of 'the member of the assembly' is mentioned in connection with the Horse sacrifice in the S. Yv. It is expected that the member of the assembly should flourish along with other most desired and essential objects which are necessary for the development of the kingdom. This indicates what an important role was played by the Sabhā as a popular institution ; its members as public repesentatives were influential even though the state was headed by a king. Again, in the Puruṣamedha chapter[6] the member of the assembly is mentioned as 'Sabhācara'.

He is desired to be created by the Lord Himself for administering law and justice. The 'Sabheya' and 'Sabhācara' of the S. Yv. may be equalled with 'Sabhāsad' of the present day assembly.

The administration was no doubt run by the monarch, but the existence of Sabhā or public assembly as an essential feature of the Government, proves that the spirit of democracy was there behind the monarchal type of administration of that period.

(B) ADMINISTRATIVE ORGANISATION.

The reference to various Government officials in the S.Yv. indicates the gradual development of the Administrative Organisation of that period.

The King's cabinet was formed by persons technically known as Ratnins (jewels). It comprised the chief priest, the chief queen (Mahiṣī), the ministers (Mantrins), the Senānī, the Sūta, the Grāmaṇī, the Kṣtra, the Samgrāhitṛ and the Bhāgadugha. The king had to depend on these officials for the smooth functioning of different administrative affairs.

The priests or purohitas generally stood as the guide and philosopher of the monarch. With their impartial and disinterested vision, they used to guide the king to the right path and direct him to adopt the policies befitting the welfare of the kingdom.

The function played by the chief priest can be compared to the function played by the Chief Minister. The minister (Mantrin) is referred to in the S. Yv.[7] as an epithet of Rudra, one of the most powerful deity. From this, it appears what a powerful position was held by the minister in the administrative machinery of that period.

Just as the king used to seek the advice of the ministers in times of peace, so he had to deliberate with the Senānī or commander-in-chief in matters of warfare either of offensive or defensive type. The ministers were, therefore, in charge of administrative affairs while the Senānī was in charge of military affairs. Both the army (Senā) and its commander (senānī) are mentioned in the Śatarudrīya chapter of the S. Yv.[8] The term senānī also occurs in another chapter of the S. Yv.[9] The army consisted of four forces viz. elephantry, cavalry, chariot and infantry. These four fources were technically called 'Patti'[10] and its commander was known as pattipati or senānī.

From the participation of the chief and other queens in the monarchal sacrifices (Aśvamedha & Rājasūya etc) it can be well imagined what an important official status they used to occupy in the Vedic state.

Rathakāra,[11] the chariot maker and Sūta[12] or Kṣattṛ, the charioteer held position of superintendents of conveyances and communication. All of them are mentioned in Śatarudrīya and Puruṣamedha chapters of the S. Yv. Grāmaṇī[14] was the head of the village or the representative of the royal unit. He was the leader both for civil and military operations. In the S. Yv., he is certainly found to be connected with Senānī, but in the S.B. he is ranked as inferior to Sūta or charioteer. The Saṃgrāhitṛ and the Bhāgadugha are mentioned for the first time in the Yajurveda and Brāhmaṇas. These two terms are, however, differently interpreted. Saṃgrāhitṛ, according to some, means the charioteer[15] while according to others, it means the treasurer. Bhāgadugha is interpreted by Mahīdhara[16] as 'the distributor' while Sāyaṇa renders it as 'the collector of taxes'. It is better to take the second interpretation of these terms and thereby the Saṃgrāhitṛ would stand

12

for such an official as holding the charge of treasury and the Bhāgadugha for one entrusted with the collection of taxes and revenue. Another official ranked as superintendent of gambling is mentioned as Akṣa-rāja in the S. Yv. in lieu of Akṣavāpa. His duty was to supervise the gambling hall and to collect taxes from the gamblers.

Besides the Ratnins or chief officials, some other officers of lower rank are also mentioned. They are—the Karmāra[17] who was in-charge of industry, the Vratapati or assembler of various races, the Gṛtsapati,[18] the head of the intellectual class and the Sthapati[19] or artisan entrusted with the duties of house-building.

(C) CRIMES AND PUNISHMENT

Varieties of crimes and criminals mentioned in the Śatarudrīya chapter of the S. Yv. indicate the increase in crime during that age. The said chapter mentions cheats, pilferers, thieves, house-breakers, pick-pockets, night-rangers, highway-men, cutthroats, robbers armed with swords, maranders equipped with bows and arrows, swindlers and gangsters. The terms Kuluñca, Stena, Stāyu, Muṣṇāt, Taskara, used in this chapter singnify different types of thieves.[20]   Thieves, according to Mahīdhara, were chiefly classified into two categories :—visible (prakaṭa) and disguised (aprakaṭa). Visible thieves were known as Taskara and thieves in disguise were called Stena and Stāyu.

The terms Nisaṅgina, Giricara, Uṣṇisin and the like bespeak different types of gangsterism. Besides these various kinds of thieves and robbers, the Puruṣamedha chapter of the S. Yv.[21] mentions also other vices and criminals such as—Unchaste woman (Ayogu), harlot (Puṃścali), gambler (Kitava), adulterer (Jāra), paramour (Upapati), a lustful woman bent on arousing passions (Smara-kārī), and cow-killer (Go-ghāta) etc.

Severe punishment was prescribed for these criminals and the king as the head of the administration used to wield the rod of punishment. Some of the verses of the S. Yv.[22] draw our attention to this matter. The language of these verses is figurative ; the tusks, teeth and jaws of the king symbolise his policy of punishment, discipline and diverse means of suppressing the evil-minded people. 'Just as grass is laid in the jaws of an animal to be chewn, so wicked persons were placed at the disposal of the king for punishment'. 'Just as everything put in the mount of fire is burnt, so boisterous enemies, thieves and robbers were placed at king's disposal for the punishment'.

As regards civil procedure, voluntary arbitration appears to be the earlier form of judicial procedure in which the plaintiff (the Praśnin), the defendant (Abhi-praśnin) and the arbitrator or judge (praśna-vivāka) figured. These three personages were referred to in the puruṣamedha chapter of the S. Yv.[23]

Certain expiatory rites were prescribed as natural punishment for some crimes. So one indulging in excessive drinking of liquor (Surā) had to perform the Sautrāmani sacrifice as an expiation. Similarly, the slaying of a Brāhmaṇa by a king was expiable by the performance of Aśvamedha.

(D) WARFARE ARMY AND WEAPONS

From the references to varieties of weapons and missiles, their manufacturers and different classes of soldiers, it can be guessed that in the period of the S. Yv. warfare reached an advanced stage.

The king after due consultation with the commander-in-chief declared war either for defensive or for offensive purposes. Being the head of the state he had the responsibility to protect his subjects and kingdom from some oppressing forces like Rākṣasas, demons, or Dasyus. Again, for establishing his superiority or paramountcy, a mighty king used to engage in warfare against the contemporary rival kings. There is, however, no mention of any particular king resorting to war in the S Yv. but it is recorded that Indra, the warrior defeated Vṛtra with his famous weapon Vajra and also subdued another powerful demon named Namuci with the help of twin Aśvins.[24] In the coronation ceremony, the king is asked to follow the ideal of Indra as a warrior. As Indra did not hesitate to take the help of Aśvins, so should earthly king seek the help of the nobility and common-people in times of war. In the S. Yv., Lord Rudra is alluded to as the most powerful war-god. He is described to be identified with the army and the chief of Army.[25] He with his terrific fight and thundering sound makes the enemy weep in the battle-field.[26]

ARMY.

The terms Senā and Senānī correspond to army and its chief. The position of the commander-in chief (Senāni or Senāpati) was the most dignified one as he was regarded as one of the Ratnins or jewels of the royal establishment. So far as the ceremony of royal consecretion is concerned, the position of Senānī, seems to be superior even to that of chief priest or chief queen. From the reference to Aśvapālas i.e. the band of soldiers engaged in the protection of sacrificial horse, we can know how many divisions of the army existed at that period.

A hundred royal princes clad in armour, a hundred warriors armed with sword, a hundred sons of heralds and headmen of villages bearing quivers filled with arrows, a hundred sons of attendants and charioteers bearing a hundred horses, used to accompany the sacrificial horse.[27] Thus, it is seen that the divisions of army consisted not only of the people belonging to the military class but also of the people belonging to the different walks of life.

The Śatarudrīya hymn of the S. Yv. refers to various types of soldiers who appear to be the various manifestations of Lord Rudra. Rudra also appears as their protector and guide. Epithets befitting good soldiers are ascribed to Rudra. He is termed 'Senānī', 'Senāpati' (commander-in-chief) and 'Pattinām Pati' (chief of army). He is 'Āśu-senāḥ' and 'Āśu-rathaḥ' i.e. his army marches with great speed and his chariot runs most swiftly. The thirtyfifth verse of the hymn concerned runs thus :—

'Homage to Him (Rudra) who wears a helmet and to him who bears a cuirass (Kavacin), salutation to Him who wears mail and defensive armours (Varman) and to Him who possesses strong hold on elephants back to fight therefrom (Varuthin), homage to the far famed one whose army if renowned (Śruta-senā), homage to the skilled drummer (Dundubhya) and to the efficient player on military musical instruments (that encourage the soldiers).'[28]

These passages thus illustrate how the well organised army of that period marched to the battle-field being equipped with good conveyances, defensive armours and sharp weapons, exhilerated by the sound of drums.—The then army technically known as 'Patti' consisted of infantry, cavalry, charioteers, and elephantry.

WEAPONS AND MISSILES :

Various types of weapons and missiles were used in the Śukla-Yajurvedic period. The great demand for weapons and missiles is evident from the reference to various sorts of manufacturers of different types of weapon. It seems that manufacturing of weapons and missiles formed an established profession of a certain section of people. The Iṣukāra (the manufacturer of Shafts), Dhanuṣkāra (the maker of bows), the Jyākāra (maker of bow-string) and Rathakāra (the builder of conveyances like chariot etc.) are illustrations in point.[29]

A long list of weapons enumerated by the Śatarudrīya hymn of the S. Yv. There, it is mentioned that 'thousands of varieties of weapons are in possession of Rudra.'[30] He is described to be equipped with Heti (weapon), Pināka (colossal), Dhanu (small bow), Iṣu (arrow), Vajra (thunder-bolt), Khaṇga (scimitor), Asi (sword), Niṣaṅga (a kind of sabre), Iṣudhi (quiver), Śara (thin arrow), Āyudha (missile), Sātadhanu (hundred bows) ; he wields weapons to be hurled and weapons to pierce.[31]

REFERENCES

1. Dr. R. K. Mukherjee—'Hindu Civilisation', Ch. V
2. Vedic Index, p. 426 (Vol. II)
3. S. Yv. III. 45 ; XX.17, XVI.24
4. S. Yv. III.45 XX.17 (Sabhāyāṃ pakṣapātādi yadenaḥ'—Mahidhara)
5. S. Yv. XVI.24
6. S. Yv. XXX.6

7. S. Yv. XVI.19
8. S. Yv. XVI.26 ; XVI.17
9. S. Yv. XV.15
10. S. Yv. XVI.19 ('Hastyaśvarathapadātisaṃkhyā pattiḥ...'—Uvaṭa).
11. S. Yv. XXX.6 ; XVI.17
12. S. Yv. XVI.18 ; XXX.6
13. S. Yv. XVI.26 ; XXX.13
14. S. Yv. XV.15 ; XXX.20
15. Mahīdhara and Sāyaṇa on S. Yv. XVI.26
16. 'Bhāgaṃ dugdhe Bhāgadughastaṃ Vibhāgapradam'—Mahīdhara on S. Yv. XXX.13
17. S. Yv. XVI.7, XXX.7
18. S. Yv. XVI.25
19. S. Yv. XVI.19
20. S. Yv. XVI.21, 22
21. S. Yv. XXX.5, 9, 18
22. S. Yv. XI.77-80
23. S. Yv. XXX.10
24. S. Yv. XI.34
25. S. Yv. XVI.26
26. S. Yv. XVI.19...'Nama ucchairghoṣāya ākrandayate'...
27. Mahīdhara on S. Yv. XXII.19
28. S. Yv. XVI.35
29. S. Yv. XXX.6-7
30. S. Yv. XVI.53...'Sahasrāṇi sahasraśo hetayaḥ'.
31. S. Yv. XVI.16-23.

BOOK III

THE RELIGIO-PHILOSOPHICAL ASPECT

CHAPTER I

THEOLOGY

(A)   NUMBER AND NAMES OF DEITIES.

In the pluralistic Vedic pantheon, a good many number of deities are met with. But opinion differs as regards the exact number of these deities. The number of gods in the Rgveda is usually stated to be thirty-three and this number is variously expressed :……'trayaḥ ekādaśa' (R.V. IX.92.4). In another passage of the Rgveda, gods are said to be 'three hundred, three thousand, thirty and nine.[1] This passage reappears in the S. Yv. (XXXIII.7) In the other passages of this Saṃhitā, gods are numbered as thirty-three.[2] From this, it appears that the S. Yv. just follows the R.V. in determining the number of gods. Again, in another Śukla-Yajurvedic verse we get the number of deities as 'three, eleven and thirtythree'.[3]

In the R.V., deities are seen to be classified into three groups as the deities of heaven, of air or atmosphere and of the earth.[4] With this view in mind, Yāska, the author of Nirukta, divides the vedic gods into three classes. According to him only three gods such as Agni, Vāyu or Indra and Sūrya represent all the deities of earth, atmosphere and heaven respectively.[5] In support of such threefold classification, we may refer to a Śukla-Yajur-vedic verse[6] where it is told that eleven deities reside in heaven, eleven on earth and eleven in atmosphere.

The S. Yv. mentions the following deities :—

1. *Celestial deities*   : Dyaus, Varuṇa, Sūrya, Savitṛ, Mitra, Viṣṇu, Vivasvat, Puṣan, Bhaga, Ādityas, Uṣā, Aśvins etc.

2. *Atmospheric deities* : Indra, Maruts, Vāyu & Vāta, Rudra, Parjanya, Āpaḥ, Tvaṣṭa, Prajāpati & Viśvakarman.

3. Terrestrial deities :   Agni, Soma, Candramā, Bṛhaspati &
                             Pṛthivī etc.

Some prominent deities belonging to the above mentioned three regions are mentioned together in a verse of the S. Yv.[7] which runs thus :-

'Agni, Vāta, Sūrya, Candramā, Vasus, Rudras, Ādityas, Maruts, Viśvedevāḥ, Bṛhaspati, Indra and Varuṇa—are all gods.'

In another verse, gods like Agni, Soma, Āpaḥ, Savitṛ, Vāyu, Viṣṇu, Bṛhaspati, Mitra and Varuṇa—are invoked.

Two other verses refer to such gods as Indra, Vāyu, Bṛhaspati, Mitra, Agni, Pūṣan, Bhaga, Ādityas and Maruts together.

DUAL & GROUP DIVINITIES.

A number of verses of the S. Yv. are devoted to the praise of dual and group divinities. The most important pairs are Dyāvā-Pṛthivī, Mitra-Varuṇa, Indra-Varuṇa, Indra-Agni, Indra-Vāyu, and Indra-Bṛhaspati. All these names are combined as dual compounds. The characteristic feature of dual deities is that the epithets and functions more properly belonging to one god are applied equally to the other. For example, although Indra is the chief Vṛtra-slayer and Soma drinker, these epithets are applied to Agni as well as Varuṇa when they are associated with Indra. Group deities such as Maruts, Rudras, Ādityas, Vasus and above all Viśvedevāḥ (all gods) are already mentioned. It was convenient practice to invoke either a single god or any number of them under the title—Viśvedevāḥ (all gods). It appears almost certain that this device was suggested by the necessity of invoking all the gods to the sacrifice.[10]

GODDESSES.

Allusions to 'deva-patnīs' or wives of gods are found in the S. Yv. XXVI, 20,24 where they are invoked along with Tvaṣṭṛ, but their names are not mentioned. The names of the goddesses of the Ṛgveda such as—Aditi, Sinīvālī, Sarasvati, Iḍā and Bhārati reappear in the Y.V. More emphasis is, however, laid on the role of Sarasvatī as the goddess of speech than on her role as the goddess of river.   As a goddess of river she is mentioned only once.[11]

From the above enumeration of deities, it can be said that the theology of the S. Yv. does not fundamentally differ from that of the R.V.   The names of the deities of the R.V. reappear, only we notice a shift in the emphasis laid on them.   Thus, Viṣṇu who is a mere form of Sun-god and Rudra who appears primarily as a malignant deity in the Pantheon of the R.V., rise in importance in the Y. V.   Here, these two deities are not of minor importance but are accorded universal veneration.   Rudra is no longer a dreadful figure, he is now a benevolent deity—'the god of the people'.   This is indicated by a number of litanies addressed to him in the Śata-rudrīya hymn.   He is called the "great god" (Mahādeva) and he already bears the epithet—'Śiva'—propitious, current to the present day.   Viṣṇu rises to high importance as he is constantly identified with sacrifice.   Similar is the case with Prajāpati, the lord of creation.   This minor god of the Ṛgvedic pantheon, becomes the chief god and Viśvakarman, the creator of the world, is often identified with him.   He is also identified with Hiraṇyagarbha, the cosmic energy.   Among goddesses, Sarasvatī, the goddess of speech viz., Iḍā and Bhārati takes a more adorable position in the Śukla-Yajurvedic pantheon.   Brahmaṇaspati, the lord of prayer, becomes the leader of hymns and organiser of rites.   He is often eulogised for protecting the followers of vedic rites from the violence of uncharitable persons.[12]   He is again requested to make the sacrificer endowed with different capacities for the acquisition of Soma hymns.[13]

The peculiarity of the Yajurvedic theology is that here even the materials of the sacrifice such as—the twig of Palāśa (S. Yv. I. I.), the Sieves (S. Yv. 1.3), the vessel (S. Yv. 1.6), the sacred water (S. Yv. 1.7), the Kṛṣṇājina (S. Yv. 1.14) etc., and above all the sacrifice itself are deified.   Sacrifice was ascribed the greatest importance at this period.   So its impact on theology was quite natural.

(B) CHARACTERISTIC FEATURES OF SOME DEITIES.

We shall now bring out briefly the characteristic feature of

some of the prominent deities of the S. Yv. except Rudra &
Viṣṇu who will be dealt with in the Chapter under the heading—
'Emergence of Popular Religious Cults—Viṣṇu Cult, Rudra-Śiva
Cult'.

SŪRYA

Sūrya, the Sun-god, is described as the self-existent, most
excellent and self-effulgent.[14]   He is often described as the eye of
Mitra, Varuṇa, and Agni.   He is the protector of the sky, earth
and atmosphere and the resplendent one, the soul of all that
moves and all that moves not.[15]   The shining and wind-
urged Sun grants full life to the sacrificer, protecting and nourishing his subjects, he variously sheds his lustre.[16]

In order to illuminate the World, the Sun, present in all
created objects, spreads his rays wonderously.[17] The cloud disappears when the sun sets forth his bright lustre and this natural
phenomenon is imagined by the poet seer as the slaying of Vṛtra
by Indra.[18]   The sun is worthy of veneration as he destroys darkness, produces light and illuminates the whole Universe.[19]   The
sun-rise was most desirable to the Aryans because they believed
that it would absolve them of sin and from blame.[20]   The beneficient sun is described as the well-wisher of all, foremost of all
gods, unconquerable, ubiquitous and effulgent.[21] Being enamoured
of his immense greatness, the poet seer praises him with the
following words :—

'O Sun, thou art great, truly indestructible, omniscient god.
As thou art great indeed thy greatness is admired, yea, verily thou
god art great'.[22]

SAVITṚ

The very name Savitṛ which means the stimulator was derived
from the morning twilight. Macdonell[23] concludes that Savitṛ
was originally an epithet of Indian origin applied to the sun as the
great stimulator of life and motion of the world. Like the sun,
the adorable and wise Savitṛ brightens the sky after dawn and
stimulates all creature—men and animals to their won activities.[24]

Being inspired by Savitṛ, the sacrificer proceeds to sacrificial rites.[25] It is the inspiration of Savitā that enables the sacrificer to collect the most essential Soma plants.[26] The all-producing god Savitā is invoked to be gracious so that the sacrificer can achieve the merits of sacrifice.[27] Through the grace of this Lord, the sacrificer can attain both the worldly prosperity and the heavenly bliss. He is the true-inspiring lord whose command is followed by Indra and Bṛhaspati. The highest heavenly regions attached to these gods will, therefore, be attainable to the devotees of Savitā [28]

Not only in religious rites but in administrative affairs too, Savitā acts as an inspirer. Through his inspiration, the king proceeds to rule his subjects.[29]

He is all pervading.[30] With his glory he pervades the worldly creatures, generated by him.[31]

Savitā is endowed with powers of purification like Agni. He is asked to purify his invoker on every side.[32] He is also eulogised for purging vices, preventing calamities and for granting virtues.[33]

He is described as the possessor of golden arms[34] and golden eyes.[35] With his luminous lustre, he pervades the eight quarters, three worlds and seven rivers.[36] The gold-handed Savitā, the inducer of happiness and prosperity, sends away disruptive elements like Rākṣasas etc.[37]

The vedic seer earnestly prays to the god Savitā, the creator of universe, the developer of intellect, for granting him the power of intellect.[38]

The manifold merits of this Lord are described in some verses with such words as given below :—

'O lord Savitā, the fulfiller of our noble desire, our impeller through ommipresence, direct rightly our sacrifice ; you are the protector of the learned, the bringer of friends, the promoter of truth, the giver of wealth and the leader to the achievement of heaven'.[39]

"We praise Savitā, the procurer of comforts, the distributor of wondrous wealth, the creator and seer of men"[40]

The most famous and sacred Gāyatrī or Savitṛ mantra which is recited at the beginning of vedic study and in the daily prayers by the Brahmin still today, is addressed to the Lord Savitā. This supreme prayer holds such a dominant position that every school of thought in Hinduism presses it into service attaching different significance to it. Its importance in the vedic lore can be well-imagined from the repeated reference to it in the R. V. and the Y. V.[41] It runs as follows :—

"We meditate upon that adorable effulgence of the resplendent vivifier, Savitṛ, may He stimulate our intellects".[42]

VARUNA

Varuṇa is the great lord of the laws of nature and his ordinances which govern gods, men and things alike cannot be transgressed. Consequently, he is called 'dhṛtavrata'—one whose ordinances are fixed. He has, thus placed the air on the tree-tops, milk in the cows and strength in the swift horses, wisdom in human hearts, fire within waters, the sun in heaven and Soma on the mountain.[44]

He is like Indra designated as a universal monarch (Samrāṭ) at whose command the firmament and the atmosphere remain stable and the earth widens herself and the creation of the worldly things starts.[45] Prof. Mocdonell says that 'Varuṇa's character resembles that of the divine ruler in a monotheistic belief of an exalted type.'[46]

The sun is often spoken of as the eye of Mitra and Varuṇa. In a passage[48] Varuṇa is described as the king of water.

Varuṇa is ever merciful to penitents. Through his grace even those who have sinned become his beloved. In most of the hymns to Varuṇa, we find, therefore, the prayers for the foregiveness of sin, filled with confession of guilt and repentance.

Varuṇa grants protection and happiness to his devotees. He provides wealth and strength for the sake of sacrificers.[49] Like Aśvins, Varuṇa is also renowned for his experience in medical science. He is mentioned as the Lord of physicians.[50]

Varuṇa was undoubtedly one of the most important deities in the R. V. But his importance waned to some extent in the pantheon of the S. Yv. and other later Vedic literature. The reason behind such waning of Varuṇa's importance is the attribution of eminence to such gods as—Prajāpati, Rudra and Viṣṇu. In Purāṇas and other post-Vedic literatures, he is mentioned only as a lord of water and sea, probably through his connexion with 'Vāri' (water) and 'Varṣ' (to rain).

AŚVINS

The Aśvins are the inseperable twins. They are bright, young, yet ancient, multi-formed, beautiful, agile, strong and they possess wisdom and power. Yāska gives their derivation as follows :— 'They are called Aśvins because they pervade everything, the one with moisture, the other with light'.[51]

By far the most important characteristic of the Aśvins is, however, their power of healing and helping. They are recognised as divine physicians. In the R. V. they are mentioned as healers and helpers of so many persons and sages like—Kali, Cyavana, Bhujju, Viśpalā, Rjraśva and so on. In the S. Yv, they are, however, specially mentioned as the healers of Indra. When Indra lost his vigour by the drink of adulterated Surā, Aśvins came forward and cured him of his importance ; just as a father protects his son, so Aśvins saved Indra from the clutches of the demon Namuci.[52] There is an allusion to an expiation rite called Sautrāmani which was held in favour of Indra in which Aśvins, the divine physicians were present along with Sarasvatī, the goddess of speech and through their treatment Indra was able to regain his lost vigour.[53]

The connexion of Aśvins with Uṣas and their association which Sūrya are often described in the R. V. In the S. Yv., however, they are described as more closely associated with Sarasvatī. We find them either mentioned as co-physicians or invoked as deities with Sarasvatī in a good number of verses of the S. Yv.

The Aśvins are wedded to truth, they are the chastisers of the wicked and they are equipped with horses and cows. Through their grace, it is believed, no malicious foe will be able to do any harm to their devotees.[54]

The Aśvins are invoked for coming to the sacrifice with a chariot, lustrous like the Sun.[55]   Like other gods, they are also fond of Soma and are often invited to drink it.[56]   They are invoked to grant wealth and protection to their worshippers.[57] With a mind full of devotion, their worshippers extol them with such words :—

'O Asvins, the truthful, come along with thirtythree gods to this sacrifice for enjoying honey. Wipe out our sins, ward off our enemies, prolong our life and help us in our noble deeds.'[58]

INDRA

Indra is the national god of the vedic Aryans. The major parts of his activities are connected with the struggle against the natural forces. In the words of Macdonell—'Indra is primarily the thunder-god, the conquest of the demons or draught or darkness and the consequent liberation of the waters, or the winning of light, from his mythological essence. Secondarily, Indra is the god of battle, who aids the victorious Aryan in the conquest of the aboriginal inbabitants of India.'[59]

Indra, otherwise called Maghavan, is the most powerful god. He allows injuries to be inflicted on the enemy of his devotees,[60] who seek his help in the battle-field.[61]   He is primarily a thunder-god by whom the rain is made to come down on the earth.[62]

His chariot is generally drawn by two tawny horses[63] which are variously described[64] and often said to be yoked by the power of prayers.[65]   Indra, the protector and sustainer, ascending his chariot drawn by tawny horses, approaches his devotees for their rescue.[66]

He is described as the best promoter of happiness.[67] Though gods in gerneal are fond of Soma, Indra is pre-eminently addicted to it. Drinking the Soma-juice again and again, the valorous Indra subdues the enemy and wins the riches for the sacrificer.[68]

This mighty god is described as the powerful central Ruler (Samrāṭ).[69] There is none mighter than him. He pervades the whole world and sustains the creatures by transporting his own lustre into the three lustrous phenomena—sun, air and fire.[70]

In the battle-field Indra's aid is highly solicited. He is urged to dispel the enemies and disgrace the person who seeks to cause injury to his invoker.[71]

The most heroic war-god, Indra, strikes terror in the heart of the enemies and subdues hundreds of them. The Aryans begged his grace at the time of fighting against the Rākṣasas.[72] The 'Destroyer of Vṛtra'[73] and 'Wielder of thunderbolt'[74] are the most common epithets to Indra.[75] So the Vedic seer praises Indra with the following strain :—

"We invoke you, Indra, who are the destroyer of Vṛtra and capable of destroying the enemies." Indra,[76] is urged to subdue the enemies and drag them to the hell enveloped in darkness.[77]

AGNI

In the Vedic pantheon, Agni the fire god, appears as the nearest and dearest one. In the Ṛgveda, he is next to Indra in importance. In the Y. V. his position is no less important. In the sacerdotal period of the Y. V. great emphasis was laid on the performance of sacrifice and no sacrifice was possible without the presence of fire. From this, the importance of fire-god in the Yajurvedic pantheon may be ascertained. We find, therefore, in the S. Yv. a good number of verses devoted to Agni as prayers to the great deity.

The process of lighting fire was to rub against one another forcefully two sacrificial sticks—the upper one (Uttarāraṇi) and the lower one (Adharāraṇi) or two stones. Agni is, therefore, known as 'the son of strength'.[78] It is said that Atharvan first discovered fire out of water and thereafter the sages of this earth churned him out.[79] Bhṛgu is also mentioned as the discoverer of Agni in the forest.[80] The sacrifice is the abode of Agni.[81] For the welfare of sacrificers, Agni was kindled by sages like Bhṛgu in the midst of woods.[82]

Agni knows well the function of the Hotṛ priest and acts as the messenger between gods and mortals.[83] He carries the gods to the sacrifice and again leads them back to their places in time.[84] As an expert charioteer, he brings the deities in his chariots drawn

14

by fast galloping horses.[85]

Various appelations are attributed to Agni. He is described as Vājajit[86] (the generator of food grains), Gṛhapati[87] (the lord of houses). Vratapati[88] (the lord of penances), Jātaveda[89] (omniscient), Kavyavāhana[90] (the bearer of oblation to departed fathers). He is designated as Vaiśvānara who is indestructible, shining, non-violent, producer of rains, purohita and well wisher of five races.[91] He is referred to as Kavi (the most intelligent one), Vājapati (the lord of food grains) and bestower of most valuable gems.[92] He is called the thousand-eyed one (Sahasrākṣa).[93] The numerical figure seven appears to be a favourite attribute of Agni. 'Seven breaths are the fuels of Agni ; seven flames are his tongues ; seven organs of perception are his sources of wisdom ; seven beloved mansions belong to him ; seven priests in seven-fold manner pay him worship'.[94]

Alluding to the three forms of Agni, it is advised that one should avoid in a Yajña, the use of fire that burns the corpses, and should use the fire that ripens the raw commodities and endows us with nobler qualities.[95]

Three births of Agni are also alluded to. First he is born in the sky as the sun ; secondly, he takes birth in the earth as 'jāta-veda' or fire, and thirdly, he comes out of water as 'Vāḍavā'.[96] He possesses some other characteristics :—'As an earthly fire, Agni takes the position of a son of strength because he is produced by the forceful friction between two sticks. He is Varuṇa because of his stay in water ; in the cloud he takes the form of lightning and as the sun, he rises in the sky'[97] The all pervading nature of Agni is repeatedly referred to.[98] Agni pervades the three regions—earth, atmosphere and heaven and purifies all objects.[99] His lustre has been equalified with that of Brahman, because he has come out of Brahman Himself.[100]

Agni is regarded as an ever-beneficient deity. His beneficient nature is revealed in a number of Śukla-Yajurvedic verses.[101] He is the best bestower of wealth ; so he is prayed to earnestly for bestowing riches to the sacrificer.[102]

Agni with his burning and ever-illuminating lustre removed

darkness and dampness.[103] He is asked to destroy Rākṣasas and other evil forces who created disturbance in sacrificial performances.[104] Agni endows his sacrificer with the merits of sacrifice.[105] He betows offspring, wealth, prosperity and food to the sacrificer.[106]

Like Indra, Agni is described as the destroyer of Asuras. He takes possession of three castles made of iron, silver and gold of Asuras in Heaven.[107] He devours the enemies in the battlefield and brings booty for his worshipers.[108] The epithets 'Killer of Vṛtra' and 'destroyer of the castles of demons', assigned to him stand to prove his valourous nature comparable to that of Indra and Rudra.[109]

The manifold qualities of Agni are described in a verse[110] where he is invoked as the envoy of all deities, knower of his own function, expert, good accomplisher of any work, protector of all beings and possessor of sacred tongues in the form of blazing flames. Again, he is described as the most adorable one, the nourisher of plants and herbs.[111]

He is urged to cast away the evil forces like demons, enemies and illness through his prowess.[112] In addition to the general domestic welfare rendered by him, Agni plays a very important part as a purifier and protector, second only to that played by Varuṇa. He is frequently invoked to keep men sinless, blameless and free from hatred :—

'O Agni, dissuade me from sin and establish me firmly in righteousness. May I enjoy the pleasure of final beautitude by leading a virtuous life'. (S. Yv. IV. 28)

'O Agni, the knower of our actions and thoughts, lead us to salvation through the path of virtue ; keep away all crooked sins from us'. (S. Yv. V. 36 ; VII. 43)

'O Agni, the lord of penances, through your grace may we attain truth crossing the bounds of non-truth' (S. Yv. I. 5).

To the praise and invocation of other remaining deities, the following Śukla-Yajurvedic verses, as stated against their names are specially devoted.

Soma	: IV. 26-27, 34, 37 ; V. 7 ; VI. 25-26, 33 ; VII. 14.21 ; XXVI. 16, 17 ; XXXIV. 20.
Mitra	: XXXV. 10 ; XXXVI. 9
Vāyu	: XXVII. 27, 30-34.
Bṛhaspati	: XXXVI. 2 ; VI. 8 ; IX. 26 ; XII. 89 : XVII. 40 ; XXV. 19 ; XXVI. 3 ; XXVII. 7-8.
Ādityas	: VIII. 3-4 ; XXXIII. 81, 83.
Viśvedevāḥ	: VII. 33-34.
Bhaga	: XXXIV. 39.
Pūṣan	: XXXIV. 41-42.
Brahmaṇaspati	: III. 28-30 ; XVII. 52 ; XXXIV. 56-58.
Tvaṣṭr	: VIII. 14 ; XXI. 55 ; XXVII. 20 ; XXVIII. 9 ; XXIX. 9.
Prajāpati (Hiraṇyagarbha)	: XXII. 1.3, 26-27, 65 ; XXVII. 25-26 ; XXV. 10-12 ; XXXI. 19-20.
Uṣas	: XXXIV. 40
Sarasvatī (Iḍā & Bhāratī)	: (i) as a river god., XXXIV. 11. (ii) as Vākdevi-goddess of speech.........IX. 29, 30 ; XX. 63, 68, 75, 84-86.
Sinivālī	: XXXIV. 10

REFERENCES

1. R. V. III.9.9...'Trīṇi śata trī-sahasrāni Agniṃ trimśacca devāḥ nava cāsaparyān'
2. S. Yv. XXXIV.47, XX.11
3. S. Yv. XX.11...'Traya devā ekādaśa trayastrimśāḥ surādhaśaḥ...'
4. R. V. X.158.1...'Sūryo no divaspātu, vāto antarikṣāt Agnirana Pārthivebhayaḥ'
5. Nirukta VII.5...'Tisra eva devatā iti Nairukta-Agniḥ Pṛthivīsthānaḥ, Vāyurvā Indro vā antarikṣasthānaḥ, Sūryo dyusthānaḥ'
6. S. Yv. VII.19...'Ye devāso divyekādaśa stha pṛthivyāmadhyekādaśa stha. Apsukṣito mahinaikādaśa stha...'

7. S. Yv. XIV.20 'Agnirdevatā vāto devatā sūryo devatā...Varuṇo devatā'
8. S. Yv. XXII.6
9. S. Yv. XXXIII.4-5
10. Macdonell—'Vedic Mythology', p. 130
11. S. Yv.XXXIV.II 'Pañcanadyaḥ Sarasvatīmapi yanti sasrotasaḥ.
      Sarasvatī tu pañcadhā so deśohabhavatsarit'
12. S. Yv. III.30
13. S. Yv. III.28
14. S. Yv. II.26
15. S. Yv. VII.42
16. S. Yv. XXXIII.30
17. S. Yv. XXXIII.31
18. S. Yv. XXXIII.35
19. S. Yv. XXXIII.36
20. S. Yv. XXXIII.42...'Adyā deva Udita Sūryasya niraṃhasaḥ pipṛta nira-
    vadyāt...'
21. S. Yv. XXXIII.40
22. S. Yv. XXXIII.39...'Vanmahā asi Sūrya Vadāditya mahā asi. Mahaste
    sato mahimā panasyate addhā deva mahā asi...'
23. Macdonell, Vedic Mythology, p. 34
24. S. Yv. XII.3
25. S. Yv. II.12
26. S. Yv. V.39
27. S. Yv. VIII.6-7
28. S. Yv. IX.10
29. S. Yv. IX.39
30. S. Yv. II.13
31. S. Yv. XI.6
32. S. Yv. XIX.43
33. S. Yv. XXX.3
34. S. Yv. XXXIV.25 'Hiraṇyapāṇi'
35. S. Yv. XXXIV.24 'hiraṇyākṣaḥ'
36. S. Yv. XXXIV.24
37. S. Yv. XXXV.26
38. S. Yv. XXII.11.14
39. S. Yv. XI.8 'Imaṃ no deva savitayajñaṃ praṇaya...Svarjitaṃ.
40. S. Yv. XXX.4 'Vibhaktāraṃ havāmahe vaseścitrasya rādhasaḥ. Savitāram
    nṛcakṣasam'
41. R. V. IV.53.2 ; 54. 2 ; 110.3 ; S. Yv. III, 35, XXII.9 ; XXXVI.3
42. 'Tatsaviturvareṇyaṃ bhargo devasya dhīmahi, Dhiyo yo naḥ pracodayāt'
43. S. Yv. X.27
44. S. Yv. IV.31

45. S. Yv. IV.30

46. Macdonell, Vedic Mythology, p. 3

47. S. Yv. VII.42 ; XIII.46

48. S. Yv. XIX.94

49. S. Yv. XX.71

50. S. Yv. XXI.40

51. Nirukta XII.1.   'Aśvinau...Yad vyāsnuvate sarvaṃ rasena anyo jyotiṣā anyaḥ'

52. S. Yv. X.34 ; XX.59

53. S. Yv. XIX.21

54. S. Yv. XX.81-82

55. S. Yv. XXXIII.73

56. S. Yv. XXXIV.28

57. S. Yv. XXXIV.30

58. S. Yv. XXXIV.47

59. Macdonell, Vedic Mythology, p. 54

60. S. Yv. III.34

61. S. Yv. III.46

62. S. Yv. III.46

63. S. Yv. III.52

64. S. Yv. VIII.34

65. S. Yv. VIII.33

66. S. Yv. XX.47-50

67. S. Yv. VII.37

68. S. Yv. VII.12

69. S. Yv. VIII.37

70. S. Yv. VIII.36

71. S. Yv. VIII.44

72. S. Yv. XVII.33-39

73. S. Yv. VIII.33

74. S. Yv. X.22

75. S. Yv. XXVI.10

76. S. Yv. VIII.68

77. S. Yv. XVIII.70

78. S. Yv. XV.28...'Sahasputramangiraḥ'

79. S. Yv. XV.22

80. S. Yv. III.15

81. S. Yv. XXXIII.3

82. S. Yv. XXXIII.6

83. S. Yv. II.9

84. S. Yv. VIII.19

85. S. Yv. XIII.36-37

86. S. Yv. II.7
87. S. Yv. II.27 ; X.23
88. S. Yv. II.28
89. S. Yv. XXVII.22
90. S. Yv. XIX.64-66
91. S. Yv. XXVI.6-9
92. S. Y . XI.25
93. S. Yv. XIII.47
94. S. Yv. XVII.79...'Sapta te agne samidhaḥ sapta jihvāḥ
      Sapta ṛṣayaḥ sapta dhāma priyāṇi,
      Sapta hotrāḥ saptadhā tvā yajanti
      Sapta yoniraprṇasva ghṛtena svāhā.'
95. S. Yv. I.17
96. S. Yv. XII.18
97. S. Yv. XII.22
98. S. Yv. XI.23-24
99. S. Yv. II.27
100. S. Yv. III.9
101. S. Yv. XII-57-60 ; XV.38-39
102. S. Yv. IX.28
103. S. Yv. XI.26
104. S. Yv. I.8
105. S. Yv. XII.66
106. S. Yv. XII.110, XXXIV.13
107. S. Yv. V.8
108. S. Yv. V.37
109. S. Yv. XI.33
110. S. Yv. XI.36
111. S. Yv. XI.43
112. S. Yv. XI.49.

CHAPTER II

MONOTHEISTIC TENDENCY

Behind the pluralistic vedic pantheon, a monotheistic tendency generally grew-up even in the Ṛgvedic period. The plurality of gods could not satisfy the intellect of the Ṛgvedic seers. So, there arose a tendency to identify one god with another or throw all the gods together. Systematization took the form of the classification of gods into different categories or of the amalgamation of them all into one comprehensive group of the 'All Gods'. This systematization was but a step forward towards more logical monotheism. All personal gods having personal attributes were regarded as the manifestations of one Supreme Absolute Impersonal Godhead. Yāska, the celebrated author of Nirukta considers one Impersonal Ātman to be the source of all the gods. According to him—'All gods are but the limbs of one Supreme Soul—that one Supreme self is invoked variously'.[1] In a famous Ṛgvedic hymn, this monotheistic conception is thus clearly expressed :—

"The wise name the one Existing Reality (Ekam Sat) variously, viz. Indra, Yama, Mātariśvān etc."[2]

Many gods are, therefore, comprehended as different embodiments of the universal Spirit.

From the study of the S. Yv. also, it appears that a similar monotheistic train is flowing behind its pluralistic theology. The basic conception behind the Śukla-Yajurvdic pantheon is nothing but a monotheistic one. The fact is well-observed in the following mantras :—

'The oblation is for one Absolute Godhead'.[3]

'The God who is the giver of spiritual force and physical strength, whose ordinance is obeyed by the whole world, at whose control are all the gods, at whose support lies the immortality and transgression of whose law is death. May we pay homage to Him, the Absolute Godhead'.[4]

The Yajurvedic seers were aware of the fact that the Godhead is Supreme and Absolute and therefore uncomparable. Hence they proclaimed—'there is no image of that Supreme one'.[5]

Different gods are nothing but the manifestations of His great glory. This turth is outlined thus :—

'That God is Agni, He is Āditya. He is Vāyu, He is Candramā, He is light. He is Brahma as He is great, He is Apa being all pervading. He is Prajāpati as He is the guardian of His creatures'.[6]

This monotheistic idea of the S. Yv. is conveyed by one of its upaniṣads—the Bṛhadāraṇyaka upaniṣad.[7] In answer to a question put by Śākalya regarding the innumerable number of deities mentioned in the Vedas, Yājñavalkya states that it is Hiraṇyagarbha who expands Himself into many deities and contracts them into one. The one God has different names, forms, activities, attributes and powers, owing to differences of function. People practise different kinds of meditation, perform different rites, and thus acquire different grades of mental culture. The various gods are but parts of one Cosmic Energy, Hiraṇyagarbha or the World Soul.

REFERENCES

1. Mahābhāgyād devatāyā eka eva ātmā vahudhā stūyate.
   Ekasyātmanohanye devāḥ pratyaṅgāni-bhavanti''—Nirukta VII.4
2. R. V. I. 164.46...''Ekaṃ sat viprā vahudhā vadanti
                     Agniṃ Yamaṃ Mātariśvānamāhuḥ''
3. S. Yv. XXII.34...'Ekasmai svāhā...'
4. 'Ya ātmadā valadā yasya viśva upāsate prasiṣa yasya devāḥ.
   Yasya chāyāmṛtaṃ yasya mṛtyuḥ kasmai devāya haviṣā vidhema'.—
   S. Yv. XXV.13
5. S. Yv. XXXII.3...'na tasya pratimā asti...'
6. S. Yv. XXXII.1...'Tadevāgnistadādityastadvāyustadu candramaḥ.
                     Tadeva śukram tad Brahmā ta āpaḥ sa prajāpatiḥ'.
7. B. U. III.9.1.28

15

CHAPTER III

ORIGIN OF BHAKTI CULT

The Bhakti Cult or the cult of devotion which attained a distinct shape in the age of Purāṇas, had its root in Vedic eulogies. Though the term Bhakti in the technical sense is not present in the Vedic hymnology, still the aroma of devotion may be smelt in some Vedic passages. If Bhakti means faith in personal god, love for him, dedication of everything to his service and attainment of Mokṣa or liberation by personal devotion, surely we find all these in Varuṇa-worship[1] or in the eulogy of Rudra. With a self-surrendering attitude and with a mind filled up with reverence, the Vedic seer urges Varuṇa to absolve them from sin. The earnest appeal of a truly devout heart can be seen in the following Ṛgvedic eulogy to Varuṇa.

"How can I get near to Varuṇa? Will he accept my offering without displeasure? When shall I with a quiet mind see him propitiated"?

"Was it for an old sin, O Varuna that thou wishest to destroy thy friend who always praises thee? Tell me, thou unconquerable Lord and I will quickly turn to thee with praise, freed from sin".[2]

Emphasising the importance of Varuṇa worship in the evaluation of Bhakti Cult, Dr. Radhakrishnan observes—"The theism of the Vaiṣṇavas and Bhāgavatas with its emphasis on Bhakti, is to be traced to the Vedic worship of Varuṇa, with its consciousness of sin and trust in divine forgiveness".[3]

This attitude of devotion towards Varuṇa is also retained in the S. Yv. A more reverential attitude is seen in this period to the popular deity Rudra. Rudrādhyāyī or the hymn ascribed to Rudra, referring to the different epithets and qualities of Rudra-śiva, exhibits the heartfelt devotion of the worshipper by means of his repeated salutation to that Lord It will suffice to quote here a passage from that celebrated hymn.

"Homage to God, the source of happiness and the source of delight. Homage to God, the bestower of happiness and the bestower of delight. Homage to the Auspicious, homage to the most auspicious God."[5]

After a thorough study of this hymn, we may safely conclude that Śaivism or devotion to Lord Śiva as the personal god, has its inception in the Śukla-Yajurvedic period.

A tendency is seen in different Bhakti Cults to chant the prayer of a personal god enumerating as many names and epithets of his as possible. So, we find a thousand names of Viṣṇu, a thousand names of Śiva or a hundred and eight names of lord Kṛṣṇa and so on in later literatures. 'The beginning of this kind of prayers we find in the Śatarudrīya, the enumeration of the hundred names of god Rudra in section XVI of the S. Yv. (Vājasaneyī Saṃhitā) and in the Taittirīya Saṃhitā IV. 5.

The spark of Bhakti Cult as seen in the Vedic period got developed to some extent in the Upaniṣadic period till it fully developed in the age of Purāṇas. There are some passages in different Upaniṣads which bear the reference to genuine Bhakti sentiments. As for example, it is said in the Bṛhadāraṇyaka Upaniṣad :-

'Just as man being embraced by his beloved wife, forged everything external or internal, similarly the man being embraced by the Wisest Soul, becomes unaware of everything external or internal.'[6]

The Taittirīya Upaniṣad declares :—'He (Brahman) is full of love, so associating with Him everyone becomes delighted'.[7] In the words of Rabindranath Tagore, the great Bengali poet :—'the Love or Bhakti-Cult had its beginning in India as concomitant of Brahmavidyā.'[8]

Thus, the prayers based on devotion or Bhakti are seen as existing in different Upaniṣads and this sets aside the opinion that the Bhakti-Cult had its origin in the Paurāṇic age.

We may trace the origin of the Bhagavat religion, a special Bhakti Cult of Vaiṣṇavas, in the age-old Vedic Cult of worshipping the deity Bhaga. In the S. Yv., Bhaga is invoked as the bestower of blessing. The seer praises him with such words as :—

"May Bhaga, verily be bliss-bestower, and through him may he become bounteous ; gods may attend us. As such, O Bhaga, all with might invoke thee ; as such be thou art leader in this world."[9]

Bhaga gradually came to mean goodness and according to the Sanskrit grammar, the god possessing goodness comes to be known as Bhagavat. The worship of such a god constitutes the Bhāgavat religion.

The Pāśupata system, a theology centring round Śiva-Paśupati which developed in the Mahābhārata period, has its origin in the S. Yv. This system is nothing but the development of the Rudra-Śiva Cult of the S. Yv. In the Śatarudrīya hymn of this Veda, Rudra is expressly designated as Paśūnāṃ Pati, the Lord of Cattle.[10]

REFERENCES

1. Dr. Radhakrishnan—Indian Philosophy—Vol. I, p. 108
2. "Uta tvayā tanvā saṃvade tat kadā dhartarvaruṇe bhūvāni…"
   (R. V. VII.86.2)
   'Kimāga āsa Varuṇa jyeṣṭhaṃ yat stotāraṃ jighāṃsasi sakhāyam
   Pratanme vo co dūlabha svadhā vo hava tvānena namasa tura iyām"—
   (R. V. VII.86.4)
3. Dr. Radhakrishnan—Indian Philosophy—Vol. I, p. 78
4. S. Yv. XVI
5. "Namaḥ Śambhavāya ca mayobhavāya ca namaḥ śankarāya ca.
   Mayaskarāya ca namaḥ śivāya ca śivatarāya ca" (S. Yv. XVI.41)
6. 'Yathā priyayā-striyā sampariṣvakto na vāhyaṃ kiṃcana veda nāntarame-
   vāyaṃ puruṣaḥ prājñenātmanā sampariṣvakto na vāhyaṃ kiṃcana
   vedanāntaram…(B. U. IV.3.21)
7. T. U…'Raso vai saḥ Rasa hyevāyam ıabdhvā nandī bhavati'
8. Bhārātvarse Itihāser Dhārā
9. 'Bhaga eva bhagavā astu devāstena vayaṃ Bhagavantaḥ syāma
   Taṃ tva bhaga sarva ijjohaviti sa no bhaga pura eta bhaveha'
   (S. Yv. XXXIV.38)
10. S. Yv. XVI.28…'Paśupataye ca namaḥ'
    S. Yv. XVI.18…'Paśūnāṃ pataye namaḥ'

CHAPTER IV

EMERGENCE OF POPULAR RELIGIOUS CULTS

(A) VISNU CULT

The popular religious cults of modern India viz., the Viṣṇu Cult and the Rudra Cult evolved in the age of the Y. V. and through a gradual development in the Brāhmaṇic period attained a distinct shape in the age of Purāṇas.

It has been already pointed out in our discussion of Theology that deities like Viṣṇu and Rudra rose in importance in later Saṃhitā period. In the Ṛgveda, Viṣṇu holds a subordinate position. He is invoked there as a mere solar deity in five or six independent hymns. In the Y. V., Viṣṇu appears not only as a Sun-god but also as upholder of sacrificial rites and oblations, deliverer of the people from distress and bestower of riches and children to his worshippers. As a manifestation of Sun-god, he is referred to in the R. V. and the S. Yv. as the god of three strides.[1] The following verses are worthquoting in this regard :—

'Now will I tell the mighty deeds of Viṣṇu of him who measured our the earthly regions, who propped the highest place of congregation, thrice setting down his foot and widely striding'. (R. V. I.54.1 ; S. Yv. V. 18)

'Viṣṇu, the undeceivable protector strode three steps, thenceforth—establishing his high decrees'. (R. V. I. 22. 18 ; S. Yv. XXXIV. 43).

The three strides of Viṣṇu are but the three stages of the Sun viz., the rising, the culminating and the setting. Macdonell remarks—'Viṣṇu's three strides undoubtedly refer to the course of the Sun as it passes through the three divisions of the World— earth, air and heaven'.[2]

The presence of Viṣṇu in the three regions of earth, air and heaven is clearly mentioned in the following verse of S. Yv.

"By Jagatī metre in the sky strode Viṣṇu, by Triṣṭup metre in the air and by Gāyatrī metre upon the earth and thereby is excluded the man who hates us and whom do we hate" (S. Yv. II.25)

Viṣṇu is thus admittedly identified with the Sun in its activity of traversing the whole universe. The three steps of Viṣṇu can well be explained by a consideration of both the diurnal and the annual motions of the Sun.[3] He takes the first step in the morning at the time of rising, the second step in the meridian sky at midday and the third step in the evening when he sets. When we consider the annual motion of the Sun, Viṣṇu covers two-thirds of the year or eight months by his two-strides and four months by his third stride. This natural phenomenon was interpreted in the Paurāṇic Mythology as the conquering of the three worlds with three strides by the Vāmana avatāra or dwarf incarnation of Viṣṇu.

Viṣṇu is expressly called the intimate friend of Indra.[4] He is the associate of Indra in his fight with Vṛtra.

According to Nirukta, Vṛtra is nothing but cloud. It envelops the sky with darkness and holds up water. Indra with his lightning shaft pierces the cloud which then comes downwards in the form of rainy water. This natural phenomenon generally occurs in the rainy season,—the time for Viṣṇu to take his third stride according to the View point of the annual motion of the sun and counting the year from Śarat or Autumn. This gave rise to the idea of Indra's association with Viṣṇu in his fight with Vṛtra. The later Paurāṇic legend of Viṣṇu which describes him as placing his third step on the head of Vali, the Asura king, and sending him downwards, is only an expansion of the Vedic legend of Indra and Viṣṇu vanquishing Vṛtra and laying him low.

Viṣṇu, the solar deity of the R. V. was held in high esteem and became a popular deity in the post-Ṛgvedic period, especially, in the period of the S. Yv. He became more popular in the age of Brāhmaṇas and won the greatest popularity in the age of Purāṇas onwards. Observing the growing popularity of Viṣṇu in the post-Ṛgvedic period, Dr. Keith opines :—"In the later Saṃhitās and the Brāhmaṇas we find that Viṣṇu is assuming an importance in the minds of the priests which gave him undoubtedly the leading place in the living faith of the Brāhmaṇas."[5] In the Yajurvedic period, sacrifice was regarded as the most popular means for achieving both earthly and heavenly bliss.

That very sacrifice is seen to be identified with Viṣṇu.[6] The S. Yv. mentions Viṣṇu as the lord of the sacrifice[7] and as the personified sacrifice.[8] The ceremony for the preparation of the 'Yūpa' or sacrificial stake begins with an offering to Viṣṇu and a verse chanted in his praise as he is the sacrifice and the stake belongs to him.[9] Viṣṇu, being the sacrifice, the sacrificial hearth (Havirdhāna) also belongs to him.[10] He is further identified with the sacrificer. It is thus, expressed—'Viṣṇu's refuge is the sacrificer's refuge'.[11] He is again regarded as the guardian of sacrifice and oblations.[12] Mahīdhara and Uvaṭa on explaining a passage of the S. Yv.,[13] takes Viṣṇu to mean 'the pervading sacrifice'. According to Dr. Jogiraj Basu—'This identification of the sacrifice with Viṣṇu which ultimately led to the identification of the sacrificer with the God Viṣṇu indicates the growing position and reorientation of this deity'.[14] Through the performance of sacrifice which is identified with Viṣṇu the sacrificer longed for the identification with Viṣṇu or the total absorption in that deity. This idea has given birth to the modern Vaiṣṇava faith which holds that a devotee can attain Viṣṇu-loka or the highest realm of Viṣṇu by means of profound devotion to that lord.

According to modern Viṣṇu Cult, Viṣṇu assumes different incarnations at the end of each deluge for the protection of His creation. He is the sole resort of all creatures. He is the 'Antaryāmin' or the inner self of all creatures. We find these characteristic features of Viṣṇu expressed much earlier in the Śukla-Yajurvedic verses. The Yajurvedic seer after ascribing the appellations viz.—'Nibhūyupa' and 'Sipiviṣṭa to Viṣṇu' eulogises him with the following words—'Hail to Viṣṇu. Hail to Viṣṇu Nibhūyupa. Hail to Viṣṇu Sipiviṣṭa'.[15]

According to Mahīdhara, the title Nibhūyupa means, preserved by means of repeated incarnation as Fish, Tortoise etc. According to the same commentator, Sipiviṣṭa, a title of Viṣṇu, means one existing in all creatures as their 'Inner-self'. Again as an illustration of Viṣṇu as the resort of all, we may cite the following passage :—

"For this mighty deed, is Viṣṇu lauded......He within whose three extended paces all living creatures have their habitation".[16]

It is clear from the above discourse that the Viṣṇu-Cult, the popular religious cult of modern India had its origin in the Saṁhitā period. This Cult, however, attained a distinct shape in the Paurāṇic age through a gradual development in the Age of Brāhmaṇas. The dwarf incarnation (Vāmana avatāra) of Viṣṇu is distinctly mentioned in the Brāhmaṇas. 'Vāmana (dwarf) is Viṣṇu'—says the T. B.[17]

In the S.B.[18] it is said that 'men are Viṣṇus'. The origin and development of the concept of Fish-incarnation (Matsya-avatāra) may be traced in the S.B. (I.8.1.1). The name Nārāyaṇa occurs for the first time in the S.B.[19] though there it is not connected with Viṣṇu. In the T.A.,[20] Nārāyaṇa appears as the deity, etermal supreme, and lord, and is referred to as Hari. The same Āraṇyaka elsewhere mentions Viṣṇu also by his too wellknown epithets— Nārāyaṇa and Vāsudeva.[21] The Mahābhārata clearly identifies Nārāyaṇa and Vāsudeva as Viṣṇu. Thus in the Bhīṣma Parvan of the Mahābhārata, Vāsudeva, Nārāyaṇa and Viṣṇu are used as synonymous terms.

Some scholars[22] hold that the word Vaiṣṇava occurs for the first time in the later part of the Mahābhārata. But interestingly this term is met with far earlier in the S. Yv.,[23] though it is used there not to mean the worshipper of Viṣṇu but to mean anything related to Viṣṇu.

(B) THE RUDRA-ŚIVA CULT

The origin of Rudra-Śiva Cult may be traced back to the eulogy of Rudra (Śatarudrīya or Rudrādhyāyī) in the Y. V. Śiva is but a synonym of Rudra. Rudra is the dreadful or terrific one while Śiva is the most benevolent one. How the malevolent aspect of Rudra turned into Śivatva or the benevolent aspect is an interesting point to note here.

In the R. V., Rudra occupies a subordinate position having

only three entire hymns sung in his praise. His position in the R. V. is less important than that of other deities like Agni, Varuṇa or Indra, but in the Y. V. his importance rises to a height. An entire chapter of the Y. V. called Rudrādhyāyī or Śatarudrīya has been devoted to his praise. With a little bit of variation, this Rudrādhyāyī occurs in different recensions of the Y. V. The XVIth chapter of the S. Yv. Saṃhitā and the Vth and VIIth prapāṭakas of the IVth kāṇḍa of the T. S. are known as Rudrādhyāyī.

In the R. V. Rudra is mainly regarded as a god of destruction. The word Rudra may be said to have been derived thus : ('Roda-yati iti Rudraḥ').—'Rudra is He who causes bewailing and whose action leads people to mourn and lament'. Although two quite opposite characters such as, destructive and beneficient are simultaneously attributed to Rudra, the former one i.e. his male-volent nature predominates in the hymns of the R. V.

He is represented as discharging brilliant shafts towards both Heaven and the Earth[24] as the slayer of cows and men with deadly weapons. He is called the 'man-slaying' (Nṛghna).[25] 'Rudra is indeed the one malignant deity of the R. V.'—observes Dr. Mac-donell.[26] From the perusal and careful analysis of many Ṛgvedic verses,[27] it appears that the Ṛgvedic Aryans used to regard this deity as the generator of diseases and affliction. People tried to propitiate him so that he might abstain from inflicting on them diseases and sufferings. In their bid to win his favour the men feigned to be ignorant of his malevolent action and prayed to him to avert their sufferings. Hence, He is invoked as the healer of disease[28] and best of physicians.[29] All the eulogies and invoca-tion pertained to him in the R. V. are nothing but the outcome of fear and not at all the sincere love and devotion. Because anything fearful and destructive cannot be the subject of love and veneration. Naturally a tendency grew in the Aryan mind to ascribe benevolent aspects to this deity so that he might be the subject of reverence and adoration. As a result, Rudra has turned to be a popular deity like Viṣṇu in the post-Ṛgvedic period.

The XVIth chapter of the S. Yv. saṃhitā containing sixty six verses, points out clearly the two diametrically opposite characters

16

of Rudra viz., his benignant and malignant aspects. These two apparently contradictory characteristics of Rudra are transcended in his all-compassing comprehensive form.

The deity represents both the darker powers and the benign powers of nature. His benignant form is termed 'Śivatanuḥ' and 'Aghora'[30]—non-terrific as opposed to his malignant form called Ghora, Bhima, Ugra etc. meaning terrific and awe-inspiring. Since he represents the evil force of nature, Rudra is described as living far away from human habitation as the lord of forests and protector of hunters, highway robbers, night-rangers, thieves, pilferers, cheats, pickpockets, outcasts etc. He is eulogised as the presiding deity of thieves, of swordsmen, archers and robbers armed with swords.[31] He is the protector of swindlers and house breakers who roam about in the mountains putting on turbans.[32] Rudra is also the lord of soldiers, army and commander-in-chief. All sorts of fierce weapons and sharp missiles are associated with him. He holds bow, arrows, thunderbolt and various deadly weapons. The epithet that is constantly applied to Rudra as Saṃhatṛ or destroyer of the universe at the time of dissolution traces its origin in this Śatarudrīya chapter of the S. Yv. He is called 'Bhavasya hetiḥ'·—'the destroyer of the universe'.[33] The seer prays to this deity to take pity on him and 'not to kill his father and mother, and not to injure the persons dear to him,[34] not to kill the people and other created beings of the world'.[35]

In his benignant aspect he appears in this chapter of the S. Yv. as the healer of diseases, the lord of medicinal herbs and is termed 'the principal heavenly physician'.[36] Prayer is offered to him to bestow healthy minds to all men and to free them from the deadly disease, tuberculosis.[37] The same Rudra who is saluted as the protector of night rangers, hobgoblins, cuthroats, thieves, non-Aryan tribes and outcasts in his malevolent aspect is also eulogised as the all-powerful deity who can kill 'the venomous serpents and female demons'.[38] Being the lord of fields and plains, he is also the lord of cattle (Puśūnāṃ patiḥ) that graze about in those fields. In the Post-Vedic age 'Paśupati' became a special appellation of this god. Not only the term 'Paśupati' but also such epithets as

Kapardin, Sītikaṇṭha, Nīlagrīva, Gaṇapati, Bhava, Śarva, Pinākin, etc. which accompany the description and conception of Rudra or Śiva in the Purāṇas occur in this chapter of S. Yv.[39] The epithet 'Tryambaka' also occurs in S. Yv.[40] It is surprising to note that even the epithets of Kṛttivāsa—'One who puts on the garment of hide'[41] and of Giriśaya—'One who resides on the mountain'[42] are met with in the Śatarudrīya hymn.

The deity is also invoked as the lord of direction (Diśaṁ Patiḥ), lord of paths (Pathināṁ Patiḥ), lord of nourishment (Puṣṭi-nām Patiḥ), lord of food (Annanāṁ Patiḥ), lord of fields (Kṣetrānāṁ Patiḥ), lord of trees (Vṛkṣānāṁ Patiḥ), lord of herbs (Oṣadhinām Patiḥ), lord of animals (Satvānām Patiḥ), of horses (Aśvapatiḥ), lord of commoners (Gaṇapatiḥ), of hunters (Śva-patiḥ) etc.[43] In the T. S.[44] also the god is described as haunting the hills and is closely related to the trees on which he deposits his weapons. In his benignant aspect this god is also described in the S. Yv. as the presiding deity of councillors and merchants. Thus, he inspires the Mantrins or councillors of the king with good coun-sel and grants speed to the merchants for economic welfare of the country.[46]

Again, Rudra reveals himself not only in the higher castes but also in those low castes who are placed in the lowest rank of so-ciety. The Śatarudrīya chapter of the S. Yv. merits special impor-tance for this fact as well. Salutation is offered to Rudra who reveals himself among the carpenters, chariotwrights, potters, blacksmiths, Niṣādas, Puñjiṣṭhas, or bird-catchers, Śvanis or those who roam about with dogs, and Mṛgayus or hunters.[47] Not to speak of the world of human beings, he reveals himself also in the vegetable and animal kingdoms such as in trees, medicinal herbs, shrubs, dogs etc.[48]

In the S. Yv. Rudra is described and propitiated as the supre-me Godhead who is the fountain head of all energy, all life and the whole creation. In his all-comprehensive form, the Rudra-Śiva of the S. Yv. appears as the supreme godhead, Lord of all creatures, the source of all life and energy. Both the mobile and the immobile, the sentient and the insentient, the vegetable and the animal kingdom are pervaded by him. He is described in the S. Yv. as the lord of the universe—'Jagatāṃ Patiḥ'—he who assumes all forms—'Viśvarūpebhyaḥ', the all powerful Supreme God—Bhagavān, Iśāna etc. In the later part of this saṃhitā,[49] Rudra or Śiva is designated as Mahādeva—'the great god'. This very epithet, commonly ascribed to Śiva even in modern days, indicates the growing supremacy as well as popularity of this deity in the Śukla-Yajurvedic period.

As regards the original nature of Rudra, the opinions differ. According to some scholars he represents the thunder aspect of natural phenomena while others like to identify him with the Sun-god or with the fire god. The Ṛgvedic Rudra or malevolent nature may be said to be representing the thunder aspect of nature and as such he is classed with other storm gods like Vāyu and Maruts of welkin region. The Rudra of the S. Yv., however, may be identified either with the Sun-god or with the fire god. Ascribing to Rudra the epithets like Nīlagrīva or Nīla-kaṇṭha, the Yajurvedic seer poetically identifies him with the setting Sun in the following verse :—

"The cowherd boys and the village maidens who come to the tank for fetching water witness Rudra (in the form of setting Sun) who goes down the firmament tinged all over with the crimson hue but bluish at the neck."[50]

The verse anterior to the above-quoted one clearly and unmistakably identifies Rudra with the Sun-god (Sūrya) with the following words :—

"By our supplication we shall avert the wrath of Rudra who is shining in the yonder sky in the shape of the Sun, crimson and tawny in colour, the auspicious deity whose thousand rays have pervaded the whole universe".[51] Commenting on this verse, both the commentators Mahīdhara and Uvaṭa hold that Rudra is here eulogised in the form of the Sun.[52]

From the authority of the S. B. we can also identify Rudra with Agni, the fire god. This Brāhmaṇa clearly states that Rudra is a symbol of Agni and the epithets like Śarva and Bhava ascribed to him are nothing but the two names of Agni. Śarva was a name of agni among the eastern people and Bhava was used by the Bahikas (the people of the western region) to refer the same deity.[53]

A late hymn of the S. Yv.[54] marks out the wellknown epithets of Rudra such as Paśupati, Bhava, Śarva, Iśāna, Mahādeva and Ugra alone with Agni (fire) and Aśani (lightning) and enjoins that these are all but the different names of the same deity. From this reference, the identification of Rudra with fire in the earth region and with the lightning in the atmospheric region, may be established.

DIFFERENT APPELLATIONS ASCRIBED TO RUDRA IN THE S. YV. SAMHITĀ

In the Rudrādhyāyī of the Y. V. Lord Rudra has been eulogised by different names. It is interesting to bring out the etymological meanings of some of these epithets as given below :—

1) *Rudra*[55] : (S. YV. XVI. 1)

(i) He is called Rudra because he averts pain (rut).

(ii) Or, 'Rut' may mean 'Knowledge' ; hence he who imparts knowledge is Rudra.

(iii) Or, one who causes sinners to cry with sorrows and sufferings, is Rudra.

2) *Giriśantaḥ*[56] (S. Yv. XVI. 2.)

(i) He who staying at Kailāsa (Giri) extends happiness (Śam) to creatures, is Giriśantaḥ.

(ii) Or, remaining in the cloud (Giri) extends happiness to all through rainfall.

(iii) Or, remaining in the Speech (Giri), who extends happiness.

3) *Giritra*[57] (S. Yv. XVI. 3) : Being the resident of Kailāsa (Giri) who rescues the creatures from danger.

4) *Giriśa*[58] : (S. Yv. XVI. 4) : Who sleeps at the mountainous region named Kailāsa.

5) *Nīlagrīvaḥ*[59] : (S. Yv. XVI. 7) : Because of containing poison whose throat has become bluish and appears like the setting Sun endowed with crimson rays and bluish hue.

6) *Sahasrākṣa*[60] : (S. Yv. XVI. 8) : Who like Indra possesses thousand eyes.

7) *Miḍuṣa*[61] : (S. Yv. XVI. 8) : 'mih'—means 'to water' 'to sprinkle' ; (i) who like Parjanya (Rain god) sprinkles the rainy water (ii) Or, who is a young one.

8) *Bhagavaḥ*[62] : (S. Yv. XVI. 9) : God, because Bhaga i.e. six type of divine glory belongs to Him.

9) *Kapardī*[63] : (S. Yv. XVI. 10) : One having a mass of matted hair.

10) *Śateṣudha* : (S. Yv. XVI. 13) : One having many missiles.

11) *Bhava* : (S. Yv. XVI. 28) : He who gives birth to all creatures.

12) *Śarva* : (S. Yv. XVI. 28) : One who destroys sin.

13) *Paśupati* : (S. Yv. XVI. 28) : One who protects the animal world.

14) *Śitikaṇṭha* : (S. Yv. XVI. 28) : Excluding the bluish portion whose throat is white.

15) *Sambhava, Mayobhava, Śaṅkara, Mayaskara* : (S. Yv. XVI. 41) : Rudra who generates both worldly and out-worldly happiness.

16) *Śiva* : (S. Yv. XVI. 41) : The embodiment of tranquility, the most beneficient one.[64]

REFERENCES

1. Ṛ. V. 1.22, 17-18 ; 1.154. 1: S. Yv. II.25, V.18 ; XIII.55, XXXIV.43 ; XXXVI.9
2. Macdonell—Hymns of the Ṛgveda, p. 34
3. A. C. Das—Ṛgvedic India
4. R. V. I.22.19, S. Yv. VI.4 ; XIII.33…'Indrasya Yujya Sakhā…'
5. Dr. Keith—The Religion and Philosophy of the Veda & Upanisad, p. 110.
6. S. Yv. 1.10 ; VII.20
7. S. Yv. 1.12
8. S. Yv. 1.8

9. S. Yv. V.38.41
10. S. Yv. V.21
11. S. Yv. IV.10
12. S. Yv. V.21.25
13. S. Yv. XIX.56...(Viṣṇo vyāpturyajñasya—Uvata ;
   'Viṣṇo vyāpanśīlasya yajñasya. Yajña vai viṣṇu iti śrute'—Mahīdhara)
14. Dr. Jogiraj Basu—India at the age of Brāhmaṇas—p. 192
15. S. Yv. XXII.20...('Nitarāṃ bhūtvā matsādyavatāraḥ kṛtvā pāti nibhūyu-
   pastasmai Viṣṇave. Sipiṣu paśuṣu prāṇiṣu viṣṭaḥ praviṣṭohantaryāmirupena
   sipiviṣṭa stasmai viṣṇa e'—Mahīdhara).
16. S. Yv. V.20 ; R. V. I.54.2
17. T. B. 1.2.5.5....'Vāmano vai Viṣṇuḥ'
18. S. B. V.2.5.2-3
19. S. B. XII.3.4.1
20. T. A. X.11.1
21. T. A. X.1.6...'Nārāyaṇāya vidmahe vāsudevāya.
       Dhīmahi tanno Viṣṇu pracodayāt.'
22. Viṣṇupada Bhattacharjee...Bhāratīya Bhaktisāhitya.
23. S. Yv. V.21...'Vaiṣṇavamasi'
24. R. V. VII.46.3
25. R. V. IV.3.6
26. Dr. Macdonell—Vedic Reader, p. 604b.
27. R. V. VII.46.2, I. 114.1
28. R. V. I. 43.4
29. R. V. II.33.4
30. S. Yv. XVI.2...'Yā te Rudraśivā tanūraghorāpapakāśini...'
31. S. Yv. XVI.21...'Namo vañcate parivañcate...Vikṛntānāṃ pataye namaḥ"
32. S. Yv. XVI.22...'Namo uṣnīṣine giricarāya kuluñcānāṃ pataye nama'
33. S. Yv. XVI.18
34. S. Yv. XVI.15
35. S. Yv. XVI.3...'Mā himsiḥ puruṣaṃ jagat...'
36. S. Yv. XVI.5...'Prathamo divyo bhiṣak...'
37. S. Yv. XVI.4
38. S. Yv. XVI.5
39. S. Yv. XVI.28
40. S. Yv. III.60 "Tryambakaṃ Yajāmahe..."
41. S. Yv. XVI.51
42. S. Yv. XVI.29
43. Dr. Jogiraj Basu—India at the age of Brāhmaṇas, pp. 196-197
44. T. S. 4-5-1-3
45. S. Yv. XVI.19...'Namo mantrine vānijāya'
46. Dr. Jogiraj Basu—India at the age of Brāhmaṇas, p. 198

47. S. Yv. XVI.27
48. S. Yv. XVI.28
49. S. Yv. XXXIX.8
50. "Asau yohavasarpati nīlagrīvo vilohitaḥ
     Utainaṃ gopā adṛśrannadṛśrannudāhāryah so dṛṣṭo mṛḍayati naḥ"
     (S. Yv. XVI.7)
51. "Asau Yastāmro aruna nīlagrīve vilohitaḥ.
     Ye cainaṃ Rudra abhito dikṣu śritaḥ sahasraśohavaiṣāṃ īḍa īmahe"
     (S. Yv. XVI.6)
52. "Ādityarūpenātra Rudraḥ stūyate".
53. S. B. I. 7.3.8...'Agnirvai sa devaḥ. Tasyaitāni nāmāni
                      Śarva iti yathā prācyā ācakṣante.
                      Bhava iti yathā vāhīkāḥ. Paśūnāṃ pati
                      Rudrohagniriti, tānyasyāśāntānyevetarāni nāmāni,
                      Agnirityeva śāntatamam'
54. S. Yv. XXXIX.8
55. (i) 'Rut duhkhaṃ dravayati Rudraḥ (ii) Yadvā ravanaṃ rut jñānaṃ rāti
     dadāti Rudraḥ jñāne bhāve kvip tugāgāmaḥ (iii) Yadvā pāpino narām
     duhkhabhogena rodayati Rudraḥ'.—Mahīdhara.
56. 'Girau Kailāse sthitaḥ saṃ sukhaṃ prāninām tonoti vistārayati iti giri-
     śantaḥ. Giri vāci sthitaḥ śaṃ tanotiti vā, girau meghe sthito vṛṣṭidvārena
     saṃ tanotiti vā.—Mahīdhara & Uvaṭa.
57. "Giritrah-girau kailāse avasthitah trāyate bhaktān iti giritraḥ."
58. 'Girau parvate kailāsākhye śete iti Giriśaḥ'—Uvaṭa.
59. Viṣadhāranena nīla grīvā kaṇṭho yasya ; astamaye nīlakaṇṭha iva āditya-
     rūpaḥ Rudraḥ"—Mahīdhara.
60. "Sahasrākṣīnī yasya Indrasvarūpaḥ."
61. "Miha secane'—sektā vṛṣṭikartā parjanyarūpaḥ. Taruṇo vā."—Mahīdhara.
62. 'Bhagaṃ ṣaḍvidhamaiśvaryamasyāstīti Bhagavaḥ'—Mahīdhara
63. 'Kapardo jaṭājuṭohasyāstīti Kapardī Rudraḥ'—Mahīdhara
64. "Śivaḥ kalyāṇarūpo niṣpāpaḥ"—Mahīdhara.
     "Śivaḥ śānto nirvikāraḥ"—Uvaṭa.

CHAPTER V

(A) FORMS OF SACRIFICE

In accordance with the characteristic variations, vedic secri-
fices may be divided into five heads, viz, Homa, Iṣṭi, Paśuyāga,
Somayāga and Satra. Each type of sacrifice has again, two vari-
ants—Prakṛti or model and Vikṛti or modification. The Prakṛti is
treated as the main sacrifice from which Vikṛtis are derived. Hence,
Vikṛtis are treated as Aṅgas or accessories. Prakṛtis or models of
the above mentioned five types of Vedic sacrifices are—Agnihotra,
Darśapaurṇamāsa, Daikṣā or Prājāpatya Paśu, Agniṣṭoma and
Gavāmayana respectively. Only excluding Gavāmayana and
Prājāpatya Paśu, all other Prakṛtis are discussed in the S. Yv.

We shall, however, limit our discussion on the following rites
and sacrifices on which the ritualistic text of the S. Yv. contains a
good number of mantras in its different chapters.

i)	*Darśapaurṇamāsa* :	the Prakṛti or model of the Iṣṭi-type of sacrifice. (S. Yv. I. 1-3 ; II. 1-28 ; III. 1-8.)
ii)	*Piṇḍa-Pitṛyajña* :	(S. Yv. II.29-34)
iii)	*Agni-hotra* :	the Prakṛti or model of the Homa-type of sacrifice (S. Yv. III. 9-10)
iv)	*Cāturmāsya* :	(S. Yv. III. 44).
v)	*Agniṣṭoma* :	the model of Soma-yāga, (S. Yv. IV-VIII), these chapters deal with man-tras relating to Agniṣṭoma and some other mantras relevant to Agniṣṭoma.
vi)	*Vājapeya* :	(S. Yv. IX. 1-34)
vii)	*Rājasūya* :	(S. Yv. IX. 34-44 ; X. 1-30)
viii)	*Agnicayana* :	(S. Yv. XI-XVIII)
ix)	*Śatarudrīya* :	Homa : (S. Yv. XVI)
x)	*Sautrāmaṇī* :	(S. Yv. XIX-XXI)

xi)	*Aśvamedha*	:	(S. Yv. XXII-XXV)
xii)	*Puruṣamedha*	:	(S. Yv. XXX-XXXI)
xiii)	*Sarvamedha*	:	(S. Yv. XXXII-XXXIII).
xiv)	*Pitṛmedha*	:	(S. Yv. XXXV.)
xv)	*Prāyaścittam*	:	(S. Yv. XXXIX)

DARŚAPAURṆAMĀSA :

Darśapaurṇamāsa is the model for the Iṣṭi-type of sacrifices. This sacrifice has been discussed at the very beginning of the S. Yv. and the S. B. Darśa means the new moon or amāvasyā and purnamāsī means the full moon. From this, it appears that the sacrifice which is performed in the full moon and new moon days is known as Darśapaurṇamāsa. The ceremony spreads over two days in the full moon and two days in the new moon.

On the first day of the new moon the ceremonies are in the main preparatory, making ready for the fires, and taking of a vow by the sacrificer. For offering the milk mess or curd to Indra on that day, a twig of Palāśa wood is cut to drive away the calves from the Cows, for milking the latter.

Curd is to be prepared in the night of the dark moon so that it can be offered to the deity on the following day i.e. Pratipada and for this reason the calves are to be separated from their mothers in the morning of the dark moon day with the branches of Palāśa or Śamī wood. The branches are to be cut with the utterance of such mantra—'Iṣe tvā urje tvā'. The milk after being sieved is poured in an earthen vessel and some juice is to be mixed with it for transforming it to curd. The mantra for this curd-preparatory rite is—'Indrasya tvā bhagaṃ Somenātanacmi'—'that oblation for Indra, I make hard with Soma'. Then the sacrificer in presence of Agni takes the vow of leading a truthful life (S. Yv. I.5). The ceremonies of the second day include the preparation of rice, its huskings and pounding, the cooking of the cakes, the preparation of the altar, the girding of the wife of the sacrificer, the looking at the pot of butter, the covering of the altar with the grass and the setting up of the partitionary sticks which are intended to keep off evil spirits. At the end of these preliminaries the real sacrifice begins.

In the full moon performance the three principal oblations are offered to different deities. The first one consisting of rice-pap (purodāśa) is offered to Agni, the second oblation, characterised as 'Upāṃśu-yāga', is offered to one of the four deities viz.— Viṣṇu, Prajāpati, Agni or Soma, the third one consisting of rice-pap is meant for Agni and Soma. In the new moon, first oblation of rice-pap is offered to Agni, the second oblation of curd and the third of milk are offered to Indra.

The new moon and full moon sacrifices comprise six oblations in all. Some indispensable rites connected with these sacrifices such as Prayāja, Anuyāja, Patnīsaṃyāja are performed in both the full moon and the new moon ceremonies. The concluding offering known as Agni siṣṭvakṛt is an offering to the fire-god (Agni). In this closing ceremony all gods are invoked.

A householder who is married and has established the Gārhapatya fire in his abode is entitled to celebrate the Darśapaurṇamāsa sacrifice. For effecting this performance, four priests viz. Hotṛ, Adhvaryu, Agnidhra and Brahman are required. This sacrifice may be performed either regularly in every full moon and new moon days without any desire or occasionally with certain desires.

AGNIHOTRA :

It is the model or Prakṛti of the Homa type of sacrifices. In the S. Yv. a single hymn occurs in relation to Agnihotra.[1] In this sacrifice two oblations are made—one to the fire-god in the evening with the utterance of—'Agni-Jyoti jyotiragni Svāhā' (the fire is the light and the light is the fire)—and the other to the sun-god in the morning with the utterance of this verse—'Sūryah jyotih jyotih suryah Isvāhā'. The head of the family if married, has the right to perform Agnihotra. He should offer the oblations in every morning and evening throughout his life without any break. In case he becomes physically incapable, he must then get it done by his son or by a priest. Milk is regarded as the main oblation in this sacrifice and therefore a milch cow is reared for this purpose. Some other secondary items of oblation consist of—gruel, rice, paddy and butter.

Some propitiatory formulas and verses relating to Agnihotra are called the Agni-upasthāpana mantras or the verses meant for the adoration of the fires (S. Yv. III. 11-43). In these verses the fire is adored as the protector, the nearest one, the lord of the house and the best bestower of wealth.

CĀTURMĀSYA :

Cāturmāsya or the four monthly rites include the Vaiśvadeva, performed at the beginning of spring, the Varuṇa-praghāsa during the rainy season and the Śākamedha in the autumn. Internal features of these rites emphasise the connection with the seasons. These rites include five inaugural oblations and an invocation of the Maruts. The S. Yv. contains a mantra of the second rite i.e. of the Varuṇa-praghāsa. In this rite the wife is asked—'With what lover she moves' ? At this, the wife replies that she offers oblations to Maruts, the destroyer of malignant persons and the betaker of Karamba oblation. Then follows an expiatory ceremony in order to get rid of all sorts of sins committed to any sphere of life.

AGNIṢṬOMA :

Agni-stoma or Jyotiṣṭoma is the model of all Soma sacrifices. It is the simplest type of one day Soma sacrifice in which the offering of Soma-juice is the main oblation. This offering is made thrice in a day—in the morning, at midday and in the evening. The morning oblation goes by the name of Prātaḥsavanam, the midday libation is termed Mādhyandina Savanam and the twilight one the Tṛtīya Savanam. Every year in the spring, this sacrifice is to be performed by an initiated one with his wife. The rarely available Soma creeper is procured from distant land with great care ; it is generally purchased in exchange of cows. Now-a-days due to the non-availability of Soma, another creeper called 'Putikā' is used as its substitute. The Agniṣṭoma is so called because the last of the Samans used on the day is addressed to Agni.

SAUTRĀMAṆĪ :

A sacrifice originally instituted to expiate and counteract the evil effects of excessive indulgence in Soma drink. The prototype of the sacrifice is the cure of Indra by Sarasvatī and the Aśvins when he was suffering from over-joviality in his beverage. The name is derived from Sutrāman, the good deliverer or protector, Indra. The ceremony is prescribed as a means of obtaining general eminence, of reinstating a dethroned king, of ensuring victory for a Kṣatriya, of acquiring cattle and wealth for a Vaiśya. It concerns mainly the offering, to the Aśvins, Sarasvatī and Indra, of Surā, a spirituous liquor concocted of śaspa (husked rice), tokman (green barley), and lāja (parched grain) ground up with some roots to serve as yeast, and the liquor of two 'Odanas' or messes of rice and Śyāmāka or millet boiled in water, the mixture being called Māsara.

PURUṢAMEDHA : (Human Sacrifice)

Puruṣamedha is a Ahina-type of Soma sacrifice consisting of five days' sacrificial performances. It is generally performed in the tenth full moon days of the month of Chaitra. The offering is usually made by a Brāhmin or Kṣatriya with a desire to overcome all beings. For this offering, there are twenty three Dīkṣās, twelve upasadas and five Sutyas (Soma days). According to S. B., the five days meant for this rite are—Agniṣṭoma followed by an Ukthya and Atirātra, again an Ukthya then an Agniṣṭoma. The first day is identical with the feet of the sacrifice, the second day with the knee, the third day with the waist, the fourth day with the body and the fifth day with the head of sacrifice.

The peculiarity of this sacrifice is that instead of animals human beings are offered as oblations. The offering is, however, not actual but symbolical. Altogether 198 human victims of different castes and occupations are tied to eleven stakes and are symbolically offered. The offering starts with mantras to Lord Savitṛ saying : 'Deva Savitā…………tanna āsuva…'etc. (S. Yv. XXXI. 1-3).

With different desires in mind, the sacrificer seizes different victims. Thus for example, he seizes a Brāhmaṇa for priesthood, for nobility he seizes a Rājanya, for Maruts he seizes a Vaiśya, for religious toil he seizes a Śudra and so on. (S. Yv. XXX.5). None of these human victims is strangled to death or dissected. All of them are released from the stakes with the utterance of sixteen mantras (Puruṣa-Sūktānuvāka).[2] In the Xth maṇḍala of the R. V......., these mantras are also met with. Then, with six verses following the sacrificer worships the Sun-god.[3] After that, the sacrificer gives away everything in his possession to the priests and retires to the forest unseen by anybody.

The spirit underlying the Puruṣamedha is, therefore, not violence but renunciation. The erudite commentator Mahīdhara odserves : 'After the performance of Puruṣamedha, one has to resort to renunciation'.[4] Without understanding the true purport of the word Puruṣamedha, Western scholars like Griffith, Colebrooke, Weber, Wilson, Muir, Oldenberg and Maxmuller consider that actual human slaughter existed in early Vedic age. Indian Scholars like Dayananda Saraswati, Chinnvaswami Sastri and Dr. Jogiraj Basu do not agree with this view. According to them the sacrifice was quite symbolical and actual slaughter of human beings is not heard in any passage of Saṃhitā, Brāhmaṇa or Śrauta texts. Refuting the possibility of human slaughter in Puruṣamedha, the S. B. clearly states in such words as :—

'If human beings are actually offered (as victims) in that case, man would eat man's flesh ;—and as this is not possible, human victims are released after Prayagni-karaṇa ceremony'.

Puruṣamedha, therefore, does not mean actual human sacrifice; it means, on the other hand, the perfection of man for the sake of spiritual as well as worldly advancement.

SARVAMEDHA (all sacrifice)

The whole XXXII Ch. consisting of 16 verses and the first fifty four verses of the XXXIII. Ch of S. Yv. are devoted to the offering of Sarvamedha. It is a ten-day Soma sacrifice performed for the sake of universal success and prosperity. The spirit behind this sacrifice as its very name indicates is the total renunciation. After performing this ceremony the sacrificer has to leave his home and retire to the forest for the rest of his life. In spirit, therefore, this ceremony may be considered higher and more important than even Puruṣamedha.[6]

THE AGNICAYANA :

The Agnicayana or the piling of fire is a rite performed optionally together with the Soma sacrifice. It begins with an annual sacrifice of an original type. The preliminaries extend over a year and include among other things—the digging and preparation of clay for bricks, the baking of bricks, the ceremonial concerning the fire. The actual ceremony starts with the building of the fire altar which is made in five layers with 10,800 bricks in all, bearing different names.

A small golden image of a man, a symbolic of Agni and a living tortoise are burried in the lowest layer of bricks. In the centre of the construction a naturally perforated stone is placed and the whole is levelled off by means of a layer of earth. The period of this operation varies from a few days to a year. After the construction of the altar, 425 libations are offered to Rudra. The fire is brought with great pomp in the form of a fire brand which is placed on a vessel of milk on the central stone. Then comes a number of libations for Vaiśvānara, for the forty nine winds, for Agni, for the months etc. It is only after all this the great Soma ceremonies take place. The performer of the Agnicayana rite is subject to certain restrictions : he may not go out in the rain, nor eat the flesh of birds, the altar being deemed to be of bird form, nor have relation with a woman except of his own caste.

PRĀYAŚCITTAM (Expiation)

Prāyaścittam i.e. expiations are provided in the case of error concerning instrument, place or time, honorarium, or wife, fault of inattention (omission, alteration, performances of acts or recitation of formulae in a wrong order) or accident (extinction of the fire, breaking of any sacrificial utensils, theft or harm of the Soma, sickness or death of the sacrificer).

The S. Yv. after a detail discussion on various rites and sacrifices, brings out an account of Prāyaścittam or expiations in its XXXIX th chapter—the chapter that marks the closing of the ritualistic discussion of this Saṃhitā.   In this chapter we find some expiations, prescribed in case of breaking sacrificial utensils such as—Gharma, a milk pot and Mahāvīra, a large earthenware which is used in the Pravargya type of Soma sacrifice.   As an expiation for breaking of Mahāvīra, deities like Prajāpati, Aśvins, Maruts and Pūṣans are to be invoked.[7]   If the gharma is broken in the first day of the sacrifice, the Savitā is to be invoked, Agni is addressed for the breaking of gharma on the second day, Vāyu for the third, the Sun for the fourth and so on.[8]

REFERENCES

1.   "Agnirjyotirjyotiragniḥ svāhā Sūryo jyotirjyotiḥ Sūryaḥ svāhā.
     Agnirvarco jyotirvarcaḥ svāhā Sūryo varco jyotirvarcaḥ svāhā.
     Jyotiḥ Sūryaḥ Sūryo jyoti svāhā"—S. Yv. III.9.10
2.   S. Yv. XXXI.1-16
3.   S. Yv. XXXI.17-22
4.   'tat puruṣamedhānantaraṃ sanyāsa eva'—Mahīdhara on S. Yv. XXX.22
5.   'Puruṣa mā santistapa yadi saṃsthāpayisyati puruṣa eva puruṣamat syati'—
     S. B. 1-6-2-13.
6.   R. T. H. Griffith—White Yajurveda, p. 314
7.   S. Yv. XXXIX.5
8.   S. Yv. XXXIX.6

CHAPTER VI

(B) THEORY OF SACRIFICE

Yajña or sacrifice may be said to have been the backbone of the Vedic society. In the development of life and culture of the Aryan people, sacrifice played a very vital role. It was the sacrificial ceremonial round which developed all sorts of knowledge. It is true not only of religious but also of scientific knowledge. Remembering the great contribution of the sacrifice in the field of various types of knowledge a scholar observes :

'Sacrifices had a multiple purpose. The Yajñas were the open air observatories, academies and laboratories from which emanated knowledge from time to time—the sciences developed in this context were—phonetics, grammar, linguistics, geometry, astronomy, cosmology, biology, medicine, surgery and anatomy besides agriculture, diary and dietetics.'[1] Moreover, the sacrifice was regarded by Vedic seers as the source of both spiritual and material achievement. Sacrifice was the medium by which different deities embodying natural phenomena were propitiated and through their propitiation, the sacrificers were granted wealth and long life in this world and heavenly bliss in the other world.

Sacrifice was also regarded as the source of creation. By His self-immolation in the first cosmic sacrifice, the one Supreme god, the Primal Puruṣa manifested Himself into this diversified world.

That cosmic sacrifice has been described in detail in the Hymns of creation known as Puruṣa-Sūkta and in the first sixteen verses of the XXXI-Chapter of the S. Yv.[2] The description runs thus :

'The whole creation consisting of the Vedas, four castes, animals both wild and domestic, sprang from the self-sacrifice of the Primal Being, Puruṣa. His vivisected limbs were offered in the sacrifice and different objects of creation came into existence from the different organs of His body. Thus the Brāhmaṇa sprang

18

from His mouth, the Kṣatriya from His arm, the Vaiśya from his thigh and the Śūdra from the feet. The Moon was created from His mind, the Sun from His eye, Indra and the fire from the mouth and the wind from His vital breath. The welkin region was born from His navel, the firmament sprang from His head, the earth from His feet and the directions or quarters from His ear.'[3] Thus, the sacrifice is the source of creation. The whole Universe sprang from the sacrifice. Primal Puruṣa who was one and undivided before sacrifice, became many afterwards. This fact underwent reorientation in the Upaniṣadic Age and became one of the fundamental doctrines of Upaniṣadic philosophy which upholds that the diversified world is nothing but the manifestation of one Absolute Reality.[4]

Not only was the world originated but also sustained by the sacrifice. The Yajurvedic as well as Bhāhmaṇa texts consider the sacrifice to be the sustainer of the Universe. As the upkeep of the universe depends on sacrifice, it is called in the S. Yv. 'the navel of the universe.'[5] The same idea is maintained in the T. B.[6] while the S. B. regards the sacrifice as the 'source of Ṛtam or cosmic principle,'[7] and the A. B. as the 'fountain of all good deeds, acts of piety'.[8] A well-performed sacrifice as the source of cosmic principle extends its influence over natural forces and regulating them favourably generates timely and sufficient rainfall. Thus good cultivation and abundant food production are ensured. Creatures living on earth absolutely depend on food for their livelihood and for that of the future generation. Sacrifice is, therefore, at the root of the sustenance of whole creation. This fact is well-reflected in the Manu-Saṁhitā Ch. III and in the Bhagavat-gītā Ch. III. Thus declares the Manu Saṁhitā :

'Offerings reverentially offered in fire in a right śāstric way, rightly goes up to the solar region, thence due to regular taking of mundane moisture, timely rain comes down, crops grow thereby and people are born and grown up thereby.'[9]

Almost in the same tone the Bhagavat-gītā declares :—

'From food creatures come into being, from rain is the birth of food, from sacrifice rain comes into being and sacrifice is born of work'.[10]

In order to achieve worldly and other-worldly bliss, the help of sacrifice is believed to be indispensable. Hence sacrifice is regarded as the highest of all rites and rituals. The word 'greatest deed' is ascribed as an appellation to sacrifice in the S. Yv.[11] 'Sacrifice is the greatest of all deeds'—declare the S. B. & the T. B.[12] Sacrifice is again considered to be the sure means to lead sacrificers to heaven. It is often compared to a strong and defectless vessel with hundred oars which will definitely carry the sacrificer to the havenly abode.[13] The sacrifice is according to the A. B. 'the vessel by which one can easily cross'.[14] Ramendra Sundar Trivedi has brought out a book entitled "Yajñakatha". Therein he rightly holds that the duties of a householder may be equalled with 'Yajña' and the inner significance of Yajña lies in renunciation.[15]

The sacrificer invoked different deities in the sacrifice with a view to achieve manifold results of the sacrifice. The life, the life breath, the eyes and ears are desired to have strength through the practice of sacrifice. This view is expressed in the following verse of the S. Yv.

'May life prosper through the sacrifice. May breath prosper through the sacrifice. May the eye prosper through the sacrifice. May the ear prosper through the sacrifice. May the back prosper through the sacrifice. May the sacrifice prosper through the sacrifice.'[17]

The multifarious results of the sacrifice are alluded to the XVIIIth Ch. of the S. Yv. The vedic poet hopes that each and every desirable object will flourish through the practice of sacrifice. Through the grace of sacrifice, all his bodily organs such as breath, voice, ears, eyes and mind etc. will be stimulated.[18] Through the grace of sacrifice, one desires to attain long life, immortality, happiness and vivacity.[19] Moreover, all sorts of agricultural products, flowers and trees, rain etc. will flourish through the grace of sacrifice. As a result of sacrifice various minerals such as iron, tin, copper etc. will be abundant. Along with the growth of material prosperity, the spiritual attainment of the sacrificer will earn him heaven so that he may live there happily as the subject of Prajāpati with other divine beings.[20]

Among gods, Agni (fire) is directly related to sacrifice, because no sacrifice can be performed without Agni. As Agni is the nearest visible god and is easily accessible, so he is taken as the best medium for propitiating any other god. Any sacrificial offering meant for any god has to be offered first to Agni in the sacrifice and from there the essence of these offerings reaches the god concerned. Agni, thus maintains a link among the sacrifice, the deity concerned and the sacrificer. No god can be directly propitiated without the medium of sacrifice which, again, must be purified by Agni, the fire god. Agni is, therefore, eulogised for carrying all the sacrificial offerings to the desired deity and for placing the sacrificer among gods in heaven in consequence of his admirable sacrificial performances.[21] Next to Agni, other deities like Indra, Brahmā, Bṛhaspati and Viśvedevāḥ are invoked for placing the sacrificer in the highest realm of heaven.[22]

Reverence for and faith in the sacrifice also count a great deal. No sacrifice can be well-accomplished without Śraddhā or faith. Any sacrificial fee given unto the priest with reverence and the sacrifice performed with faith help the sacrificer to Truth. 'By giving the sacrificial fee one gains faith and of faith comes the knowledge of Truth'[23]......declares the Śukla-Yajurvedic text.

According to Uvaṭa and Mahīdhara,[24] the word Truth or Satya, here refers to Infinite knowledge—the knowledge of Brahman, the absolute. As the attainment of Truth or Absolute Reality is possible by means of Śraddhā or faith, its importance in the sacrificial ceremonial is well-established.

Among Saṃhitās, the Yajurveda claims the nearest relationship with sacrificial ceremonial. The A. V. has no direct bearing on sacrificial ceremonial. The S. V. deals solely with one part of the ritual, the Soma sacrifice. The Y. V., on the other hand, supplies the formulas for the whole sacrificial ceremonial. In the R. V. Gods are the objects of devotion, sacrifices are regarded as the medium only to make the god favourably disposed. In the Y. V. on the other hand, the sacrifice has attained the principal position.   Referring to the relative emphasis of sacrifice in the Y. V., Dr. Macdonell observes :—

"In the Y. V. the sacrifice itself has become the centre of thought and desire, its correct performance in every detail being all important.   Its power is now so great that it not merely influences, but compels the gods to do the will of the officiating priest."[25]

The importance of sacrificial ceremonial has been felt in the subsequent development in the Brāhmaṇas.   For any type of sacrificial discussion, therefore, the attention should be paid to the Y. V. next to the Brāhmaṇas only.

REFERENCES

1. Pandit Ganga Prasad Upadhyaya—Śatapatha Brāhmaṇa.
2. T. A. III.12
3. R. V. X.90 ; S. Yv. XXXI.1-16
4. Dr. Jogiraj Basu—India At the Age of Brāhmaṇas, p. 145.
5. S. Yv. XXII.62...'ayaṃ yajña bhuvanasya nābhiḥ'
6. T. B. 3.9.5.5...'Yajña vai bhuvanasya nābhiḥ'
7. S. B. 1.3.4.16...'Yajña va r̥tasya yoniḥ'
8. A. B. 1.5.2...'Sukr̥tasya yoniḥ (Yajñāḥ)'
9. 'Agnau prāstāhuti samyagādityamupatiṣṭate
   Ādityajjāyate vr̥ṣṭiḥ vr̥ṣṭerannaṃ tataḥ prajāḥ'—Manu-Saṃhitā III
10. 'Annād bhavanti bhūtāni parjanyādannasambhavaḥ.
    Yajñad bhavati parjanyo yajñaḥ karmasamudbhavaḥ'
                                   —Bhagavat-gītā.III.14
11. S. Yv. I.1...'Śreṣṭhatamāya karmaṇe'
12. S. B. 1-7-1-5 'Yajño vai śreṣṭhatamaṃ karma'
    T. B. 3-2, 1.4 'Yajño hi śreṣṭhatamaṃ karma'
13. S. Yv. XXI.7...'Sunāvamāruheyamasravantimanāgasam.
                Śatāritram Svastaye'—
14. A. B. 1-3-2...'Yajña vai sutarma nauḥ'
15. R. S. Trivedi...'Yajñakathā (Ramendra Sundar Racanavali), p. 624
16. S. Yv. III.5
17. "Āyuryajñena kalpatāṃ prāṇo yajñena kalpatāṃ cakṣuryajñena kalpatāṃ śrautraṃ yajñena kalpatāṃ pr̥ṣṭaṃ yajñena kalpatāṃ yajño yajñena kalpatām..." S. Yv. IX.21

18. S. Yv. XVII.2.3.29
19. S. Yv. XVIII.6
20. S. Yv. IX.21, XVIII.29…"Prajāpateḥ prajā abhūma svardevā aganmamṛta
        abhūma…"
21. "Yatra dhārā anapetā madho ghṛtasya ca yaḥ
      Tadgni vaiśvakarmāna svardeveṣu no dadhāt" (S. Yv. XVIII.65)
22. 'Dhamacchadagnirindro Brahmā devo Bṛhaspatiḥ
      Sacetaso viśvedeva yajñam pravantu naḥ subhe" (S. Yv. XVIII.76)
23. '…dakṣiṇā śraddhāmāpnoti śraddhayā satyamāpyate' (S. Yv. XIX.30)
24. "Śraddhayā satyaṃ jñanamanantaṃ Brahmāpyate prāpyate"—Mahīdhara
                                                            on S. Yv. XIX.30

      "Satyaṃ jñanamanantam Brahma…"Uvaṭa on S. Yv. XIX.30
25. Dr. A. A. Macdonell—A History of Sanskrit Literature, p. 153.

CHAPTER VII

THE PHILOSOPHY BEHIND THE WORSHIP OF VEDIC DEITIES AND SACRIFICE.

Many people think that the Saṃhitā or Mantra portion of vedic literature is burdened only with ritualistic speculations and so it has no scope for bringing out any philosophical or metaphysical ideas. According to them, the source of the later Indian philosophy or any kind of philosophical thought may be traced only in the Upaniṣadic or concluding portion of Vedic literature. But this is not wholly true. We find even in the earliest Saṃhitā—in the hymns of Ṛgveda many traces of philosophical speculations of no mean order. The philosophy in India, according to Dr. Keith,[1] shows its beginning often in the expression of scepticism. Different questions regarding the true nature of gods like Indra and that of human being, arose in the mind of Vedic seers in that early age. The Ṛgvedic poet thus exclaimed—'who is Indra, who ever saw him ?—or asserted that he did not exist at all.'[2] or such questioning arose—'I do not know what kind of thing I am, mysterious, bound my mind wanders'.

The assertion based on the unity of the gods and of the world is one of the basic problems of philosophy and this assertion is made with emphasis in a hymn of R. V. (1.164).

The idea of unity is further developed and explained in another hymn of the R. V. which is popularly known as Nāsadīya Hymn (R. V. X. 129). It is a hymn of creation. It exhibits not merely the questioning the nature of universe but an effort to enter into detail. The hymn commences with an assertion : 'in the beginning there was no atmosphere, nor sky, nor anything that is beyond ; what covered everything and where and for whose enjoyment ? Was there water, unfathomable and deep ? There was neither death, nor immortality, nor night, nor day. There was nothing else in the world besides the one which breathed without wind, by its own power'—This assertion of the Ṛgvedic seer exhibits the existence of the One, Absolute Reality who holds the phenomenal world within Him. Many more hymns from the R. V. may be illustrated as to point out their philosophic characteristics.

But as regards the hymns of the Y. V. many scholars opine that these are mainly of liturgical character based on sacerdotal mechanism and hence are lacking in any philosophical thought. This, however, can not be totally admitted when we enter into the realm of the Śukla-Yajurvedic hymns. In this samhitā, rites and rituals play no doubt the predominant part, still in it there are some hymns which in the garb of sacrifice and worship of deities contain some higher thoughts of philosophic speculations.

One of the remarkable features of this Samhitā is that it exbihits different philosophical problems or Upanisadic thoughts even in the midst of its Karma-Kānḍa or ritualistic portion.

The last adhyāya (Ch. XL.) of the S. Yv. has, however, no direct connections with the sacrificial ceremonial. It is regarded as an Upanisad-Īśāvāsyam or simply Īśā by name and professedly designed to fix the proper mean between the one exclusively engaged in sacrificial acts and those entirely neglecting them. It belongs at all events to a very advanced stage of speculation as it assumes the One, Single Lord (Īśā) of the Universe. Other parts, too, of the S. Yv. have in later times been looked upon as Upaniṣadas on account of their observation on philosophical speculations. These are, for example, the sixteenth chapter (Śata-rudrīya), the thrity first Ch. (Puruṣa Sūkta), the thirty second (Tadeva) and the beginning of the thirty fourth Ch. (Śiva Saṃkalpa).

Let us now try to expound the philosophical ideas as contained in the above mentioned chapters of the S. Yv.

ĪŚOPANIṢAD :

As constituting the concluding chapter of the Vājasaneyī Samhitā, the Īśopaniṣad is also named as the Vājasaneyī-Samhitopaniṣad. It is the single specimen of Samhitopaniṣad or upaniṣad inseparably attached to the Samhitā portion in the Vedic literature.

It is interesting enough to note that within the short space of eighteen verses only this upaniṣad upholds all the principal philosophical ideas. This upaniṣad commences with the declaration that the whole universe in diffused with the spirit of God through and through.[3]

That All-pervading Lord is luminous, bodiless, devoid of injuries and sinews, pure, unpierced by sin and self-existent. The upaniṣad teaches that one should desire to live the full span of life and to utilise the same to realise this true nature of self and be free ; without this realisation of self, it warns, life would be lived in darkness and sorrow and rendered meaningless and sterile.[4] The upaniṣad then goes on to say that a man who sees all beings in the self, and sees the self as existing in all beings, in fact, for whom all beings and everything exist has become the Self—how can there be sorrow and delusion for him ?[5] How can there be hatred which is born of the sense of separateness ? Such things can not be, their roots consisting of ignorance being burnt in the fire of spiritual awareness.

The verses 9 to 14 of this Upaniṣad seek to resolve the opposition between work and worship, between action (avidyā) and systical contemplation (vidyā) through hints and suggestions.

The first three of these six verses read thus :-

'They enter into blinding darkness who go in search after 'avidyā', into still greater darkness, do they enter, who betake themselves to vidyā.'[6]

'One result, they say, is obtained by vidyā, and another result they say, is obtained by avidyā ; thus have we heard from the wise ones explain it to us.'[7]

'He who knows both vidyā and avidyā together conquers death by means of avidyā and attains immortality by means of vidyā.'[8]

These hymns expound Samyagjñana or the philosophy of total vision. According to them and following three verses,[9] there should be a synthesis of the work (avidyā) and worship (vidyā)—of the worship of the Prime cause (asambhuti) and that of the Prime effect (sambhuti) by which alone one wins better result in the state of intuitive realisation.

19

The metaphysical idea of the Īśopaniṣad is highlighted by the following observation of Dr. Balvalkor and Ranade.[10] They say : 'The metaphysics of this upaniṣad takes us to a discussion of the self who is regarded as bright and incorporeal and whole, pure and uncotaminated by evil. He is the seer, the omnipresent and self-existent. It is due to this self that things have been disposed of rightly for eternity'.[11]

A little after this, we are told that even though this bright luminous self exists as the eternal background of all things, fulfilling all the conditions of the Highest Reality, His face, we learn, is hidden by a gold disc which comes like a cloud between the sun and the observer, and in this conception of the Veil 'some have detected the presene of the germs of later illusionistic speculations. Finally, as in every upaniṣad, so even in this the author insists upon the identity of the self in man, and the self in the Sun (Verse 16)—a conception which is the current coin of all upanisadic philosophy'.

(ii) *THE ŚATARUDRĪYA* (S. Yv. XVI).

This chapter has been discussed at length under the caption—'Rudra-Śiva Cult'. There we have observed, how Rudra appears as the All-pervading supreme God-Head—the basic unity behind the apparent diversities of the world and creation. This doctrine of unity, a fundamental philosophical conception, as expressed in this chapter, has undergone further development in later upaniṣads[12] specially in the Śvetāśvetara where Rudra is ranked with the position of One and Absolute.[13]

The leading feature of the Śatarudrīya is the description of Rudra-Śiva as the unified force of anything and everyting in the universe (Viśvarūpa), associating Himself with every aspect of society, activity and nature.

(iii) *THE PURUṢASŪKTA* (The hymn to Supreme being S. Yv. XXXI Ch).

This hymn is a mere repetition and addition of the original hymn of the R.V. X.90. The sage Nārāyaṇa being the seer, this hymn is named as 'Uttara-nārāyaṇa' or simply 'Nārāyaṇa Sūkta' in the S. Yv. (XXXI. 17-22) so also in the T.A (III. 13). Here the cosmic and individual self appear to be identified with the Universal self, and we find the famous doctrine of Indian philosophy that the inspired seer can become identical with the Supreme being, transferring his own individual self into the Universal self. As a result of this identification, he attains immortality or deathless state. The seer thus exclaims :-

'That Being came out of water, and out of the essence of earth too, he was above the Creator ; the divine architect Tvastar comes fashioning his form (in the shape of the world), the Universe was, at the beginning a product of the Supreme being'.[14]

'I know thal Great Being of the Sun's colour and beyond darkness ; he who knows Him thus becomes immortal here, there is no other path for attaining Him.'[15]

Here, in the above verse, it is urged that true knowledge of the Supreme Being alone leads one to the path of salvation—an idea quite akin to the upanisadic philosophy.

The Purusa is here, in this chapter of discussion seen to be identified with Prajāpati and with Brahman—the Absolute. Thus it is said that Prajāpati the creator is, in fact Brahman, the Eternal Unborn One, but for the sake of creation He with His creative force pervades the soul in the womb of all and thereby manifests Himself in various ways. The mainfested world is, therefore, nothing but His phenomenal aspect. Men of intellect can alone realise this truth—His true nature through cognition.[16]

iv) *THE TADEVA* (S. Yv. XXXII.Ch)

This chapter is considered to be an upaniṣad entitled 'Tadeva' from the first two letters. 'Tad'—here denotes the Supreme Being—the Prime cause of the Universe—the Puruṣa and is identified as in the previous chapter with Prajāpati and with Brahman, the Absolute. Alluded to the Sarvamedha or Universal sacrifice, the verses of this chapter contain in them a deep sense of philosophic speculation. The one Absolute supreme being is here described as the Self of all gods like Agni (fire), Āditya (Sun), Vāyu (air) and

Candramā (moon) etc.[17]

He is formless and All-pervading.

'For Him there is no counterpart (or image) (for) great indeed His glory'.[18]

Wise man sees that Eternal Being—the Brahman in the deepest recesses of his heart, in It the (whole) universe comes in as its a single nest, there, all this universe is gathered (at dissolution) and thrown out at creation ; that All pervading Being is woven into beings like warp and woof of a garment. That Immortal thing a wise man may expound, its glory is held in secret ; three steps of it are in the mystey ; he who knows them becomes the father's father.[19]—By three steps here are meant the three conditions—creation, continuance and dissolution of the universe of the Absolute (Brahman), the creator and the Individual self.[20] Does it not remind us of the great vedantic truth—'tajjalāniti' or 'sarvam khalvidam Brahma' ? He is our kith and kin, our father and creator. After realising Him, the gods enjoy immortality in the highest heaven. The performer of the Universal sacrifice, being free from ignorance, realise the true nature of that Supreme Reality (Brahman) and as a result unites with Him. Through his vision of knowledge he sees that Supreme soul and becomes That.[21]—We find here the germ of the Advaita philosophy which propagates—'a knower of Brahman becomes Brahman himself'.[22]

(v) *ŚIVA SAMKALPA :* (The hymn of good intent : S. Yv. XXXIV. 1-6)

The first six verses of the XXXIVth Ch. of S. Yv. constitute a hymn known as Śiva-Saṃkalpa (Right intentioned) from the concluding words of each verse.[23] Mind is the vital sense organ, the most powerful of all sense organs, but it is by nature very inconstant. All philosophical systems in India have laid great stress on the control and purification of mind. If mind is duly restrained, they believe, it earns the capacity of gathering the intuitive knowledge. An impure and fickle-minded man cannot proceed even a step towards the path of knowledge. In the VIth chapter of the Bhagavatgītā, we see, how Lord Kṛṣṇa stresses the need of controlling the mind for the right purpose.   In far old days of the S. Yv. the seers were aware of the necessity for mind's purification and restraint.   They believed that the auspicious mind, like a good charioteer, would lead them surely to the path of realisation. So, they repeatedly urged in a couple of verses that their mind should be of good intent.   They exclaim thus :-

'That mind, the divine, mounts far when man is wakeful and returns to him when he is asleep ; the light of all lights (sense of all senses)—may that Mind of mine be of good intent'.[24]

'By which the virtuous, thoughtful and wise persons perform the duties in sacrifice and intellectual activities, that which is the peerless spirit stored in living creatures, may that my Mind be moved by auspicious resolve'.[25]

'That which is wisdom, intellect, and firmness—that which is the immortal light within all beings—without which man can do no single action, may that my Mind be of beautiful intent'.[26]

'Whereby coupled with immortal God, the past, present and future—all are comprehended, with which the sacrifice with its seven priests grows, may that my Mind be of noble resolve'.[27]

'In whom the Ṛks, Sāmans and Yajus are estabished like spokes within a cart's nave, in whom all the thought of beings is woven—may that my Mind be moved by right intention'. (S. Yv. XXXIV. 5)

'As a skillful charioteer drives with reins the horses, so does the mind direct the man. It dwells in heart, is immortal and swiftest—may that Mind of mine be right intentioned'. (S. Yv. XXXIV. 6).

The mind of right intention as mentioned above may be equated with Buddhi or intelligence which in the Kaṭha-Upaniṣad is also described as the charioteer, the body being the chariot.[28]

Besides the above-mentioned chapters of the S. Yv. containing philosophic contents, we may quote some verses from some other chapters of the S. Yv. which though assigned to different sacrifices and worship of deities contain in them specimens of ture philosophy.

Thus, for example in connection with the Horse sacrifice, we find some theosophic riddles known as Brahmodyas in the S. Yv. Ch. XXIII. In such riddles is displayed an endeavour to solve some basic problems of philosophy. One such riddle runs thus :—

'What are things which the Supreme being (Puruṣa) hath entered in ? What are the things which He hath contained in Him ?—The solution of the problem is given thus :

Within five elements hath the Supreme being found entrance. He pervades all the creatures as their Inner self. So He is present in all and all are present in Him. (S. Yv. XXIII. 51-52)

Again, while celebrating a sacrificial rite known as 'Vasa-graha', the sacrificer expresses his realisation about the existence of All-powerful Supreme Reality in his heart with such words as :

'He (the Supreme Reality) is the Lord of living beings, upon whom the worlds depend. He is mighty—greater than space. Hence I realise Him, I realise Him in my heart'. (S. Yv. XX.33).

From what has been discussed above, it may safely be observed that the S. Yv. in the midst of its various sacrificial rites contains some specimens of genuine philosophy. And if any such argument is levelled aganist the S. Yv. that it displays only mechanical sacerdotalism and no philosophy, may instantly be refuted.

ESCHATOLOGY

The optimistic nature of the Vedic Aryan used to incite them to enjoy a life full of pleasure and prosperity and free from diseases. Poverty and diseases generally stand as obstacles in achieving a delightful life. Hence in numerous passages of the S. Yv. different deities are invoked for offering them riches in the form of cattle, sons and healthy life. Premature death was regarded as another hindrance towards the full enjoyment of life. The Vedic Aryan would therefore, nourish the desire for spending the full-span of life being endowed with vigour, health and prosperity. While performing sacrifices, the sacrificer used to express his desire for a long life with a body imbued with a sound physique through the proper functioning of all sense organs.[29] While invoking Lord Rudra[30] and Varuṇa,[31] prayers are offered not to cut short the life of the sacrificers. Their desire for running a full race of life covering hundred years is expressed in many passages of this Veda. The following passages illustrate the point clearly :

'O Gods, may we live a life covering hundred years. Let not our bodies decay before that period in which old age our sons become fathers in turn. Break ye not in the midst our course of fleeting life'. (S. Yv. XXV. 22).

'Through the grace of God, may we see a hundred years, may we live a hundred years, may we listen for a hundred years, may we speak for hundred years.'[32]

This prayer is met with in a more detailed and emphatic form in the Taittirīya Āranyaka.[33]

From the above discussion, it can be deduced that Vedic Aryans of this period were not at all indifferent to wordly life, on the other hand, their attitude towards worldly life was quite inspiring. They were desirous of spending a lengthy but successful life in a world where, in their view, only the sweetness would ever flow.[34] There was no negative attitude or escapist mentality.

Though advocating for a lengthy stay on this world, the Aryans of this period were quite aware of the fact that they could not stay here for good. A time would come when they would find no alternative but to respond to the call of death which would take them away from this known world to an unknown sphere. That unknown world was conceived as Heaven or Hell.

They believed that Heaven was meant for those who had lived life of righteousness and piety on earth—whereas hell was meant for those who had spent their life-period in an evil manner committing various misdeeds and sinful acts. Though we do not find here any trace about the immortality of soul—a conception firmly established in the Upaniṣads, still we can have an idea that the Yajurvedic thinkers believed in the existence of life of men and animals hereafter. Death here means life hereafter. What will be the position of the creature after death ? To this, the thinkers of Yajurveda answer that pious would go to heaven and the sinners would be thrown into a region full of darkness—a place popularly known as Naraka or hell.

Heaven is imagined as a place where there is a constant flow of happiness. The never failing streams of honey and butter flow in that heavenly region.[35] Gods are referred to as the common dwellers of heaven, so after death the virtuous deserve to reach there in the midst of gods.[36] The most vital longing was to attain the highest bliss.[37] In most of the sacrificial performances, prayers were sent to different deities for granting the boon for an easy access to Heaven.[38]

Sacrifice and Heaven are interrelated—the former being treated as the means to the attainment of the latter. Sacrifice is treated as one that leads to Heaven,[39] that touches the firmament.[40] 'It is the eternal sacrifice through which our forefathers attained the high Heaven and through due performance of which may we also reach to that illustrious Heaven.'—This is the reflection of the Vedic sacrificers. After the attainment of Heaven through the influence of sacrifice one becomes a divine being—the subject or the Lord of creation or Prajāpati.[41]

It has already been told that hell is conceived as opposed to Heaven, just as the darkness is the opposite of light. As the Heaven is imagined to be a place for the pious—the hell will naturally be meant for the sinners. There is, however, no clear reference to the character of hell and its terrific nature as described in the Purāṇas. In some verses of S. Yv., a region enveloped in darkness is alluded to and gods are asked to drag the evil doers to that region.[42] From this, it can be conceived that the region of blinding darkness will surely stand to mean hell as opposed to Heaven which is described as a place flooded with pure light (Jyotiruttamam). In order to escape the path of hell, one must by all means try to be sinless. A number of verses of this Veda express this feeling of the Vedic Aryans.[43]

Let God Savitā, the inspirer of all, send far away all vices and calamities and grant us virtue.[44] In some other passages the Sungod is propitiated to discard the effects of sinful acts or violence committed in villages or in forests by killing the animal or by creating disturbances in religious performances[45] or by telling a lie in an assembly. It is urged that the grace of gods would expiate the sins committed knowingly or unknowingly.

However desirable the Heaven may be and however profitable may be the association with the divine beings there, it can not, in the view of the Yajurvedic thinkers, give permanent relief to the departed being. Because after a certain period on expiry of his spiritual attainment, he will have to be reborn in this world in accordance with the law of Karma. Death will come again in its natural course. This endless cycle of birth and death possesses a great problem and causes endless sorrows and sufferings. An ardent desire naturally sank deep in the heart of Vedic people to get rid of sufferings caused by the recurrent cycle of birth and death. Some of the Śukla Yajurvedic verses draw our attention to this fact.

Lord Rudra is invoked in a verse for [47] liberating the sacrificer from the shackle of birth and death. This liberation or emancipation is possible only through the knowledge of Supreme soul. By cognition, the individual being emerges into the supreme soul and attains immortality.[48] With full conviction, the Yajurvedic seer proclaims that he has realised the Supreme Being, refulgent like the Sun after casting aside the veil of ignorance ; and this knowledge, par excellence, can only rescue him from the clutches of death, for salvation there is no other path than this.[49] It is notable that the same view regarding final emancipation and beautitude occurs in the Upaniṣads. The last chapter of the S. Yv. which is best known as Iśopaniṣad points out that mere knowledge without rites or mere rites without knowledge cannot lead a person to the path of liberation. Knowledge and dispassionate action redeem a person from the whirlpool of birth and death. Salvation can be attained by knowledge while death can be overcome by Action or religious rites.[50] The later Upaniṣadic doctrines based on liberation, thus have their source in the Śukla Yajurvedic propagation on this point.

Yama, the presiding deity over death is eulogised in a number of verses in the R. V., but in the S. Yv., he is rarely mentioned. In a passage he is invoked as the lord of death[51] and in another passage he is being praised with Aṅgiras and other departed fathers.[52]

In the R. V.,[53] the idea of hell is nascent. There are referen-

20

ces to eternal punishment in a region of deep darkness. The references describe a deep subterranean region or a pit. There is no such term as 'Naraka' nor is there any description of infernal harrowings.

In the A. V., the idea of hell is clear. It mentions 'Naraka-loka' as distinct from 'Svarga-loka'. Naraka-loka is a subterranean cavern enveloped in blinding darkness. The harrowings of hell are also described. Those who injure Brahmins are believed to sit in streams of blood.

REFERENCES

1. Dr. A. B. Keith—Religion & Philosophy of the Veda & Upanisads
2. R. V. II.12.5 ; VIII.103.3
3. Īśā vāsyamidaṃ sarvaṃ yatkiñca jagatyāṃ jagat.
   Tena tyaktena bhuñjithā mā gṛdhaḥ Kasyaviddhanam—S. Yv. XL.I (Īśā-1)
4. "Asūryā nāma te lokā andhena tamasāvritāḥ.
   Tāṃste pretyābhigacchanti ye ke cātmahano janāḥ."—S. Yv. XL.3 (Īśā-3)
5. "Yasmin sarvāni bhūtānyatmaivabhūdvijānataḥ.
   Tatra ko mohaḥ kaḥ śoka ekatvamanupaśyatah."—S. Yv. XL.7 (Īśā-7)
6. "Andhaṃ tamaḥ praviśanti yehavidyāmupāsate.
   Tato bhūya iva te tamo ya u vidyāyāṃ ratāḥ."—S. Yv. XL.9 (Īśā-9)
7. 'Anyadevāhurvidyayā anyadāhuravidyayā.
   Iti śuśruma dhīrānāṃ ye nastadvicacakṣire'...S. Yv. XL.10 (Īśā-10)
8. "Vidyāṃ cāvidyāṃ ca yastadvedobhayaṃ saha.
   Avidyayā mṛtyuṃ tīrtvā vidyayāmṛtamaśnute"—S. Yv. XL.11 (Īśā-11)
9. S. Yv. XL.11-13 (Īśā-11-13)
10. History of Indian Philosophy, Vol. II, Creative period
11. S. Yv. XL.8 (Īśā-8)
12. C. U. III.7.4 ; B. U. III.9.4
13. "S. U. 3/2..."Eko Rudro na dvitīyāya tasthuḥ."
14. S. Yv. XXXI.17 ; T. A. III.13
15. 'Vedāhamatam puruṣaṃ mahāntamādityavarṇaṃ tamasaḥ parastāt.
    Tameva viditvāti mṛtyumeti nānyaḥ panthā vidyate ayanāya.'
                           S. Yv. XXXI.18 ; S. U. 3/8 ; K. U. I.ii.20
16. S. Yv. XXXI.19
17. 'Tadevāgni stadāditya stadvāyu stadu candramāḥ
    Tadeva śukraṃ tad Brahma tā āpaḥ sa prajāpatiḥ"—S. Yv. XXXII.1
18. "...na tasya pratimā asti yasya nāma mahadyaśaḥ"—S. Yv. XXXII.3 ;
                                                         S. U. IV.19

19. S. Yv. XXXII.9..."trīni padāni nihita guhāsya...pitāsat"
20. "Trīni padāni...sargasthiti pralayah, vedāh kāla vā Brahmantaryāmivijñanātmā vā"—Mahīdhara on S. Yv. XXXII.9
21. S. Yv. XXXII.10..."Sa no vandhurjanitā sa vidhāta...dhāmnadhyairayanta".
22. "Brahmavid Brahmaiva bhavati"
23. "...tanme manah śivasankalpamastu"
24. S. Yv. XXXIV.1
25. S. Yv. XXXIV.2
26. S. Yv. XXXIV.3
27. S. Yv. XXXIV.4
28. K. U. I.iii.3
29. "Āyuryajñena kalpatām prāno yajñena kalpatām cakṣuryajñena kalpatām śrotram yajñena kalpatām vāk yajñena kalpatām mano yajñena kalpatām..."
    S. Yv. XVIII.29
30. S. Yv. III.60
31. S. Yv. XXI.2
32. "Taccksurdevahitam purastāchukramuccarat. Paśyema śaradah śatam jivema śaradah śatam śrnuyāma śaradah śatam pra bravāma śaradah śatamadīnāh syāma śaradah śatam bhūyaśca śaradah śatāt"—S. Yv. XXXVI.24
33. T. A. IV.42
34. S. Yv. XIII.27-29
35. S. Yv. XVIII.65...'Yatra dhārā anapetā madho ghrtasya ca yah'
36. S. Yv. XVIII.64-65...'svardeveṣu no dedhāt'
37. S. Yv. XXXVIII.24 ; XX.21 ; IX.10
38. S. Yv. XV.52 ; XVIII.61, 65
39. S. Yv. XXXIII.85..."divasprśam"
40. S. Yv. XXVII.30 'duviṣṭhaṣu'
41. S. Yv. XVIII.29 ; IX.21
42. S. Yv. XVIII.70 ; VIII.44...('śatrumadharam nikrṣṭam tamo narakam gamaya prāpaya'—Mahīdhara).
43. S. Yv. XXX.3
44. S. Yv. XXX.3
45. S. Yv. XX.16-18 ; III.45
46. S. Yv. XXXVIII.20 ; XXVII.9
47. S. Yv. III.60
48. S. Yv. XXV.13
49. Vedāhametam puruṣam mahāntamādityavarnam tamasah parastāt"—
    S. Yv. XXXI.18
50. S. Yv. XI.14
51. S. Yv. XXXIX.13
52. S. Yv. XXXVIII.9
52. R. V. VII.10.11 ; VII.104-17 ; II.29.6 ; IX.73.8-9 ; IV.5.5 etc.

CHAPTER VIII

COSMOGONY

Cosmogonical or cosmological hymns of the S. Yv. bear affinity to those of the R. V. as most of the hymns of the S. Yv. dealing cosmogony have been borrowed from the R. V.

Prajāpati, the manifested form of the Absolute reality, is described in a verse of the XII Ch. of the S. Yv.,[1] as the creator of Heaven and Earth as well as of the Primeval water out of which all the creatures of the world sprang up. In the next chapter,[2] the same Prajāpati, renamed as Hiraṇyagarbha is referred to as the sustainer of the three regions—heaven, earth and atmosphere. He who stood alone before the creation is described to be the Lord of all that were created afterwards. The process of creation is dealt with elaborately in some verses of the S. Yv. in Ch. XIV.[3] There we find how Prajāpati, the Lord of creation, after realising the necessity of manifold creation praises the Supreme Soul (Paramātman) with the help of different organs of his body viz.—speech, breath, hands etc. and thereby gradually the creation starts. Different deities emerged to guide the different created elements.

After creation, Prajāpati himself stood as the guide of human beings ; Brahmaspati, Bhūtanātha, Mahādeva and Dhātr̥ appeared to sustain the Vedas, the five elements (earth, water, air, fire and ether), and seven sages respectively. In this way the different seasons, months and years, persons belonging to different castes viz. Brāhmaṇa, Kṣatriya, Vaiśya and Śudra, animals both domestic and wild, trees and all other creatures came into being. Several deities such as—Aditi, Indra, Varuṇa, and others emerged as the lords of these evolved objects. In the S. Yv. (XXIII.63) we have an account of the creation of the world by an Omnipotent God who generated initially the Hiraṇyagarbha or Prajāpati—His creative agent out of the vast cosmic water pervading the universe.[4]

Cosmic water is thus regarded as the source of creation. In the beginning the universe was nothing but a limitless vast expanse of water. On this water was floating an embryo or golden egg out of which was generated the Primal being or Prajāpati.[5] The Brāhmaṇa of this Veda viz. Śatapatha also recounts the legend of cosmic waters and golden egg in the sixth Brāhmaṇa :

'Verily in the beginning the universe was water, nothing but an illimitable expanse of water. Out of this cosmic water a gold egg was produced while floated on the face of the deep for a whole year'.

Within the term of a year the Primal Being Prajāpati was produced therefrom rending asunder the shell of the gold egg. At the end of the year Prajāpati uttered 'bhūḥ' and the world assumed the form of this earth, he uttered 'Bhuvaḥ' which became the air and the word 'Svar' uttered by him became the sky.

Not only the cosmic water, but the space (dyauḥ) is regarded as the first created element of the universe from which other elements of the universe came into being. This idea is met with in some verses[6] of 'Brahmodya' type in the Aśvamedha chapter of the S. Yv. where the Hotṛ priest puts forward the following question to the Adhvaryu priest :-

'What was the first conception ?'—To this a quick repartee comes from the Adhvaryu—'The sky (space) was the first conception.'

This observation of the S. Yv. that the sky is the first created element is also endorsed in the Brāhmaṇa and Upaniṣads.[7] It will not be out of place to note that the findings of modern science announcing the space to be the 'pre-condition of creation' agree with this view of the S. Yv. belonging to hoary antiquity.

In conformity with the cosmogonic view of the R. V., the seers of the S. Yv. upheld the sacrifice as another vital source of creation. The universe emerged out from the first sacrifice that was performed by the great God, the Primal Being called Puruṣa.

This cosmic sacrifice is dealt with in detail in the XXXI Ch. of the S. Yv., otherwise knows as the Puruṣamedha chapter which is, as it were, the replica of the Puruṣasūkta of the R. V.[8] As the first sacrifice was performed at the dawn of creation consisting of four Vedas, four castes, animals both wild and domestic, different seasons sprang from the Self-sacrifice of that Primal Puruṣa. From the different organs of that dedicated Puruṣa different elements of the universe evolved out of this Primal sacrifice. Thus, from His mouth, arms, thigh and feet originated—the Brāhmaṇa, Kṣatriya, Vaiśya and Śūdra respectively. The moon was generated from His mind ; the Sun from His eye ; the fire from His mouth, the wind and vital breath from His ear. The welkin region was born of His navel, the firmament was created from His head, the earth came into being from His feet and the quarters from His organ of hearing. [9]

This idea that holds the sacrifice as the factor of creation also finds place in the subsequent Brāhmaṇa. The S. B. asserts—'All beings are born of the sacrifice'. [10] The self immolation of the Puruṣa stood as a pre-condition of the creation of the universe with its multifarious objects.

The divergent elements of the universe both sentient and insentient are nothing but the emanation of the Primal Puruṣa who stood single without a second as an indivisible whole before the process of creation started through the cosmic sacrifice. That Puruṣa held within Himself the entire creation in the form of an embryo or seed. Then, he manifested Himself as the Virāṭ in the entire gross and material creation. In yet more divisible forms He appeared as individual objects of creation.

A monistic trend in cosmology that propagates the existence of One Supreme Godhead named as Puruṣa, underlying all the diversities of the universe, leads to develop the fundamental doctrine of the Upaniṣad which asserts the oneness of the Absolute Reality in the words :—'Whatever is seen here or whatever exists therein, all that is—He.' [11] 'This one has become all' [12]—This one and Absolute, the sole cause of creation is termed as Brahman in the Upaniṣads. Another Upaniṣadic doctrine that propagates the One to be the creator, sustainer and lastly destroyer of every worldly object [13] traces its germ in the following cosmogonic hymn of the S. Yv.

"The great Being who sacrifices unto Himself all this universe at the time of the end of the cycle of creation, is the great seer, the Omniscient and the Great gatherer. Such is our father who again becomes the creator.

Because at the end of each cycle of creation the only existent Being is the Great Being who gathers unto Himself all, this creation that emanated from Him."—(S. Yv. XVII. 27).

A few more verses may be cited from this Veda as an illustration of monistic trend in cosmogony.

The S. Yv. (XIII. 18)[14] asserts the bases of all creation thus :- 'What was His support at the time of creation ? The significance is that there was not and could not be any outside support as He exists by Himself and there cannot be any support to the supporter of all—'what were the materials which He, the Viśvakarman, created' ? As the potter collects his wheel, stick and clay to turn out earthenwares of different shapes, did He also collect materials for His work ?—To this, the answer comes in this way that the Non-dual, One God Himself becomes the maker as well as the material of creation. He who is naturally present as the soul of all creatures, is described to be the possessor of everything extended everywhere.

His mouth is everywhere ; His arms spread out everywhere and so are His thighs and feet. With His arms and feet moving, He performs all works and thus produces the space and earth.[15]

As regards the bases of creation and all embracing nature of the creator, a query is conched in the following verses[16] :—

'What was the tree, growing in which forest that He felled and joined to produce the space and the earth ? O, Ye sages, do you ponder over and interrogate yourself as to wherein He takes His stand to uphold the universe' ?

The significance underlying this query brings out the fact that the Supreme creator Himself is the tree ; He is the forest and He Himself is the source from which the creation evolved, nothing exists, can exist or existed at all beyond or beside Him.

REFERENCES

1. "...Janitā yaḥ pṛthivyā yo va divaḥ ..yaścāpaścandrāḥ prathamo jajāna..."
    S. Yv. XII.102
2. S. Yv. XIII.4-5
3. S. Yv. XIV.28-31
4. "Subhūḥ svayambhū prathamohantarmahatyarṇave.
    Dadhe ha garbhamṛtviyaṃ yato jātaḥ prajāpatiḥ".—S. Yv. XXIII.63
5. S. Yv. XXVII.25
6. S. Yv. XXIII.11-12 ; 53-54
7. S. B. 13-5-2-17 ; T. U. 2-1-3 : C. U. 'Ākāṣo vai nāma-rūpayornirvahitā".
8. R. V. X. 90
9. S. Yv. XXXI.1-15
10. S. B...'Yajñad vai prajāḥ prajāyante'
11. "Sarvaṃ Khalvidaṃ Brahma"
12. "Ekam vai idaṃ vibabūva sarvam"
13. "Tajjalāniti"
14. "Kiṃ svidāsīdadhiṣṭhānamārambhanaṃ katamat svid kathāsīt.
    Yato bhūmiṃ janayan Viśvakarmā vi dyāmāurnon mahinā
    viśvacakṣāḥ"—(S. Yv. XVII.18)
15. "Viśvataścakṣuruta viśvatomukho viśvatobāhuruta viśvataspāt.
    Saṃ bāhubhyāṃ dhamati saṃ patatrai dyāvābhūmi janayan deva eka"—
    S. Yv. XVII.19
16. "Kiṃ svidvanaṃ ka usa vṛkṣa āsa yato dyāvāpṛthivī niṣṭhatakṣuḥ.
    Manīṣiṇo manasā pṛcchatedu tadyadadhyatiṣṭhad bhuvanāni dhārayan"—
    S. Yv. XVII.20.

CHAPTER I

FLORA AND FAUNA

(A) THE FLORA

In the midst of sacrificial and other discussions, the S. Yv. has incidentally mentioned varieties of flora. Agriculture and forestry were notable professions of the Aryans belonging to that period. They being the civilised people, settled down to pastoral life— evolved working knowledge of the things that formed their imme diate environment ; and plants which formed an important item of environment were utilised by them to the best of their advantage. Their food and drink ingredients mainly consisted of plant-products and plants which they cultivated in the fields and gardens. These were cultivated plants pertaining to village (Grāmya), while there were many indigenous plants pertaining to natural forests (Āraṇya). The household furniture and means of conveyances like boats, chariots etc. were made of wood. Wooden vessels were also used. Certain plants and herbs were essentially needed for preparation of medicines. Wooden plough constituted the major instrument of cultivation. The plants thus played an important part in the Aryan life and necessarily the necessity was felt for the study of plant and plant life.

The plant world was mainly divided into two categories—Oṣa dhi or Virudha (shrubs and herbs) and Vanaspati or Vṛkṣa (trees in general). The S. Yv. and the T. S.[1] narrate the different parts of a plant as follows :—the root (mūla), the panicle (tula), the stem (kāṇḍa), the twig (valśa), the flower (puṣpa) and the fruit (phala). The different plants referred to in the R. V. are as follows :- Vanas pati, Auṣadhi, Anna (Food-grains), Virudha, Durvā and Kuśa (grass), Muñja (reed grass), Vetasa and Veṇu (cane and bamboo). The A. V.[2] classifies the plants under the following heads :—those that expand (prastṛnatiḥ), those that are bushy (stambinīḥ), those that have only seath (eka-śungāḥ), those that creep (pratanvatiḥ), those that have many stalks (amsumatiḥ), those that are knotty (kāṇḍinīḥ) and those that have spreading branches (viśākhāḥ).

We shall now enumerate here the list of some trees, shrubs, and other plants mentioned in the Vājasaneyī Samhita or S. Yv. in an alphabetical order with their botanical (Latin) synonyms, characteristics and uses.

Vedic Name	Indian synonym and family	Reference to the S. Yv.	Characteristics and uses.
Aṇu	Panicum millaceum (Gramineae)	XVIII. 12	a kind of food-grain (cina) used as fodder.
Apāmā-rga	Achyranthes aspera (Amarantaceae)	XXXV. II	A cleansing plant or a wiping plant used for medicinal & ritualistic purposes.
Avokā	Blyxaoryzetorum	XVII.4; XXV.1	an aquatic plant like sedge (Śaivāla) used in the ritual.
Badara	Zizyphus Sp. (Rhamneae)	XIX. 22.90; XXI. 30	a kind of fruit tree.
Durvā	Cynodon dactylon (Gramineae)	XXII.20	used in the sacrificial and medicinal purposes.
Gavīdh-uka	Coix Lachryma (Gramineae)	XV.5	Kernal used as food & medicine.
Godhu-ma	Triticum Vulgare (Gramineae)	XVIII.12; XXI 29;XIX.22.89	Wheat food.
Karka-ndhu	Zizuphus nummul-aria.	XIX.23.91;XXI 32;XXIV.2	Jujube—a kind of fruit.
Masūra	Lens esculenta (Legumenoseae)	XVIII.12	a kind of lentil used as food.
Nīvāra	(Grameneae)	XVIII.12	A variety of paddy— wild rice used as food.
Nygro-dha	Ficus benghalensis (Urticaceae)	XVIII.13	a kind of banyan tree, its branches or leaves were used in sacrifices.

BOOK IV

MISCELLANEOUS

Vedic Name	Indian synonym and family	Reference to the S. Yv.	Characteristics and uses.
Priya-ṅgu	Pancium italicum	XVIII.12	Panic seed used as food.
Parṇa	Butea frondosa	XXXV.4	a synonym of Pal-āśa tree ; its branches were used in Darśapaurṇamāsa sacrifice.
Śālmalī	Śālmalī malabarica or Bombax malabaricum.	XXIII.13	Silk-cotton tree.
Śyāmā-ka	Echinochloa colona	XVIII.12	Cultivated millet used as food.
Soma	Now cannot be identified with certainty or identified variously : 1. Sarcostemma brevistingma. 2. S. Intermedium. 3. Periploca aphylla 4. Ephedra Vulgaris 5. Cannibis Sativa.		Used as drinks and medicines. Its juice was essentially needed in sacrifices specially in the Soma sacrifice.
Tila	Sesamum idicum	XVIII.12	Sesamum plants and grains used as food and for medicinal & ritual purposes.
Ulapa	Imperata arundinacea	XVI.45	a kind of grass, ritual and sacrificial.
Upavā-ka	Wrightia tinctoria	XIX.22, 90 ; XXI.30	food grains.
Urvārū-ka	Cucumis melo	XII.60	Wild fruit plant
Vrīhi	Oryza sativa	XVIII.12	cultivated rice 'food'
Yava	Hordeum Gulgare	V.26; XVIII;12; XXIII.30	Barley' used as food.

Vedic Name	Indian synonym and family	Reference to the S. Yv.	Characteristics and use.
Aśvattha	Ficus religiosa	XXXV.4	a kind of banian tree. Sacredness was ascribed to it, its leave and branches were used in sacrifices.

Some plants viz. Kuśa, Udambara, Bilva (Aegle marmelos) etc. are not mentioned in the R. V. and Y.V. These are mentioned in the A. V. Another 'Khadira' is mentioned once in the R. V. (III. 53.19) but not in the S. Yv. The Nygrodha does not occur in the R. V., it occurs once in the Y. V. and twice in the A. V,[3] 'Vetasa' in the sense of cane or bamboo does not occur in the R. V. There is mention of golden reeds or 'Hiranya Vetasa' in the S. Yv.

'I look upon the flowing streams of butter : the golden reed is in the midst of Agni'.[4]

'I look upon the streams of oil descending, and lo the golden reed is there among them'.[5]

'Descend upon the earth, the reed, the rivers : thou art the gall, O Agni, of the waters'.[6]

Among flowers—Puṣkara which means blue lotus is only mentioned in the S. Yv.

'O lotus bloom fully like the extensive sky'.[7]

(B) THE FAUNA

The Vedic Indians who were a nature-loving people, studied not only the flora of their surroundings, but possessed an intense knowledge of the fauna too. The fauna or the animal world that we find in the S. Yv. specially in its XXIVth Chapter, is undoubtedly one of the richest catalogues of fauna that occurs in any ancient literature. The chapter dealing with the Horse-sacrifice contains an exact number of animals that were to be housed in the cabins, technically called 'Yūpas' and in the intermediate space with the names of deities or deified entities to which they were dedicated separately. Twentyone 'Yūpas' were necessary in the Aśvamedha sacrifice. The principal Yūpa among those was the

eleventh one, called the Agniṣṭha. About fifteen animals were to be housed in each of these cabins, all domestic animals, the total number being 327. In the spaces between the stakes 282 wild animals ranging from elephant and rhinoceros to the very bee and fly, were to be temporarily confined and to be freed at the conclusion of the sacrifice. This brings the total number of assembled animals upto 609.[8]

The collection of such a large number of animals on a particular occasion may well compare with any Zoo and indicate how deep was the interest of the Aryans of that ancient period about the wild and domesticated animal world.

Just as in a Zoo where animals are classified and housed according to a system, the animals described here were also classified and systematically placed in groups along certain posts known as Yūpas.

The XXIV Ch of the S. Yv, contains forty verses of which the first nineteen enumerate the detailed list of docile animals and the remaining verses bring out the detailed account of wild animals. In order to get a clear idea about the classification, positions and qualities of these animals, we should go through these verses in the following manner :

1. Aśva (horse), tūpara (hornless goat) and gomṛga (forest cow), these belong to Prajāpati. Kriṣṇagrīva (a black necked goat) is meant for Agni and is to be placed in front of the forehead (of the horse) ; an ewe (Meṣī) possessing the quality of speech (Sarasvatī) below his jaws ; two goats belonging to the Aśvins with marks on the lower part of the body, to his forelegs ; a darkcoloured goat (belonging to Soma and Pūṣan) to his navel ; a white and a black (belonging to Soma and Yama) to his sides ; two goats (belonging to Vāyu) to his tail ; Vehat or a barren cow (to Indra) and a Vāmana (dwarf) (belonging to Viṣṇu).

2. The red goat, the smoky red, the jujubed red—these belong to Soma. The brown, the ruddy brown, the parrot brown—these beasts belong to Varuṇa. One with white ear-holes, one with partly white, one with wholly white belong to Savitā. Beasts with white, partly white, wholly white arms belong to Bṛhaspati. Beasts

speckled with spots, with small and big spots, belong to Prāna and Udāna (Mitra-Varuṇa).

3. The bright-haired, the wholly bright haired, the jewel-haired beasts are ascribed to Aśvins. The white, the white eyed, the reddish belong to Rudra, the protector of cattle. The long eared goats belong to Yama, the Avaliptas (proud-one goats) belong to Rudra and the sky-coloured beasts belong to the clouds.

4. Speckled, transversely speckled, upward speckled beasts belong to Maruts. The beasts fond of fruits (phalgu), red haired, sharp-eyed belong to Sarasvatī. The beasts having ears like spleen, dry ears, golden ears belong to Tvastr. The black necked, the white flanked, the plump-thighed beasts belong to Indra-Agni. The animals with black marks as well as with small and large marks belong to Uṣas or Dawn.

5. Śilpa or parti-coloured female goat belongs to Viśvedevāh or All-gods ; the Rohini or red-coloured eighteen months old belongs to Vāk, goats without distinguishing marks belong to Aditi, goat of one colour known as Sarūpa belongs to Dhātar, tender aged goats and sheep (Vatsavari) belong to consorts of gods.

6. Black necked animals possess the qualities of fire. White browed animals possess the qualities of Vasus. Red-coloured animals possess the qualities of Rudras. Bright animals possess the qualities of Ādityas. The sky-coloured animals possess the qualities of clouds.

7. The tall and sturdy animals with distorted organs possess the qualities of electricity (Indra) and air (Vāyu). Animals possessing the strength of arms possess the qualities of air and sun. The parrot coloured, fast variegated animals possess the qualities of fire and air. The dark-coloured possess the qualities of cloud.

8. The variegated animal belongs to Indra-Agni, the dvirūpa or two coloured belongs to Agni-Soma ; the dwarf oxen belong to Agni-Vāyu, the Vasa or barren cows belong to Mitra-Varuṇa, partly variegated animals belong to Mitra.

9. Black-necked animals possess the qualities of fire. Animals with brown colour possess the qualities of Soma. White animals belong to air. The undistinguished animals possess the qualities

of earth (Dhātar). Tender-aged calves belong to consorts of gods.

10. Black animals used for ploughing the land belong to the earth. Smoke-coloured ones belong to the firmament. Animals, tall in size and whitish in colour belong to the sky and lightning and blotched ones to stats (Tārakās).

11. Smoke-coloured ones are procured for spring, white for summer, black for rains and red for autumn, bulky for winter, reddish-yellow for the dewy season.

12. The Tryavi (tri-avi or calves with three sheep time old i.e. 6×3 or eighteen months old calves) belong to Gāyatrī, the Pañcāvi (i.e. steers of thirty months) belongs to Triṣṭup, the Dityavāha or two year old steers to Jagatī, the Trivatsā or three year old one to Anuṣṭup, the Turya-vāha or four year old animals to Uṣnik.

13. The Ṣaṣṭhavāha or six year old animals belong to Virāj, the Ukṣan or full grown bulls to Bṛhatī, the Ṛṣava or strong bulls belong to Kakup, the anadvāh or draught oxen belong to the Paṅkti, and the Dhenu or milch cows to Atichandas.

14. Black-necked animals belong to Agni, brown animals to Soma, spotted ones to Savitā ; weaned she-kids to Sarasvatī, dark coloured ones to Pūṣan, the Pṛṣṇi or speckled cows belong to Maruts, the multi-coloured one to Viśvedevāḥ, the Vaśā or barren cows to heaven and earth.

15. Dappled animals are presumed for Indra and Agni, black ones for Varuṇa, the speckled for Maruts and the hornless for 'ka' or Prajāpati.

16. He procures the first-ling goats for Agni, Savālya or those born of one mother for Maruts, the Baṣkiha or those born after a long time for Gṛhamedhi Maruts, the Sansṛṣṭa or those born together for sportive Maruts, the Anusṛṣṭa or those born in succession to self-strong Maruts.

17. Called contemporaneous, the Eta or dappled belonging to Indra-Agni, the Praśṛṅga or with projecting horns to Mahendra and the Bahurūpa or multi-coloured to Viśvakarman.

18. The animals of peace-loving parents are smoke-coloured and of brownish hue. The animals of parents who sit on grass are

22

browny and smoky-looking. The animals of parents who know the science of fire are black and brownish looking ; the animals of fathers who know the three forces are black and spotted.

19. Called as contemporaneous, Etā, the dappled ones for Sunāsīra, white ones for Vāyu and Sūrya also.

The verse 11 associates different animals to different seasons, the verses 12 and 13 associate animals—cow or bull to various metres. From all the above quoted verses 1 to 19, we have an exhaustive enumeration of 327 domesticated animals of goat and cow groups, classified or described according to the age, stature, physical features, shades of colours and the characteristic marks of their necks and tails. The verses quoted above clearly testify to the meticulous observation of the Vedic Aryans regarding innumerable varieties and shades of colour, even various shades of each colour have been correctly described.

In the succeeding verses, we have another exhaustive enumeration of wild animals and creatures, birds and insects, totalling 282.

20 An expert in the knowledge of animals, procures Kapiñ- jalas (heath cocks or francolines) in Spring, Kalaviṃka or sparrows in Summer ; the Tittiri or partridge in the Rains, Varttikā or quails in Autumn, the Kakara (unidentified creatures) in Winter, Vikakaras in the Dewy Season.

He procures the Śiśumāra or porpoises for the sea ; the Man- ḍuka or frogs for rains ; the Matsya or fiishes for water, the Kulī- paya or ducks for Mitra, the Nakra or crocodiles for Varuṇa.

22. He finds the Hansas or wild geese for Soma ; the Balākās or female crane for Vāyu, the Krauñca or curlews for Indra-Agni, Madgu or divers for Mitra and the Cakravāka or ruddy geese for Varuṇa.

23. He procures the Kutaru or cocks for Agni, the Uluka or owls for Vanaspatis (trees). The Cāṣa or blue jays for Soma, the Mayūras or peacocks for Aśvins, and the Kapota or pigeons for Mitra-Varuṇa.

24. He procures the Laba or quails for Soma, the Kaulika (an unidentified bird) for Tvaṣṭr, the Goṣādi (Indian starlings) for gods consorts, the Kulikās for gods sisters, Paruṣnas (an

unknown bird) for Agni, the lord of house.

25. He procures the Pārāvata or pigeons for the Day, the Sicāpu (birds unidentified) for Night, the Jatu or bats for the joints of day and night, the Dātyauha or gallinules for Months, Suparṇas or great eagles for the Year.

26. An expert in the science of Earth should study Ākhu or rats for understanding the nature of ground, the Paṅkta or flied rats for firmament, the Kaśa or voles for light, the Nakula or mungoose for quarters and the Babhruka or brownish ichneumons for the intermediate spaces.

27. An expert in the knowledge of animals procures the Ṛśya or black-bucks for Vasus, the Ruru or stages for Rudras and the Nyaṅku deer for Ādityas, the Pṛṣata or spotted deer for All gods, and the Kuluṅga antelopes for Sādhyas.

28. Parasvat deer should be secured for the wealthy (Īśāna), Gaur deer for the friend (Mitra), buffaloes for the most prosperous, the Gavaya or gayals for the guardian of the virtuous (Bṛhaspati), and Uṣṭra or camels for the artisans.

29. He procures the puruṣa Hasti or male elephants for Prajāpati, the plusi or flying white ants for Vāk or eloquence, Maśaka or mosquitoes for sight, and the Bhṛṅga or black bees for hearing.

30. For swiftness like a king and air Gomṛga should be known ; a wild ram (Meṣa) for an excellent person (Varuṇa), a blackdeer for the Lord of justice (Yama) ; a monkey for a human king, the Rohit or a red doe for the tiger (Śārdula) ; a gavayī or female goyal for a Ṛṣabha or bull, a Varttikā or quail for Kṣipraś-neya or swift falcon, a Krimi or worm for Nilaṅga or a tape worm, a Śiśumāra or porpoise for sea and a Hasti or elephant for a mountain.

31. The Mayu or a kind of monkey belongs to Prajāpati, the Ula deer to the Halikṣṇa (a kind of lion), and the Vṛṣadaṁśa or cat belongs to Dhātar, the Kaṅka or heron to quarters, the Dhuṇkṣa (a kind of female bird) belongs to Agni, the Kalaviṅka (sparrow), Lohitāhi or red snake and the Puṣkarasāda or Sārasa or Indian crane to Tvaṣṭṛ, and the Krauñca or curlew belongs to Vāk.

32.   The Kuluṅga or antelope for Soma, the Āraṇya-aja or wild goat, the Nakula or mungoose, and the Śaka (might be a bird or fly) for Pūṣan, the Krosṭa or jackal for Māyu (i.e. Kinnara or monkey) the Gaura-deer for Indra, the Pidva (a kind of deer) the Nyaṅku or antelope and the Kakkaṭa or cock for Anumati, and the Cakravāka for Pratiśruta or Echo.

33.   The Suparṇa, or eagle belongs to cloud ; the birds like Ati, Vāhasa and the Dārvida, or wood-pecker belong to the air, the Paiṅgarāja (a kind of bird) belongs to Bṛhaspati, Lord of speech, the Alaja (an unknown bird) belongs to firmament. The Plava or Pelican, the Madgu or cormorant, and the Matsya or fish belong to Nadīpati or the Lord of rivers, and the Kūrma or the tortoise belongs to Heaven and Earth.

34.   The Puruṣa-mṛga or the buck belongs to the Moon, the Godhā or iguana, the Kalaka (not identified), and the Dārvāghāṭa (some type of wood-pecker, different from Dārvida) belong to the Vanaspatis (trees), Kṛkavāku or some sort of cock belongs to Savitar, the Haṁsa or swan belongs to air (Vāta), the Nakra (crocodile), the Makara (dolphin) and the Kulīpayas or acquatic birds belong to the Akūpāra or the sea, the Śalyaka or porcupine belongs to the Modesty.

35.   The Ainya or the black doe belongs to Day, the Maṇḍū-ka or the frog. Mūṣikā or female rat and Tittiri or partridge belong to the serpents, the Lopāśa or the jackal belongs to the Aśvins, the black buck to the Night, the Ṛkṣa (bear), the bat and the Suśilīkā (some unknown species of bird) belong to the other folk, the Jahakā or the pole-cat belongs to Viṣṇu.

36.   The Anyavāpa or cuckoo belongs to the Half-months, the Amṛśya or the antelope, the Mayūra or peacock and Suparṇa or eagle belong to the Gandharvas, the Apāmudra or an acquatic animal called otter belongs to the Months, Kaśyapa (tortoise), the Rohita (doe-antelope), the Kundṛṇāci (iguana) and Golattika belong to the Apsaras, the Asita or the black snake belongs to death.

37.   The Varṣābhū (frogs, different from Maṇḍūka) belongs

to Rains ; the Ākhu (vole), the Kaśa (rat) and the Mānthāla (mouse) belong to Fathers ; the Python (Ajagara) is for strength, Kapiñjala is for Vasus ; the Kapota (pigeon), the Ulūka (owl) and Śaśa (hare) are the harbingers of adversity (Nirrti) and wild ram belongs to Varuṇa.

38. The Śvitra or the white snake belongs to the Ādityas ; the Uṣṭra or camel, the Ghrniwān (a strong animal) and the Vārdhrīnasa or rhinoceros belong to thought (Mati) ; Srmara or forest cow is for the forest ; the Ruru (buck) is for Rudra ; the Kvayi bird, the Kuntaru (cock) and the Dātyauha (gallinule) possess the qualities of Vājins (horses) and the Pika or cuckoo belongs to Kāma (passion).

39. The Khaḍga (Rhinoceros) belongs to All gods, the black dog (Śva), the long-eared ass (Gardhava) and the hyena (Tarakṣu) belong to Rākṣasas : the boar (Sūkara) belongs to Indra ; the lion (Simha) to Maruts; the chameleon (Krkalāsa), the Pippaka (Female bird) and Śakuni (Vulture) belong to Śaravya, the Prṣata or spotted antelope belongs to All-gods.

From the above list of animals, birds, serpents, insects, and bees, it appears that not even a single creature of that period was left unnoticed.

According to the S. Yv. the animals are usually classified into two Groups (i) Grāmya-paśu (domestic animals) (ii) Āraṇya-paśu (wild[9] animals). Sometimes a third category is also added to as Vāyavya (creatures of air) in the Puruṣa-Sūkta in which the three categories are described thus :—Vāyavya (pertaining to air), Āraṇya (wild) and Grāmya (cattle).[10]

REFERENCES

1. S. Yv. XXII.28...'Mūlebhyaḥ svāhā, śākhābhyaḥ svāhā, vanaspatibhyaḥ svāhā. Puṣpebhyaḥ svāhā, phalebhyaḥ svāhā, auṣadhibhya svāhā'—T. S. 7-3-20-1
2. A. V. 8-7-4

3.   A. V. IV.37. 4 ; V.5.5
4.   S. Yv. XIII.38...'Ghṛtasya dhārāhabhicākaśībhi hiraṇyaye vetaso madhye-
     hagneḥ'
5.   S. Yv. (XVII.93)
6.   S. Yv. XI.29...'Puṣkare divo mātrayā varimnā prathasva'.
8.   'Atra dvāviṃśatirekādaśinaḥ saptaviṃśatyadhikāni trīni śatāni aśvādayaḥ
     sauryāntāḥ ṣaṣṭhyadhikāṃ śatadvayaṃ kapiñjalādayaḥ pṛṣatāntā āraṇyā-
     paśavaḥ—sarve militvā ṣaṭsatāni navadhikāni paśavo bhavanti. Ślokāśca...
     'Ṣaṭ śatāni nijujyañte paśūnāṃ madhyamehahani. Aśvamedhasya yajñasya
     navabhiścādhikāni ceti. Tesvāraṇyāḥ sarve utsṛṣṭavyā na tu himsyāḥ'—
     Mahīdhara on S. Yv. XXIV.40
9.   S. Yv. XVIII.14...'Gramyāśca me paśavaḥ āraṇyāśca me...'
10. 'Tasmādaśvāhajayanta ye ca ke cobhayādayaḥ. Gāvo ha jojnire tasmāt
     ajāvayaḥ Tasmāt...gramyāśca ye...' S. Yv. XXXI.86 R. V. X.90.8.10 ;
     A. V. XIX.6

CHAPTER II

CALENDAR

The observation of calender was an immediate necessity for the purpose of alloting time or period to any particular sacrificial performance. The Samvatsara or year with its different components such as Ṛtus (seasons), Māsas or Samāḥ (months) are repeatedly referred to in the S. Yv.[1] References are also made to day and night (Aho-rātra), half-month of a year (Ardha-māsa) and dawn (uṣas) indicating the period of the day etc, the joints of Day and Night (Sandhi) are also alluded to.[2] The following passage indicates how the calendar could be observed from a study of different birds.

'An expert in the science of time should study pigeons in the beginning of the day, sīchāpūs in the night, bats in the joints of day and night, gullinules for the knowledge of months, birds with beautiful plumes for realizing the beauty of the year.'[3]

'Five-year-circle' called 'Yupa' is said to be comprised of Samvatsara, Parivatsara, Idavatsara, Idvatsara and Vatsara. Referring to a rule of the science of Astronomy, Mahīdhara says— 'five years, consisting of Samvatsara etc. make a Yugo'.[4]

According to the S. B. the year or Samvatsara usually consisted of 360 days and of 12 months,[5] but sometimes the year is referred to as consisting of thirteen months. The thirteenth or intercalary month is mentioned in the S. Yv. as Aṃhasaspati.[6] While in the Taittirīya and Maitrāyani Saṃhitās (Kṛṣṇa-Yajurveda) it is mentioned as Saṃsarpa. The intercalary month of 35 dyas occurred at every six year interval.

The names of 12 months are given in their clearest form in the sacrificial texts of S. Yv. where the Agnicayana or building of fire altar is described.[7] These names are as follows :-

(i) Madhu (2) Mādhava (3) Śukra (4) Śuci (5) Nabhas

(6) Navhasya (7) Iṣa (8) Ūrja (9) Saha (10) Sahasya (11) Tapa and (12) Tapasya. There are similar lists in the descriptions of the Soma sacrifice (S. Yv. VII.30) and the Horse sacrifice (S. Yv. XXII.31)—all of them agreeing in essentials.

These twleve months of Vedic calendar correspond respectively to twelve months of our present day calendar. Thus Madhu corresponds to Chaitra (March-April), Mādhava to Baiśakha (April-May), Śukra to Jaiṣṭha (May-June), Śuci to Āṣādha (June-July), Nabhas to Śrāvaṇa (July-Angust), Nabhasya to Kārtika (October-November), Saha to Mārgaśīrṣa (November-December), Sahasya to Pauṣa (December-January), Tapas to Māgha (January-February), and lastly Tapasya corresponds to Phālguna (February-March).

In the Vedic Text, sacrifice or Yajña is often compared with year of Samvatsara because both of them have Prajāpati as their common Lord. Prajāpati is identified with Samvatsara in a passage where twelve epithets—(Vāja, Prasava, Apija etc.) ascribed to Prajāpati correspond to twelve months of a year. The Chaitra is called Vāja as there is plenty of food production in that month. The Vaiśakha is Prasava or favourable for water-sports. The Jaiṣṭha is called Apija because one loves to enjoy water-sports in that month. A good number of sacrifices such as Cāturmāsya etc. are celebrated in the month of Āṣādha ; it is, therefore, known as Kratu. As journey is prohibited in the Śrāvaṇa, it is called Vasu. The Bhādra is Aharpati because of its casting intense heat like the lord of the day (Sun). The Āśvina is regarded as Mugdha as it shades the day-light with snow. The Kārtika is Vainaśina because people takes holy baths in that month for getting rid of sin. The Mārgaśīrṣa is called Antya because of its association with Viṣṇu, the deity who remains alone even at the destruction of everything. The Pauṣa is Bhauvana as it makes the people healthy by increasing appetite. The Māgha is the Bhuvanapati or protector of all and lastly the Phālguna is Adhipati as it comes at the end of all months of the year.[8]

These twelve months are distributed into six seasons. Each season comprises two months and the name of each pair of months corresponding to each season have been thus enumerated in the

S. Yv. under the caption of "Season-Cups" (Ṛtu-grahāḥ).

The Vasanta or Spring season comprises the two months Madhu and Mādhava.[9] Śukra and Śuci are the two months of Grīṣma or Summer season.[10] The Varṣā or Rainy season is associated with two months—Nabha and Nabhasya.[11] The Śarad or the season of Autumn is concerned with the twin months like Iṣa and Ūrja.[12] The winter season or Hemanta is associated with Saha and Sahasya.[13] The sixth or last season mentioned as Śiśira or dewy winter comprises the two months of Tapa i.e. Māgha and Tapasya i.e. Phālguna.[14] References to these six seasons are also met with in the description of Rājasūya sacrifice in the S. Yv.[15]

There was the division of day and night (Ahorātra) into thirty parts or Muhūrtas. The word—Trimṣad-dhāma[16] occurring in the description of Agnyādheya ceremony and the word Trimṣad-padani[17] occurring in the description of Sarvamedha, indicate, according to Uvaṭa and Mahīdhara, the thirty muhūrtas of the day and night. According to Sāyaṇa,[18] however, the word Trimṣ-addhāma means the thrity days of months.

REFERENCES

1. S. Yv. XXII.28 ; XXVI.14 ; XXVII.1.45
2. S. Yv. XXIV.25
3. 'Anhe pārāvatānālabhate rātryai sīcāpūrahorātrayoḥ sandhibhyo jatumā-sebhyo datyauhāntsamvatsarāya mahataḥ suparṇān'—S. Yv. XXIV.25
4. 'he Agne—'Pañcasamvatsaratmaka-yuga-rūpohasi ityarthaḥ'— 'Yugaṃ bhaved vatsarapañcakena' iti jyotiḥśastrokeḥ'—Mahīdhara on S. Yv. XXVII.45
5. S. B. 1-3-5-9···'trīṇi ca śatāni ṣaṣṭiśca saṃvatsarasyāhāni'
   S. B. 1-3-5-10...'Dvūdaśa vai māsāḥ saṃvatsarasya'
6. S. Yv. VII.30 ; XXII.31...('Aṃhasaspataye trayodaśo māsaḥ...'Uvaṭa)
7. S. Yv. XIII.25 ; XIV.6, 15, 16, 27 ; XV.57
8. Mahīdhara on the S. Yv. XVIII.28
9. S. Yv. XIII.25...'Madhuśca mādhavaśca vāsantikāvṛtu...'
10. S. Yv. XIV.6...'Śukraśca śuciśca grīṣmāvṛtu...'

11. S. Yv. XIV.15...'Nabhaśca nabhasyaśca vārṣikāvṛtu...'
12. S. Yv. XIV.16...'Iṣaścorjaśca śaradāvṛtu...'
13. S. Yv. XIV.27...'Sahaśca sahasyaśca haimantikāvṛtu...'
14. S. Yv. XV.57...'Tapaśca tapasyaśca śaiśirāvṛtu...'
15. S. Yv. X.10-14
16. S. Yv. III.8...Trimśaddhāma...('Trimśaccahorātre muhūrttasta iha gṛhyante
          ...'Uvaṭa ; Ahorātrasya trimśamuhūrttā dhāmaśabdenābhipre-
          tāḥ'—Mahīdhara)
17. S. Yv. XXXIII.93...Trimśadpadāni ('Ahorātreṇa trimśanmuhūrttān krāma-
          tītyarthaḥ'—Mahīdhara)
18. 'Māsagatadinabhedena trimśatsamkhyākam'—Sāyaṇa

CHAPTER III

LANGUAGE & LITERATURE OF THE S. Yv.

(A) THE LANGUAGE OF THE S. Yv.

The language of the mantra portion of the Y. V. according to Dr. Macdonell, represents no doubt a later stage but on the whole agrees with that of R. V., though separated from that of classical Sanskrit by a considerable interval. From the perusal of the Śukla-Yajurvedic language however, this observation appears to us as partially true. The language of the S. Yv. is marked with the following important characteristics :—

(a) As in the R. V. and the A. V. the 'an'-stems of the S. Yv. are very often endingless in locative singular, e.g. 'tṛtīye dhāman' (S. Yv. XXXII. 10).

But this is not the case in the Brāhmaṇas where only two words such as—'Ātman' and 'Ahan' are endingless.

(b) The Injunctive is here frequent as in Brāhmaṇas in negative sentences with the prohibitive particle 'mā'.

e.g. 'mā no vīrān Rudra bhāmino vadhīḥ' (do not kill our father)—S. Yv. XVI. 16.

b) 'mā no aśveṣu rīriṣaḥ (do not kill our horses)—S. Yv. XVI.16.

'mā no vadhīḥ pitaram......(RV. I.8.6 ; S. Yv. XVI.15)
'mā vibhita' (A.B) ; 'ma suṣvpīhāḥ' (S.B)

c) The form 'amba'—occurring thrice in the R. V. may have a vocated meaning—'O mother'. The S. Yv. and T. S. have the vocative form—'ambe'—from a stem 'ambā' (mother)[2].

d) In the nominative singular of the word 'ari', the S. Yv. has the form—'arīs' besides the regular form 'aris' of the R. V.

e) The regular Vedic formation of the word 'tanū' in Dative and Genitive would be 'tanve' and 'tanvas' respectively, but the

S. Yv. and also the Brāhmaṇas use such forms as—'tanvai' and 'tanvas' to denote Dative and Genitive respectively.

e.g. 'Śamvastu tanvai tava' (S. Yv. XXIII.44).

f) The particles already used in the R. V. such as—'Svid', 'U', 'Uta' etc. are also met with in the S. Yv. The particles like va, vai, vava etc. which are frequently used in the Brāhmaṇas are, however, rare in the S. Yv.

g) The peculiar Aorist-form such as 'dāḥ' from the root 'dā' in second person singular is frequently met with (S.Yv. XXXVII.12).

h) The substitution of the ending 'ai' for 'āḥ' both in Ablative and Genitive singular of feminine stems (ā, ī) is another characteristic feature of the Śukla-Yajurvedic language.

e.g. Indraḥ pṛthivyai varṣīyān (S. Yv. XXIII.84), here pṛthivyai is used in lieu of pṛthivyaḥ, Brāhmaṇa prose also agrees in this respect with the S. Yv.

The language of non-borrowing passages of the S. Yv. though bearing affinities to some extent with that of the R. V. is, however, closer to that of the Brāhmaṇa texts. Moreover, the language of some Śukla-Yajurvedic verses which are lacking in special vedic rules for word formation, resembles even to that of classical Sanskrit. A Sanskritist can understand the meaning of such verses without having any special knowledge in Vedic grammar.

(B) LITERARY ESTIMATION OF THE S. Yv.

The verses of the S. Yv., of course, vary much in literary merit. Many of them display a high order of poetical excellence, while others consist of common place and mechanical verse. The degree of skill in composition is on the average remarkably high especially when we consider that here we have the poetry of so remote an age.

The XVIth Ch. or the Rudrādhyāyī of the S. Yv. represents some verses which in magnificent metaphors depict the reciprocal identicalness of Rudra and Sūrya. Rudra is identified with Sūrya or Sun-God. Rudra is titled as 'Kapardin' as he bears long matted hair and in the poetic vision of Vedic seers this mass of matted hair is nothing but the mesh of rays of the rising or setting sun. Again, Rudra as Nīlakaṇṭha is none but another manifestation of the setting sun. The setting sun reddens the western horizon and bedecks its own orb with bluish colour. The orb or midportion may be equalled with Kaṇṭha or neck. As there is bluish colour in that portion, the sun is known as Nīlakaṇṭha or Nīlagrīva and Rudra being identified with the sun is also known as Nīlakaṇṭha. This type of metaphorical identification of these two deities, affluent with poetic imagery, is reflected in verse quoted thus in translation :-

'That Rudra, the blue necked, red coloured one (the form of the Sun), goes downwards slowly (in the firmament). Beholding him thus, the cowherd boys return with their cattle and the girls with water.'[5]

As a good poet, the Śukla-Yajurvedic seer was aware of the use of Upamā (simile). This figure of speech plays a very important part in later Indian poetry. Sanskrit rhetoricians regard Upamā (simile) as the best of all figures of speech—nay, 'the mother of poets' family'.[6] Kālidāsa, the highest literary figure of the classical Sanskrit literature shows his competency in the best use of Simile.[7] The Śukla-Yajurvedic seer was also adept in this regard. Let us justify this statement by illustrating some verses from the S. Yv. where simile is properly used.

A popular trend was there to draw similarity between the familiar things. It is, therefore, seen that mother goes in comparison usually with water or with 'Ukhā', the sacrificial cooking pot. Water being of the beneficient nature is compared with loving mother in a verse which runs thus :

'Just as mothers with their longing love feed the children so, O water, with thy beneficial juice nourish us.[8] The cooking pot named 'Ukhā' is placed on fire for the preparation of sacrificial offerings. It is desired that the Ukhā would contain within it the heat of fire, just as a mother bears her son in her lap.'[9]

'The Ukhā made of clay contains fire in it just as a mother conceives the child in her womb'.[10]

The sacrificial remainings or ashes, thrown into water go in comparison with a child in mother's womb.[11]

In a good poetic style, the seer describes how the sacrificial fire, kindled early in the morning removes darkness and spreads its light in all directions. In this matter, fire follows the process of the Sun which after rising shines beautifully in the sky before dawn, removes darkness with its lustre, pervades the universe and fills with splendour all material objects.[12]

Again, in another verse,[13] the manifold beneficient character of the fire-god is beautifully described.

The following passage illustrates a beautiful simile wherein medicine is compared to a strong person and the disease, to the enemy.

'O medicines, when you creep in a patient, part by part, joint by joint, you destroy his pulmonary disease, as a strong man destroys delicate bodily parts of his foe' (S. Yv. XII. 80).

Adorned with a number of similes, the following verse brings out a beautiful poetic imagery :

'With fuel fire is kindled, just as a calf is delighted at the sight of its mother's arrival or as one is endowed with intellect at the arrival of dawn and the glow of one's intellect soars high over the sky like the flight of birds over the branches of trees' (S. Yv. XV. 24).

The chapter XVII of the S. Yv. contains a number of verses which in a beautiful manner make a poetic appeal. In such a verse, the spontaneous flow of the pure speech and that of knowledge go in comparison with the flow of rivers and with the quick race of the deer respectively.

'From the depth of the heart, purified by the mind, our speeches will flow as streams flow to the ocean. The waves of knowledge pass as swiftly as a deer runs through the fear of a hunter' (S. Yv. XVII. 94).

In order to describe as to how uninterruptedly the flow of ghee falls from the ladle to the sacrificial fire, the Yajurvedic poet seer displays such a beautiful imagery :—

'Just as the waves of a currentful river being favoured by the forceful wind rush down the rapids, just as the swift running horse, breaking aside the battle fields, falls upon the ememy, watering the earth with perspiration arising out of his endeavour to kill the enemy, so does the flow of ghee fall from the ladle' (S. Yv. XVII. 95).

Again, with the help of simile, the poet seer depicts as to how the flow of butter reaches to the fire and how it is accepted by the fire.

'Just as woman of high character, of the same frame of mind, gently smiling, be inclined towards their husbands, so does the flow of butter pervading the fuel reach to the fire' (S.Yv. XVII.96).

Here we see the beautiful poetic imagination by which women and their husbands go in comparison with butter and fire respectively.

The next verse also exhibits poetic exuberance :

'As maidens deck themselves with gay adornments and exhibit their beauty to join their husbands, so the flow of butter always proceeds towards that place where Soma is being pressed and sacrifice performed' (S. Yv. XVII.97).

Again, drawing a beautiful simile, the poet seer expresses his desire that he will please the god with the utterance of prayers just as a calf attracts its mother-cow by making lows.[14]

The employment of simile in the following passage is also noteworthy :—

'...Just as an ideal housewife gives all delicious things to her husband so also Agni bestows his treasures upon the sacrificer.'[15]

Again, for explaining the eagerness of his mind at the time of god's prayer, the seer draws out the poetic imagery in this way :—

'Just as a non-milked cow eagerly longs for her calf, so do we eagerly pray for thee (Oh god Indra).'[16]

In a poetical style rich in simile, the seer narrates, again, in another passage as to how the ideal of ancestors led the seven divine sages to the performance of sacrifice.

'Just as a charioteer controls the reins of a horse and drives it to his desired place, so the seven divine sages after following the path of their ancestors started the great sacrifice with the help of stoma, metre etc.'[17]

Here, in the above passage, the particle 'na' is used in lieu of 'iva' to express similarity.

(C) REFERENCE TO METRES IN THE S. Yv.

In a number of verses of the S. Yv., the seven principal Vedic metres such as Gāyatrī, Uṣṇik, Anuṣṭup, Bṛhatī, Paṅkti, Triṣṭup, and Jagatī along with some allied metres such as Virāṭ, Dvipada, Kakup and Ati—are referred to. We, however, get the name of seven principal metres altogether in a verse of the S. Yv. (XXIII. 33). Different metres are again alluded to different deities. It is, thus, said[19] that the metre Gāyatrī is represented by Agni, Indra represents the Triṣṭup and the Viśvedevāḥ (all gods) represent the Jagatī metre. Lord Viṣṇu is famous for his three strides. It has been described in a verse that the first foot of Viṣṇu placed in heaven was in the form of Jagatī, the second foot placed in atmosphere was in the form of Triṣṭup and the third foot placed on earth was in the form of Gāyatrī.[20]

Different results are attached to different metres in the following way :—

'Through the Gāyatrī metre one may develop the power of perception.'[21]

'Through the Vedic verses in Uṣṇik metre, one may develop the power of breath.'[22]

'With Vedic verses in Anuṣṭup metre, one may acquire the strength of soul.'[23]

'With Vedic verses in Bṛhatī metre one may cultivate in him the power of hearing.'[24]

'With the aid of Paṅkti metre one may be filled with heroism and affluence.'[25]

'With the aid of Triṣṭup metre one may develop the power of enjoying happiness.'[26]

'With the verses in Jagatī metre, strength of over-powering the enemy may be developed.'[27]

'With the verse in Virāṭ metre one develops beauty in the soul'.[28]

'With verses in Dvipada metre one may establish fortune and strength in the soul.'[29]

'With the aid of Kakup metre one may acquire fame.'[30]

'And so, with the aid of verses in Ati metre one may possess sway.'[31]

We shall quote here some verses from the S. Yv. illustrating different metres :—

a) The *Gāyatrī* stanza consists of three octosyllabic verses $(8 \times 3 = 24)$.

e.g. "Yo vaḥ śivatamo rasa
stasya bhājayateha naḥ.
Gaśaoṭriva mātaraḥ'. (XI.11)

```
- - u u        ()    u - u -
- u - u        ()    u - u -
u u - u        ()    u - u -
```

b) The *Uṣṇik* consists of 28 syllables being divided into three feet, either the first two or the last two of which are treated as hemistich : $(8 + 8 + 12)$ $(12 + 8 + 8)$

e.g. "Idaṃ viśvā avivrdhantsamudravyacasaṃ giraḥ.
Rathītamaṃ rathīnāṃ satpatiṃ patiṃ" (XVII.61)

```
u - - - u - u -       ()    u - - uu - u -
u - u - u - - - u - u -
```

c) The *Anuṣṭubh* stanza consists of four octosyllabic verses divided into two hemistichs : (8×4)

e.g. 'Tato virāḍajāyata virājo adhi puruṣaḥ.
sa jāto atyaricyata paścādbhūmimatho puraḥ'.
(XXXI.5)'.

```
u - u - u uu       ()    u - - uuu - -
u - - - u - uu      ()    - - - uu - u -
```

d) The *Triṣṭubh* stanza consists of four verses of eleven syllables divided into two hemistichs :

e.g. 'Yasminnṛcaḥ sāma yajumṣī yasmin pratiṣṭhita
rathanabhāvivāraḥ.
Yasminścittaṃ sarvamota prajānāṃ tanme manaḥ

śivasankalpamastu'.

    - - u - - u u - u - u   ()   u - u - u u - - u - -
    - - - - - u - - u - -   ()   - - u - u u - - u - u

e) The *Bṛhatī* is 36 syllabic metre consisting of four feet :
(8 + 8 + 12 + 8)

e.g.   'Śrudhi śrutkarṇa vahnibhirdevairagne sayāvabhiḥ.
                Āsīdantu varhisi mitro aryamā prātaryavāṇo
                adhvaram'-(XXXIII.15)
                u - - u - u -   ()   - - - - u - u -
                - - - u - u u - - - u - ()   - - - - - - u -

f) The *Paṇkti* metre consists of five octosyllabic verses divided into two hemistichs : (8 × 5 = 40)

e.g.   'Asau yastāmro aruṇa uta babbruḥ sumaṅgalaḥ.
                Ye cainaṃ rudra abhito dikṣu śritaḥ sahasraśoha-
                vaiṣāṃ heḍa īmahe'. (XVI.6)
                u - - - u - u () u u - - u - u -
                - - - - u u - () - - u - u - u - () - - - u - u -

g) The *Jagatī* metre consists of four verses of twelve syllables
divided into two hemistichs :-

e.g.   'Sapta te agne samidhaḥ sapta jihvā
                       sapta ṛṣayaḥ sapta dhāma priyāṇi.
                Sapta hotrāḥ saptadhā tvā yajanti
                       Sapta yonirapṛnasva ghṛtena svāhā' (XVII.79)
                - u - - - u u - - u - - () - - u u u - - u - - u - u
                - u - - - u - - u - u - () u - - - u - - u - u - -

h) The *Atyaṣṭi* a variety of Ati metre comprises of four
Gāyatrī and three Jagatī verses i.e. 68 syllables in all.

e.g.   'Jyaiṣṭhyam ca ma ādhipatyaṃ ca me manyuśca me
                bhāmaśca mehamaśca mehambhaśca me jema ca me
                mahimā ca me varimā ca me prathimā ca me varṣimā
                ca me drāghimā ca me vṛddham ca me vṛddhiṃśca
                me yajñena kalpantām'. (XVIII.4).

i) The *Kakubh* is a 28 syllabic metre divided into three feet.

REFERENCES

1. A. A. Macdonell—A History of Sanskrit literature, p. 152
2. Macdonell—Vedic Grammar, p. 78
3. —   Ibid......p. 84
4. cf S. Yv. XXXII.14-16, XXIII.46, XXIII.10, XIII.28-29
5. S. Yv. XVI.7...'Asau yohavasarpati nīlagrīvo vilohitaḥ
          Utainaṃ gopāḥ adṛsrannadṛsrannudāhāryaḥ...'
6. 'Upamā kavivaṃśasya mātaiveti matirmama'—
7. 'Upamā Kālidāsasya...'
8. 'Yo vaḥ śivatamo rasastasya bhājayateha naḥ
   Gaśatoriva mātaraḥ'—S. Yv. XI.51, XXXVI.15
9. 'Mātā putraṃ yothopasthe sāgni bibhartu garbha ā'—S. Yv. XI.57
10. S. Yv. XII.61...'Māteva putraṃ pṛthivī puriṣyamagniṃ sveyonavabhārukhā...'
11. S. Yv. XII.35...'māteva putraṃ bibhṛtāpsvanat'
12. S. Yv. XI.13
13. S. Yv. XII.22
14. S. Yv. XXVI.11
15. S. Yv. XXVI.12...'...mahiṣīva tvadrayistvadvāja udīrate'
16. S. Yv. XXVII.35...'Abhi tvā śūra nonumohadugdhā iva dhenavaḥ...'
17. S. Yv. XXXIV.49...'Pūrveṣāṃ panthānamanudṛśya dhīrā anvālebhire rathyo
    no raśmīn'
18. S. Yv. XXI.12-22, XXVIII.24-45
19. S. Yv. V.2
20. S. Yv. II.25
21. 'Gāyatryā chandasendriyaṃ cakṣuḥ ..'—S. Yv. XXVIII.35
22. 'Uṣṇihā chandasendriyaṃ prāṇam...'—S. Yv....XXVIII.36
23. 'Anuṣṭubhā chandasendriyaṃ balam...'—S. Yv. XXVIII.37
24. 'Bṛhatyā chandasendriyaṃ śrotram ..'—S. Yv. XXVIII.38
25. 'Paṅktyā chandasendriyaṃ śukram...'—S. Yv. XXVIII.39
26. 'Triṣṭubhā chandasendriyaṃ tviṣim...'—S. Yv. XXVIII.40
27. 'Jagatyā chandasendriyaṃ śūṣam...'—S. Yv. XXVIII.41
28. Virājā chandasendriyaṃ rūpam...'—S. Yv. XXVIII.42
29. 'Dvipadā chandasendriyaṃ bhagam...'—S. Yv. XXVIII.43
30. 'Kakubhā chandasendriyaṃ yaśam...'—S. Yv. XXVIII.44
31. 'Atichandasā chandasendriyaṃ kṣatram...'—S. Yv. XXVIII.45

CONCLUSION

After a long traversing down the route of the Śukla-Yajurvedic era, we are now in a position to estimate, in brief, the nature of the then Aryan culture and civilisation. It is a concerted opinion that the Yajurveda in general contains formulas for the sacrificial ceremonial only. And it is generally inferred that the contents of the S. Yv. reflect only the religio-philosophical aspect of the Aryan civilisation of that period. But the fact is otherwise. Not only the religio-philosophical aspect but also the economic, political and certain other aspects viz. flora and fauna, calendar, language and literature etc. have been well reflected in those contents. This work thus presents an overall study of the then Aryan culture and civilisation which was in no sense primitive but, on the otherhand, highly developed.

Yajña or sacrifice played no doubt a vital role in the development of life and culture of the Aryan people. The function of sacrifice was not limited to the activities of ritualistic offerings and development of religio-philosophical conceptions. It was sacrifice centering on which every sphere of Aryan life developed. So, in the midst of sacrificial formulas of the S. Yv., we find the picture of Aryan life which showed signs of progress in socio-economic, political, religio-philosophical and other fields of advancement.

Aryans in this age were no longer nomadic, but were leading a settled life in states having territorial bases and geographical boundaries. In lieu of hunting, the Aryans adopted the agricultural and industrial pursuits and also cattle-rearing as means of their livelihood.

The organisation of family was practically the same as it exists in India to the present time. The Śatarudrīya hymn of the S. Yv. mentions nearly seventy varieties of profession of which some were earmarked for women. One will be astonished to find so many varieties of occupations prevalent as far back as 2000 B.C.

Aryans in that age were not lacking in ideas of government

and law. Kingship was there and it was heriditary in character.
Though monarchy was the system of government, it was free from
autocracy. The spirit of democracy prevailed behind the monarchical system of government. The public organisations, viz. Sabhā
and Samiti used to help the monarch in matters of administration
and government.

There was a marvellous achievement in the educational sphere
as well. Religious and scientific knowledge developed side by side.
The syllabus of study was extensive and directed towards making
a human being perfect in all ways.

The rigidity of caste-system and class bar gradually relaxed in
this age and intercaste marriage was in vouge. The standard of
morality was evidently comparatively high. Adultery and rape
were serious offences, while robbery, cow-killing etc. were recognised as punishable crimes.

The achievement of religious and philosophical thought is
noteworthy. New religious cults, such as the Viṣṇu cult, Rudra-
Śiva cult, Bhakti cult came into existence. Philosophical thought
was not lacking. There are some hymns in the S. Yv. which though
in form are hymns of sacrifice and worship of deities, in essence
they contain higher thought of philosophical speculation. One of
the striking features of this saṃhitā is that it embodies even in the
midst of sacrificial formulas, different philosophical speculations.

The sketch of Vedic civilisation as drawn from the critical
survey of the S. Yv. Saṃhitā, amply justifies the conclusion that
the Vedic Aryans of that age were anything but primitive. The
development of culture and civilisation is a reflection of the mental
development and it is but natural that the religion of the Vedic
people was in consonance with the development of their mental
capacities.

BIBLIOGRAPHY

A. ORIGINAL SOURCES :

Aitareya Brāhmaṇa, Anandasrama Edition, Poona, 1931
Aitareya Āraṇyaka,   „   „   „   1898
Atharva Veda Saṃhita, Ed. by. C. R. Lanman, Tr. by W. D. Whitney ; Harvard University, 1905.
Bṛhadāraṇyaka Upaniṣad, Vani-vilas press.
Bhagavadgītā, Ed. by Tilak, Poona, 1915
Bhāgavata-Purāṇa, Kumbhakonam ed ; Poona, 1926
Chāndogya Upaniṣad, Vani-vilas press.
Gopatha Brāhmaṇa, Ed. by Rajendra Lal Mitra, Delhi, 1972
Kaṭhopaniṣad, Vani-vilas press.
Kauṣitakī Brāhmaṇa, Anandasrama ed ; 1911
Kṛṣṇa Yajurveda (Taittirīya Saṃhitā), Anandasrama ed ; 1948
Kātyāyana Śrauta-Sūtra, Ed. by Madan Mohan Pathak, Varanasi, 1904
Kāṭhaka Saṃhitā, Ed. by Von Schroeder, Leipzig, 1900-10.
Maitrāyani Saṃhitā, Ed. by Von. Schroeder, Leipzig, 1881-6
Muṇḍakopaniṣad, Vani-vilas press
Māṇḍūkyopaniṣad, Vani-vilas press
Manu Saṃhitā
Mahābhārata, Calcutta ed, 1934-39
Pañcaviṃśa Brāhmaṇa Ed. by A. Vedantavagisa, Calcutta, 1869-74
Pāraskara Gṛhya Sūtra, Bombay, 1971
Padma Purāṇa, Anandasrama ed ; Poona, 1893-4
Ṛgveda Saṃhitā, (With Sayana's commentary) Vaidika Samsodhana Mandala, Poona, 1936-46
Sāmaveda Saṃhitā, Ed. by Satyavrata Samasrami, Calcutta, 1873
Śatapatha Brāhmaṇa, (With Sayana's commentary) Ed. by A Weber, London, 1885
Śvetāśvatara Upaniṣad, Vani-vilas press
Taittirīya Brāhmaṇa, Anandasrama ed, Poona, 1934

Taittirīya Upaniṣad, Vani-villas press
Taittirīya Āraṇyaka, Anandasrama ed. Poona, 1934
Vājasaneyi Saṃhitā, Śukla-Yajurveda, (Kanva recension with Sayana's commentary) Ed. by Madhava Sastri, Varanasi, 1915
Vājasaneyi Saṃhitā, Śukla-Yajurveda, (Madhyandina recension with commentaries of Uvata and Mahīdhara) Ed. by Vasudeva Laxman Sastry. Nirnay Sagar Press, Bombay, 1929
Viṣṇu Purāṇa, Ed. Jivananda Vidyasagar, Calcutta, 1882

B) SECONDARY WORKS :

A. A. Macdonell, A History of Sanskrit Literature, London, 1900
,, ,, Vedic Mythology, Strassburg, 1897
,, ,, Vedic Religion, Vol. XII, 1920
,, ,, A Vedic Reader for Students, Oxford, 1917
,, ,, A Vedic Grammar for Students, Oxford, 1916
A. A. Macdonell & A. B. Keith, Vedic Index of Names & Subjects (Vols. I & II) Matilal Banarsidass, 1958
A. B. Keith, Religion & Philosopoy of the Veda & Upanisads (Vols. XXXI & XXXII), Harvard Oriental Series, 1925.
A. Weber, History of Indian Literature, Vol. I, Calcutta University, 1962
A. S. Altekar, State & Government in Ancient India.
,, ,,   ,,   The Position of Women in Hindu Civilisation, Varanasi, 1956
A. C. Das, Ṛgvedic India, Vol. I, Calcutta, 1921
Aurobinda, On the Veda, Pondicherry, 1956
Anirvan, Veda Mimansa, Sanskrit College, Calcutta, 1956
Acharya Baladev Upadhyaya, Vaidik Sahitya Aur Samskriti, Varanasi, 1973
Beni Prasad, Theory of Government in Ancient India.
B. C. Law, Indological Studies (Part I), Indian Research Institute, 1950
Devichand, Yajurveda, New-Delhi, 1956
F. Max Muller, History of Ancient Sanskrit Literature (IInd Ed.) London, 1860
Haran Ch. Chakladar, Aryan Occupation of Eastern India.

Hemchandra Roy Choudhury, Studies in Indian Antiquities, University of Calcutta, 1932

Hemchandra Roy Choudhury, Materials for the Study of the Early History of the Vaisnava Sect, 1920

Jogiraj Basu, India at the Age of Brahmanas, Calcutta, 1969

„	„	Veder Parichaya (Ist & IInd Ed.).

Jogendranath Bagci, Veder Mantrabhāge Iśvar-O-Dārśaniktatva

		„			„		Veder Mantrabhāge Adhyātma Vidyā

K. P. Jayswal, Hindu Polity, Calcutta, 1924

Kshitimohan Sen, Bhārater Samskriti.

K. C. Chatterjee, Vedic Selections, Calcutta University, 1944

Louis Renou, Vedic India, Calcutta, 1957

M. Winternitz, A History of Indian Literature, Vol. I, Calcutta University, 1962

M. Bloomfield, Vedic Concordance, Harvard University, 1906

„	„	„	Religion of the Veda

Narayan Bapujee Udgitkar, Collected Works of R. G. Bhandarkar (Vol. II), Poona, 1929

Narayan Bhattacharjee, Atharva Vede Bhāratīya Samskrti.

P. S. Deshmukh, Religion in Vedic Literature, Oxford, 1933

Pandit S. D. Satavalkar, Go-jñana Kośa.

„	Ganga Prasad Upadhyaya, Śatapatha Brāhmana (Vols.I & II)

„	R. S. Acharya, Yajurveda.

„	Joydev Sharma, Yajurveda Samhitā (Bhasa-bhasya).

R. C. Majumdar & A. D. Pusalkar, The Vedic Age (History & Culture of the Indian People. Vol.-I). London, 1952 (IInd impression)

R. K. Mukerjee, Hindu Civilisation, London, 1936

R. C. Dutt, The Early Hindu Civilisation, Calcutta, 1963

„	„	„	Rgveda Samhitā, Calcutta, 1885-86

R. T. H. Griffith, The White Yajurveda (3rd Ed.) Varanasi, 1957

R. N. Dandekar, Vedic Bibliography (2 Vols.) Poona, 1961

R. S. Sarma, Sudras in Ancient India, Delhi, 1958

Ramendra Sundar Trivedi, Yajña Katha (Ramendra Sundar Racanavali).

Swami Dayananda Sarasvati, Satyartha Prakash.

Swami Mahadevananda Giri, Vedic Culture, Calcutta University, 1947

„ Gambhirananda, Upanisad Granthavali (Vols. I-IV)

S. Radhakrishnan, Indian Philosophy (Vol. I), London, 1958

S. K. Belvalkar and R. D. Ranade, History of Indian Philosophy (Vol. II)

S. N. Pradhan, Chronology of Ancient India, Calcutta University, 1927

Sitanath Goswami, Isopanisad.

Swami Ranganathananda, The Message of the Upanisads (Bharatiya Vidya Bhavan Publication).

T. Burrow, Sanskrit Language, London, 1955

U. N. Ghosal, Studies in Indian History and Culture.

U. N. Ghosal, A History of Indian Political Ideas.

U. N. Ghosal, The Beginning of Indian Historiography and other Essays.

U. N. Ghosal, A History of Hindu Public Life.

V. Raghavan, The Indian Heritage.

V. C. Mahazan, Ancient India.

Visnupada Bhattacharjee, Vaidik Devata.

Visnupada Bhattacharjee, Bharatiya Bhakti Sahitya, 1964

V. S. Verma, Studies in Hindu Political Thought.

INDEX